Examining
the
Great Commission

Examining
the
Great Commission

A Call to Study

Christopher Baidoo-Essien

authorHOUSE®

AuthorHouse™
1663 Liberty Drive
Bloomington, IN 47403
www.authorhouse.com
Phone: 1-800-839-8640

First published by AuthorHouse   10/14/2011

ISBN: 978-1-4670-3699-3 (sc)
ISBN: 978-1-4670-3698-6 (hc)
ISBN: 978-1-4670-3697-9 (ebk)

Library of Congress Control Number: 2011916708

Printed in the United States of America

CONTENTS

PART 1

Matthew 28:18

Authority

Introduction

All four gospel accounts give a variation of Jesus charging the apostles to proclaim the gospel to all nations. The amazing truth is that all four accounts tell the same story. In this writing, I seek to carefully analyze and understand the Great Commission. For this is now my charge as a faithful Christian: to faithfully discharge the duties that the commission requires. Furthermore, as one who seeks to teach others who seek to serve the Lord Jesus, it seems only proper for me to understand the Great Commission well in order to impart that knowledge accurately to others. As noble as the above reasons might be, they were not what set me on the track to examine the Great Commission. It all started as I was contemplating what to do with the time that had become available to me because of a contract job that had just ended.

As I was riding the bus home, weighing my options for the use of my free time, I decided to write down what I have learned about baptism over the years. I went to work studying and writing these thoughts down. I also thought it would be a great way to engage lessons from my Greek classes. As I progressed with my script on baptism, I got to a point where I was asking myself where the authority or the command to baptize the disciples originated.

I still remember the fateful day in September 1983 when I submitted to the Lord in baptism. After I made the confession in front of the whole congregation, Brother Munko and I trekked down the road to the waters of the Atlantic Ocean, where he baptized me. We went to the familiar place where I had witnessed many other disciples give up their lives to Christ in baptism. As we stepped into the ocean, there were no waves, so we went a bit farther to where the water passed our knees. If you've walked at any depth into the ocean, you know how difficult it is to stand still. That is exactly what Brother Munko and I tried to do. We were successful for a minute or so. As Brother Munko dipped me into the water, a big wave came from nowhere. This wave swept the sand from under Brother Munko's feet, which caused him to lose his balance. As a result his grasp was loosened a bit and I went down, trying not to gulp in too much seawater. If you know what a bicycle kick looks like in soccer, that is what happened to me next as we tried to gain control and balance. (A bicycle kick is the kind a soccer player attempts on the ball when it is in the air. The height of the ball is usually higher than waist level. The kick motion is such that the player leaps and his or her legs are swung in a crisscross motion simultaneously.) I still remember the whole event vividly even today as well as what happened to me when Brother

Munko and I said good-bye to each other, knowing we were now eternal brothers—brothers bound, bought, and paid for by divine blood. As I looked down the road heading home, which was straight down the hill in the distance, a joyful song—"Oh happy day that fixed my choice on thee my savior and my God . . ."—erupted in my head the rest of my way home.

About the subject on hand, as I delved into the New Testament in an effort to address the question about the origin for the command to baptize the new disciple, I realized that the Great Commission was essential to the discussion on baptism. At first I wrote about three pages and tried to shorten the discussion on the Great Commission, but the harder I tried to end the discussion, the more difficult it seemed, since I knew that more needed to be said. I decided it would be better to discuss the topic by itself before continuing with the study on baptism.

What I seek to do in this writing is to break down the commission statements and carefully examine them. After examining the separated parts of the Great Commission statements we will try to understand them all together. Since the Great Commission is the source of authority for all faithful Christians engaged in winning souls for the Lord, let us carefully investigate our Bibles to be sure that what is being discussed here is consistent with what the scripture is saying. Questions will be raised or arise as we dig into the scriptures, so let us make the concerted effort to rely on the Bible for answers to these questions. I will be using the New American Standard Bible (NASU), Updated Edition; New American Standard Bible (NASB); American Standard Bible (ASV); English Standard

Bible (ESV); and the King James Version (KJV) as my primary texts. I will also be using the literal translation of the Greek for most of the main passages when I break down the text.

What Is a Commission?

Before we go any further, let's look at what the word *commission* means. When we look up the definition for *commission* in the Merriam Webster dictionary, for example, we conclude that a commission is a reward for undertaking a business transaction or an empowerment to perform specific duties or functions. Thus we see two aspects in a commission: reward or empowerment. Common to both aspects of a commission is the underlying authority or power. Whether the authority is to dispense the reward corresponding to a task performed, say the percentage of a sale to a salesperson, or authorizing a group of people to perform a specific task, the authority associated with the commission usually comes from someone in a higher position of authority or power. An interesting observation about commissions is an implicit expectation that their tasks and responsibilities will be performed or discharged within the limits of the authority given them. Neither Jesus nor the Gospel writers dubbed the statements found in Matthew 28:18-20 or Mark 16:15-18 or the statement in the last chapter of Luke the Great Commission. I do not know who first titled these passages the Great Commission. However, given the fact that in these statements Jesus outlines specific tasks for His disciples authorizing them to make disciples, baptize them, and teach them to obey everything He, Jesus, has commanded, the title fits. Thus, we will refer to these passages as the Great Commission. Besides, this title is universally accepted and recognized among Christians.

The following are Matthew and Mark's versions of the Great Commission statement:

And Jesus came up and spoke to them, saying, "All authority has been given to Me in heaven and on earth. Go therefore and make disciples of all the nations, baptizing them in the name of the Father and the Son and the Holy Spirit, teaching them to observe all that I commanded you; and lo, I am with you always, even to the end of the age." Matthew 28:18-20 NASU.

And He said to them, "Go into all the world and preach the gospel to all creation. He who has believed and has been baptized shall be saved; but he who has disbelieved shall be condemned. These signs will accompany those who have believed: in My name they will cast out demons, they will speak with new tongues; they will pick up serpents, and if they drink any deadly poison, it will not hurt them; they will lay hands on the sick, and they will recover" (Mark 16:15-18, NASU).

Background Information—Pre-Great Commission

Preceding the Great Commission was the birth, life, death, burial, and resurrection of Jesus Christ. He had been on earth at this point for more than thirty years. Jesus Christ had walked with and taught the disciples for three years. He had overcome Satan's initial temptations. He had done many wonders, including walking on water, healing various infirmities, casting away evil spirits, telling sinners their sins had been forgiven, feeding thousands with a little boy's lunch, and many other acts that no ordinary man could have done. So let us imagine ourselves as the apostles or faithful disciples who had attended Jesus's presence regularly and heard Him teach, and saw Him heal and cast away demons. How disappointed would we have been to know that God's plan for saving His people was taking place in a way that was entirely different from what we had imagined? How would we have felt when such a powerful person yielded to His enemies without a fight? I imagine that we would have drawn our swords with Peter to defend Jesus the Savior. What would have been our reaction when Jesus told Peter to put his sword back in place while at the same time He performed an act of kindness to one of the people who was about to severely mistreat Him to His death? What a downer! How would we have felt if we had been there? Would we not have been disappointed, angry, depressed, furious, frightened, hopeless? The list is endless.

Let us place ourselves in the state of any of the eleven apostles with Jesus at Gethsemane; that is, you and I are Peter, John, James, Matthew, or any of the others. How would we have reacted to the arrest of Jesus Christ, and what emotional state would we have been in as He was condemned unjustly and given a sentence He did not deserve? What manner of confusion and disappointment would we have shown? Would we have abandoned the course of Christ and return to our previous lifestyles as some of the apostles did? Would we have felt hopeless and given up, given that we had invested three years learning from Jesus and now all seemed to be for nothing? Imagine that as Saturday rolled around, we had recovered a little from the initial shock of the Lord's death, or maybe we were still in a state of disbelief and had a million unanswered questions. What kind of Sabbath would that have been? It would be a Sabbath we would not desire to see repeated for sure. As one of these disciples, further imagine that we are just waking up on Sunday morning exhausted, emotionally wrecked and wearied by another sleepless night. Imagine that all of a sudden there is banging on the door followed by two familiar feminine voices, perhaps screaming or perhaps in an emphatic low voice not desiring to be heard by the neighbors for fear of being reported to the Jewish leaders. Imagine we are hearing the two Marys, "Mary Magdalene and the other Mary," according to Matthew 28:1, banging on the door and that they seem to be saying what sounds like "He's risen! The tomb is empty! We have seen Him with our own eyes and spoken to Him!" The two Marys like the others saw Jesus teach, heal, and do all kinds of wonders. Like the other disciples these two women were hit equally hard by the incidents leading to the death of the Lord. Imagine that as the two Marys enter, it is clear from their countenances that they are excited, and so overwhelmed with joy, they can hardly contain themselves. It takes a little bit of effort to calm them down to hear the full details of what they have just witnessed or uncovered.

After hearing their news we understood why they were excited. If we were truly there that Sunday, how would we have been affected by the first story about the risen Christ told by the two Marys? Perhaps there would more chaos in our minds, not knowing what to make of what we have just heard. Let's keep in mind that we are in the shoes of the apostles or the disciples who were close to Jesus Christ. Since we think individually and individually assess our emotions, how do we see ourselves processing the news brought by the two Marys? Do we believe them immediately or seek ways to verify their news? It is easy to criticize Thomas for doubting and saying he would not believe until he saw and examined the wounds of Jesus. But why don't we think of Peter and John as doubting when they ran to the tomb to verify what they had heard about Jesus having arisen? Once at the burial site they realized that the stone closing the tomb had been rolled away just as the two women had described. Yet, Peter ran into the tomb only to find no dead body, just the burial cloth with the bloodstains from the Lord's wounds, folded and placed in a corner. Thomas verbalized what he was thinking, but Peter and John showed their doubt by their actions, in my opinion. Why else did Jesus need to convince them that He was alive as recorded in Luke's account? As we continue to imagine ourselves in the shoes of the apostles, whatever we choose to do in processing the news of the risen Lord, let us remember that Jesus told the disciples that the events they had just witnessed were going to happen. And indeed they happened just like Jesus Christ had instructed.

Still in the shoes of the apostles, yes, we have seen the Lord raise the dead and even call them back to life as He did Lazarus, but no one had ever heard of the dead walking out of a tomb or grave alive of their own volition! Let us further imagine that Peter and John return to the group and report their findings about the empty tomb and the burial cloth folded and placed in its corner. All of this is really confusing: first the two Marys say they have seen the risen Lord, then Peter and John return from the tomb with a report that the Lord's body is not in the tomb and the burial cloth is lying inside! What if someone went and took the dead body and hid it? How can the dead walk out of the tomb alive at the will of the dead when it had never happened before? All the disciples, including the apostles, had their doubts about these stories. They had heard several stories that the Lord was arisen, and yet they did not believe it to be the case. According to Luke's record, in chapter 24, most of the disciples were still in disbelief even after hearing the story of the two Marys, the report of Peter and John of the empty tomb, and the accounts of the other disciples who had seen and communicated with the risen Lord, even to the point when Jesus stood in their midst and offered them physical proofs to help them believe. After all that, some still had a difficult time believing, so Jesus asked for food, which He was given and ate. Would we have done better if we had been one of these disciples? Can we say we would have done better remembering all that Jesus taught and that we would not be as confused? What kind of emotional discipline would we have shown had we been present on that first Sunday when the news started trickling in about the risen Savior? Would we have been emotional wrecks or emotional mixed bags, or would we have been in disbelief?

According to Luke's account Jesus had to help the disciples understand and believe that He had risen. As part of the disciples, imagine listening to Jesus as He stood in our midst offering one piece of evidence after another about these events and gently guiding our thoughts by pointing to what He had said earlier as well as what the prophets had written long ago about the Christ. Imagine that with each word spoken by Jesus the confusion, fear, emotional swings, doubt, and disbelief that made it impossible for us to think straight begin to give way to clarity. Gradually it seems that the knots formed in our minds because of all the uncertainty begin to untie. Soon, we arrive at the conclusion that He is risen just as He said! For Jesus had taught that with God, everything is possible. Gradually we begin to look back at the events that took place: the

Lord's arrest, the leaders rejecting and condemning Jesus to death, the crucifixion of Jesus, the story of the two Marys, and the fact that we are looking at Jesus eating cooked food and examining His scars. We realize that it is not only possible but also real: Jesus has risen, and our eyes are observing His physical presence. As we evaluate what has been happening and look at the Lord, the belief is not 100 percent—there is some self-doubt for sure—yet we are gaining some confidence and understanding what happened. Our countenances have improved, and all in the room have brightened up a bit. First we wonder, and then slowly but surely smiles creep in, changing the default positions of the lips of some among us, exposing their white enamels as they shine through. The atmosphere turns into a mixture of joy, disbelief, and doubt. Little by little the demeanor of some has changed from confusion to enlightenment, then from enlightenment to understanding, then from understanding to appreciation, then from appreciation to discernment, which in the case of Thomas led to the exclamation, "My Lord and my God!" when he finally saw Jesus and felt the wounds. As Americans we would have said, "You did it, Lord! You did it!" perhaps jumping up and down.

As if the emotional states the disciples found themselves in were not enough, the soldiers and the Jewish leaders devised a plan to spread a message contrary to the truth. This false story probably spread faster than the real truth of the moment. Again, imagine walking around town and hearing the false charge that the disciples of Jesus went to the tomb and stole His dead body. The false news is spreading fast like a wildfire that Jesus has not truly arisen, that His disciples stole His body. As disciples, we have let fear paralyze us and our ability to refute any of these false rumors. Never mind the physical proofs, including the empty tomb and the burial cloths left behind. Never mind that Jesus had Thomas examine the wounds in the presence of other disciples who were still in a state of disbelief. The emotional ups and downs mixed with fear have made it impossible to think clearly. Imagine that with all these pieces of evidence available to us from the initial announcement of Jesus's resurrection by the two Marys, the verification of the empty tomb by Peter and John, to Jesus revealing Himself to some of the disciples on different occasions under different circumstances, we are unable to challenge the spread of false news because we fear the Jewish leaders.

According to the first eleven verses of Luke's record in Acts chapter 1, Jesus for forty days after His suffering "presented Himself alive . . . , by many convincing proofs . . . and speaking of the things concerning the kingdom of God." Knowing exactly what was going on, it seems to me Jesus made sure that the people He was sending out to present the good news about Him to the rest of the world had enough evidence and proof to make them firsthand witnesses and not secondhand witnesses. That is, these people saw all these events take place in person with their own two eyes. In fact, they were in some ways part of the story. They saw Jesus in person. They walked with Him for three years and saw Him abused and crucified on the cross. Some went to request His dead body from Pilate so they could bury it. Pilate granted their request, and they buried the body. They struggled with the events leading to the death of Christ and after His resurrection. Some of them had taken care of Jesus and invested in Jesus in one way or another. Finally, most of these disciples saw the risen Jesus and talked to Him—or more accurately, He talked to them face-to-face, in the flesh. Mary heard Him say her name.

Thomas heard Him say to him something like, "Come near and stick your fingers in these wounds so you will believe and not doubt." He walked and talked to two disciples on their way to Emmaus. He served His disciples breakfast on the beach and talked to them. He rebuked those disciples who did not believe the news of His resurrection. Dead people don't walk around talking to and rebuking people for not believing they are alive! The only possibility is that Jesus was alive again. One might say, "What is the big deal? Lazarus died and rose again." Or, "We have heard about people coming back from the dead! Nothing extraordinary about Jesus dying and coming back from the dead!" Okay, that is true, except that Lazarus died again and is still dead, as is the case for all those who might have come back from the dead. They are all dead and are still in their graves or they will eventually return to their grave again! These same people who died and came back alive died again or will die at some point, and they will stay dead until the judgment day. But in the case of Jesus, He arose never to die again!

In rising from death never to die again Jesus robbed death of its permanency. Jesus took away the dreadful clutches with which death has held mankind hostage ever since Eden. Death has no permanence to it any longer. To those who accept the good news of Christ Jesus, death is only a matter of a long nap. Death has no permanence any longer over them.

He could have been a ghost, one might argue. Well, that might be true, but He wasn't. The fact is, Jesus once surprised the disciples when they had gathered together, perhaps to exchange and compare stories about seeing Him. Jesus surprised them by joining their meeting unannounced. According to Luke's account in chapter 24, the disciples thought they had seen a ghost and were scared. Jesus eased their fears by asking for food and having them examine His wounds. Ghosts have no flesh, so food would have meant nothing to a ghost. If Jesus had been a ghost, it would have been impossible for the disciples to have felt His wounds or seen Him with their eyes. Jesus, knowing the nature of man, made sure that those who were going to spread His good news had no doubts at all. He was solidifying not only what they had heard but also what they had seen so that the apostle John, when he was introducing his first epistle, said, "That which was from the beginning, which we have heard, which we have seen with our eyes, which we looked upon and have touched with our hands" (1 John 1:1). Jesus made the apostles and the disciples who saw Him first-class witnesses who could describe the "scene" as eyewitnesses without any doubt at all.

Within a forty-day span, Jesus made sure that if any of His disciples had any doubts about the events that had taken place before and during those days, those doubts were removed. On the fortieth day after His resurrection Jesus met with the apostles physically for the last time. As He was talking and giving His final orders, the apostles saw His whole body, His physical body, lift slowly up and up, and soon they were looking at the bottom of His feet. Soon they were gazing only at the thin air that lifted Jesus above their heads. Death did not conquer Jesus, the Messiah; He conquered death and was lifted up to heaven with an invincible lift that trumped the chariots of fire that snatched Elijah into the clouds. Only God understands the physics and the mathematics behind Christ's ascension to heaven, adding even more evidence to convict the ones among the disciples who had not yet come to the conclusion that Jesus was the Messiah.

It is these last orders that Jesus gave that we seek to look into to understand what our responsibilities are so we can faithfully do them. We now look into Matthew's account.

B: Authority—Matthew 28:18

Introduction to Matthew's Account

I have chosen Matthew's account as the focal passage for the discussion because of how well his account is partitioned. For example, one can segment Mathew's account into sections on authority and duties for the disciples. In Matthew's account, an angel got to the tomb ahead of the two Marys. He rolled the stone from the mouth of the tomb and informed the two women that Jesus was not at the present location. He invited them to look into the empty tomb and added, "He is risen just as He said." The angel further told them that Jesus was going ahead of them into Galilee where He would meet them. As if to remove all doubt about what the women had just heard and seen in the tomb, Jesus appeared in person to them as they turned to leave the tomb to go tell the others about what they had just witnessed. Jesus then confirmed the rendezvous. It was at the rendezvous that Jesus commissioned the apostles with the following: "And Jesus came and spoke to them, saying, 'All authority has been given to Me in heaven and on earth. Go therefore and make disciples of all nations, baptizing them in the name of the Father, and the Son and the Holy Spirit, teaching them to observe all that I commanded you; and lo, I am with you always, even to the end of the age'" (Matthew 28:18-20).

Even though we quote verse 18 along with verses 19 and 20 of the Great Commission, we seldom dwell on it. But I think verse 18 is a very important part of the Great Commission. One might ask, why is this verse important? I believe it establishes the authority upon which the apostles will base their work. Remember the Jewish leaders questioning Jesus about the source of His authority for doing what He did. Also earlier in His teachings, the people, after hearing Jesus teach, observed that Jesus taught not like their regular teachers, or rabbis, but like one with authority. Jesus refused to identify the source of His authority to the Jewish leaders. However, alone with His disciples He will tell them, "for I have not spoken on my own, but the Father who sent me has Himself given me a commandment about what to say and what to speak" (John 12:49). Thus Jesus made the source of His authority known.

Knowing the authority by which one performs an action adds credibility to the actions taken.

Paul said in Philippians 2 that even though Jesus was equal with God, He did not count equality with God as something to be grasped. Instead He took on the form of a servant humbling Himself, even to the death on the cross. Forty days after He was resurrected from the dead, Jesus told the same group of people, disciples or apostles, that "All authority has been given to me in heaven and on earth." The literal translation goes something like this: "have been given to me all [the whole] authority [power, rule, jurisdiction, full power, dominion] in heaven and on the earth." The words in the brackets are alternate words that can be used to replace the words followed by the brackets.

We observe these three truths about this part of Matthew's account of the Great Commission: 1) Jesus was given the authority, 2) Jesus has all authority, and 3) territories or jurisdictions covered under this authority are heaven and earth, that is the universe we see and that which we do not see with the naked eye. Before we analyze this passage, allow me to ask and find answers to the following questions: What is authority? What type of authority is Jesus referring to here? To attempt to address these questions let us pause and take some important notes about the word of God.

Authority

God's word—God's authority expressed in the past and through the law of Moses, the prophets, and in the psalms in different forms

Really, where does one begin when it comes to talking about God, authority, and the forms through which God expressed His will, say, in the Old Testament? There are many valuable lessons we can learn from the records in the Bible from Creation to Christ and beyond. I will cite a few. Take for example in the opening two chapters of Genesis where Moses narrates the Creation account as it was revealed to Him by God. Per Moses's record the Creation account revealed God speaking into existence things that were previously not in existence. God called things into existence by name, such as light, and grass. God expressed His will in these accounts by calling into existence only what He desired to come into existence and appropriately ordered them as He desired. He called into existence anything and whatever He willed to come into existence. Things He did not wish to exist or call into existence did not come into existence. If something came into existence that God had not called, that would have defied His will and power and served as proof that He was not all powerful and did not create all things. However, that did not happen and has never happened since Creation and beyond. It is profoundly important to note that nothing came into existence outside of the will of God. How would anyone know that? Well, by faith, according to Paul, who in the book of Hebrews said, "By faith we understand that the universe was created by the word of God, so that what is seen was not made out of things that are visible" (Hebrews 11:3, ESV).

Supporting Moses's accounts are the words of the prophets and the New Testament writers as they were led by the Holy Spirit: "By the word of the Lord the heavens were made, and by the breath of His mouth all their host" (Psalms 33:6, NASB).

"Lift up your eyes on high and see who has created these stars, the One who leads forth their host by number, He calls them all by name; Because of the greatness of His might and the strength of His power Not one of them is missing" (Isaiah 40:26, NASB).

"who gives life to the dead and calls into being that which does not exist" (Romans 4:17, NASB).

"by the word of God the heavens existed long ago and the earth was formed out of water and by water" (2 Peter 3:5, NASB).

"Worthy art Thou, our Lord and our God, to receive glory and honor and power; for Thou didst create all things, and because of Thy will they existed, and were created" (Revelation 4:11 NASB).

It is also worth mentioning that God since Creation has allowed things to exist that are against His will. Sin is one such example. One might ask, but there are many things that we know today that were not present at the Creation, so how can anyone say that all things exist according to the will of God? That is a good point. Question: How did all the great discoveries that have been made over the years get to be hidden for us to find them, and who put them there?

Solomon, the wisest king who ever lived, noted the following: "It is the glory of God to conceal a matter, But the glory of kings is to search out a matter" (Proverbs 25:2 NASU).

Furthermore, Daniel stated,

Let the name of God be blessed forever and ever, For wisdom and power belong to Him. It is He who changes the times and the epochs; He removes kings and establishes kings; He gives wisdom to wise men and knowledge to men of understanding. It is He who

*reveals the profound and hidden things; He knows what is in the
darkness, And the light dwells with Him. (Daniel 2:20-22 NASU)*

We humans are God's creation created in His image. God has given
us the ability to be creative not entirely independent of Him. He
opens our eyes and grants us the necessary knowledge, wisdom, and
understanding to help us uncover what He has hidden. From time to
time, God opens pockets of knowledge for us to make or create things
that will contribute to the comfort of our lives. Let's think about it for
a minute: how many of the discoveries that have contributed greatly
to our lives were directly or intentionally discovered—that is, the
discoverer set out to prove or find an atom or whatever and ended
up finding exactly that? Most of the discoveries I read about in my
science books were accidental. Although we might fail to give God
the proper credit due Him, He does not stop loving us and taking
care of our needs. Through His love for us He sees to our needs and
makes available knowledge and abilities that lead us to solutions to
our needs that He did not make available in previous generations.

We read about God expressing His will in Noah's time by using
water to wipe every living thing off the face of planet Earth, saving
only eight souls and a few animals in a boat. God expressed His
will in many other forms such as making covenants with Noah and
Abraham and protecting them. We read about God destroying Sodom
and Gomorrah on account of their sins and removing the Canaanites
from the land they had polluted with their sins. At the proper time,
God fulfilled His promise to Abraham by replacing the Canaanites
with His own people, the children of Israel. We read about several
situations where God expressed His will using His people Israel in

conquests of wars, using the prophets to heal illnesses and raise the dead. God expressed His will in preventing rainfall for a number of years and in many other extraordinary circumstances. Among these extraordinary circumstances are the prophet Elisha making poisoned food edible again using plain flour. Elisha fed a hundred men with twenty loaves with leftovers. Elisha retrieved a solid mass of iron, the head of an ax, making it float on water. An ax head floating on water is not something that is possible without an aid, but for the ax head to float up is another thing altogether. That is what Elisha made happen in the story of 2 Kings 6:1-7 in accordance to the will of God. "Then the man of God said, "Where did it fall?" When he showed him the place, he cut off a stick and threw it in there and made the iron float. And he said, "Take it up." So he reached out his hand and took it" (2 Kings 6:6-7, ESV).

Naaman was a prominent commanding officer of the Aram Army sent to the prophet Elisha for healing. The story is found in chapter 5 of 2 Kings in the Old Testament. Naaman had leprosy. A slave girl he had captured from Israel who was serving Naaman's wife mentioned to her mistress that the prophet in Israel could heal her master. When it was all said and done, Naaman agreed to go see the prophet Elisha. Naaman made the trip to Israel to see the prophet. Upon arrival in Israel, Naaman presented himself to the king of Israel with the letter from his king, the king of Aram, requiring that his commanding officer be healed. As the king of Israel didn't know what to do for Naaman, he concluded that Naaman's boss was trying to pick a fight. Elisha heard of the king's plight and asked that Naaman be sent to him. I must say that what happened next would have been humiliating to even the lowest-ranked private, let alone the commanding officer of the greatest army at the time. When Naaman came to Elisha, Elisha did not come out to greet this prominent soldier and officer. Instead he sent his servant to deliver a message to Naaman about what he needed to do to be healed. Elisha was sent to tell Naaman to go dip seven times in the river Jordan. Naaman was beside himself upon receiving the word of the prophet to go dip in the Jordan. Naaman no doubt took the prophet's action as an insult and was enraged, so he left and headed home. On the surface who could blame Naaman for his response? He had been treated very poorly by the man of God, or so it seemed. To add insult to injury, he was to go to the Jordan and dip himself in seven times. The Jordan! The Jordan! WELL! How about all those great rivers in his country? He spelled out a few of the names of those fine rivers. They surely had better-quality water than the Jordan, in Naaman's opinion. He probably had his residence near the banks of one of those great rivers with a majestic view. So he definitely could see nothing, nothing at all about the Jordan that could prompt him to dip himself into it. And definitely not at the word of a shabby and rugged-looking old man who was not courteous enough to come out and greet him! Naaman set off, heading back home and mapping out his targets for the next raid into Israel. One target was for sure and he would not miss it: the city Elisha lived in!

After some intervention and pleading by his servants, Naaman decided to go do what the prophet, the man of God, had asked him to do in order to be healed. Can you imagine what was going through Naaman's mind when he lifted his head out of the water after the first dip? The scripture doesn't say when the leprosy left him or when he was cleansed during the series of dippings. But imagine if he still saw spots of the dreadful disease on his skin after the third and fourth dips. Imagine Naaman's thoughts during the fifth and sixth dips or as he made the final dip, the seventh dip. If he still had spots on his skin or nothing had changed on his skin before the final dip, can we imagine what was going through his mind? Maybe his servants standing on the banks of the river were doing everything to calm him down to go through with the last dip. As great a man as Naaman was, let's give him a bit of credit for doing what the prophet told him. Let us also recognize Naaman for going through with dipping himself seven times without faith, since his pride could have gotten the better of him and led to him not following through with the prophet's word even at the persuasion of his servants. Now imagine as Naaman lifted his head out of the waters of the Jordan after the seventh dip and saw his skin as clean and smooth as that of a baby! Can we understand why Naaman presented himself again to Elisha, humbled by what he had just experienced? This time Elisha came out to greet Naaman, who made a great proclamation or confession before God and the prophet.

What lessons can we learn from Naaman's story, and what caused him to be healed? What healed Naaman? Was it the waters of Jordan? We have read about wonders done by God with the waters of the Jordan; remember the waters of the Jordan gathered on one side so the children of Israel could walk on dry ground as they crossed the Jordan into the land of Canaan. Or was it Naaman's obedience? Can one say that faith healed Naaman? Naaman's behavior was not a demonstration of one who believed what the prophet told him to do. Or was it the word of the prophet? I think it was the prophet's word that caused Naaman to be healed. Studying the story, we observe that everything except the prophet's word were available to Naaman at any given moment. Just coming to Israel didn't make Naaman well. Neither was dipping into the waters of Jordan (which Naaman could have done without permission from anyone). In the absence of the word of God through the prophet, Naaman would not have been made well from his leprosy. He had a very low opinion of the Jordan compared with rivers in his country, so we can safely say that there is not a chance he believed the river Jordan had healing powers. Also Naaman could have stopped dipping himself in the waters of the Jordan after the first, second, or even sixth dip, especially if he saw no improvements on his skin before the seventh dip. Yet the prophet's word said seven times. I am not sure that the number of times would have been an issue, except for the fact that the prophet said to dip seven times. The word from the prophet was not just man's word. It was God's word to the prophet. The prophet minus God's word was just like any ordinary man.

One might ask why seven times and not once or twice or five times or even ten times. The fact is, the word from God to the prophet was seven times and that was what it had to be. You see, without God's word to the prophet, which is what had been absent in Naaman's life all this time, Naaman would not have been healed. As Elisha spoke the words from God, it stood as the only choice if Naaman was to be healed in Israel. Nothing Naaman had done before seeing the prophet had brought about healing of his leprosy. So if Naaman was to be healed at all, he had to respond to God's word through the prophet by doing what he was asked to do. The power of healing was not in the waters of Jordan. Rather the healing power was in the words of God that the prophet spoke to Naaman, even if the word required Naaman to dip in the Jordan. One cannot overlook Naaman's obedience to the prophet's word that caused him to be healed, though he was furious at first. In spite of Naaman's initial disobedience, God's word and God's will was for Naaman to be healed by dipping into the waters of the Jordan. God's word stood firm and still. Naaman obeyed and was healed. He would have left Israel still a leper if he had not followed and done what God's word asked of him. It is also noteworthy that Naaman was healed though he did not believe, for belief was not required of him, only obedience. As it was, Naaman's healing depended solely on God's word spoken through the prophet. There are many other lessons we can learn from this story, but for the purposes of this study these lessons will suffice for now.

Before we move on to what this story has to do with the Great Commission, I want to make another observation about the word of God. The prophet Isaiah made this known to his generation, but it has held true since Creation before Isaiah's generation and still holds true today. In chapter 5, verses 7-11 the prophet Isaiah invites the wicked and the unrighteous to come, for God will surely forgive and pardon. He adds the following quote:

For as the rain cometh down and the snow from heaven, and returneth not thither, but watereth the earth, and maketh it bring forth and bud, and giveth seed to the sower and bread to the eater; so shall my word be that goeth forth out of my mouth: it shall not return unto me void, but it shall accomplish that which I please, and it shall prosper in the thing whereto I sent it. (Isaiah 55:10-11, ASV)

In this quote God declares that His word is like a seed in fertile ground that has received bountiful rain. Such seed will doubtlessly grow into fruition. In a similar manner God through the prophet said His word would not return to Him until it has accomplished the purpose for which it was sent. In this passage of prophecy, we see the power and effectiveness of God's words. That is, God's word has the inherent tendency and the ability to come to pass or to be fulfilled. To clarify this let's look at the encounter between the angel Gabriel and Zachariah. Zachariah disbelieved the angel's message and so he was made mute until the message he did not believe had come to pass. What is interesting to me about this encounter are the angel's words to Zachariah as he pronounced sentence on Zachariah for his unbelief. The angel said to Zachariah, "I am Gabriel. I stand in the presence of God, and I was sent to speak to you and to bring you this good news . . . because you did not believe my words, which will be fulfilled in their time" (Luke 1:19-20 ESV).

Zachariah was punished for not believing God's word, which would be fulfilled at the appropriate time. Also we learn from Hebrews 2:2 that the message spoken or declared by angels proved to be "unalterable" (NASU), "steadfast" (NKJV), "reliable" (ESV). God's word is reliable and does not change.

The passage in Isaiah teaches us many things about the word of God: 1) God's word has the inherent quality to attain the purpose for which God spoke it or sent it out. 2) God always has an intended purpose for what He says and why something He said was said. 3) God will not say A and expect B. His word will do what it was sent out to do. 4) It also serves as a very good reason why in our relationship with God we need to carefully study to understand His will and heed what God's word tells us. God's word is the only word with the ability to accomplish what it was sent forth to accomplish. One might even say that when God gives His word, a handshake is not required. God's word is good enough. It is powerful and it always has a mission that will be fulfilled.

What do all these have to do with the Great Commission? one might ask. Peter said no prophets spoke of their own accord but rather they spoke as they were directed by God. As we might notice, Jesus did not exclude Himself from this fact though He was God's Son. He told the Jews over and over again that He spoke and did as He was commanded by the Father and did as He saw the Father do. God is the source of all authority. He has it set up so that nothing escapes His notice and nothing happens without Him allowing it to take place. God is God Supreme, He is the mighty One. Thus if Jesus has all authority and it was given to Him, it was given to Him by the only one who had it all and could give to Him. God the Father is the architect of all things, and He does as He chooses.

What is authority?

When Jesus said, "All authority has been given to me," what did He mean? Was Jesus without power during His time on earth? Did He lack authority to do anything He wanted to do? Nobody has ever made such claim of possessing all authority before, so was Jesus out of His mind? What did Jesus mean? I am not sure I have answers for any of these questions, but I would like to look at some of the wonders Jesus performed and what He did while on earth and try to understand what He was saying. Before we delve into that, *Thayer's Greek-English Lexicon of the New Testament* offers four renderings for the Greek word ἐξουσία *(exsousia)* usually translated as "authority." First—the liberty to do as one pleases. Second—the physical and mental power; the ability or strength with which one is endued or possesses. Third—the power of authority and of right (this is delegated authority). And finally—the power of rule or government. Let's hold on to these definitions for a moment.

How are the three nouns *power, authority,* and *law* related to one another? According to Vine's *Expository Dictionary of New Testament Words, power* is a metonymy for "might" or "ability."—that is, power is the capability of doing anything one pleases. Now, no human, or nature or heavenly entity has unlimited power except God. God expressed that during Creation, for example. Authority on the other hand is the right or permission to exercise power. Thus authority carries an inherent limitation on the use of power—that is, one in position of authority has to be authorized, empowered, or permitted to enforce the power that is behind that authority. Paul said in the book of Romans, "For there is no authority except from God, and those which exist are established by God" (Romans 13:1, ISV).

Also, law is a set of decrees set up by custom or statute or state to provide a standard or uniform or general principle for administering justice.

To see how these three words relate let's consider a king of any land. Let's say a criminal is brought before the king's court. The king hears the case and determines that the penalty for the crime committed is death, according to the law. Now the king is in a position of authority and has the power provided by the law to condemn the criminal to the gallows to be hanged. At the same time the king, some might say, is the law of the land. That is, as the king he has the power to annul any law of the land or enforce it. Let's say that in our story the king decides to give the criminal a second chance so he shows the criminal mercy instead of giving him the punishment he deserves according to the law. The king pardons him by not condemning him or her to the appropriate sentence. In this story, we see that as one in position of authority, what the king can do in terms of the law is limited to what the law has prescribed. Separately, as one with somewhat unlimited power, the king can overrule the standard set by the law and do as he pleases. Only the king can do this, by the way. What I am trying to say here is that authority is limited in the power it can exercise, whereas power can exceed authority.

Power as the ability to perform as one desires is limited in all things except for God who is almighty. Power can be exercised beyond the bounds of authority if one has it. Jesus told the Pharisees that He had authority to forgive sins. And He forgave sins, including those of the thief on the cross. Jesus went beyond just forgiving the thief by having the just-pardoned man go to paradise with Him as they both died. This was not insignificant because the two thieves had gotten what they deserved for the crimes they had committed. According to the laws of the day, God's law and perhaps Roman law, they were to be punished in accordance with their crimes. Yet on the cross one of them asked for forgiveness and he not only got it, but was taken to paradise. Even as He shed the blood that reconciled God to mankind or rather man to God, Jesus demonstrated His authority to forgive sin. He also demonstrated His power by going beyond that authority and the law, taking the forgiven sinner to paradise. Thus in setting up authority God compartmentalized power. For example, though God is not limited in His power to do as He wills, including saving all of mankind, in revealing that "the gospel is the power of God to save" He limits Himself to allowing the authorities He has put in place to function, such as God limiting His saving abilities to the gospel, according to Romans 1:16.

Type of authority

Authority of Christ: The discussion of the authority of Jesus Christ is much broader than can be delved into here. An exhaustive discussion of this topic would require several months of study, if not years. Like most of the issues touched on in our discussions more detailed studies and prayer for insight will be required for us to fully understand the complexities entailed in understanding this topic. In this discussion we will only scratch the surface. As God is august and everything about God is vast, it is upon all of us to dedicate ourselves to consistent and serious study and prayer in matters of God and matters pertaining to our salvation so God can lead us to the proper conclusions. My encouragement thus is that we deliberately set aside time for study to increase our knowledge about God, for that is what it will take to appreciate a topic such as the authority of Christ. With that said, let each of us grab our picks, lenses, or binoculars and start digging into and searching the subject.

Let us consider a few of the ways in which God expressed His power and set up authorities: calling into existence that which before was not, that is, God's word active at Creation; punishing those who did not and do not do according to His will, that is, God's word active in condemning evildoers, which leads to death; God establishing covenants with people, that is, God's active grace and love for man, which leads to salvation; control over nature and seasons, that is, God's will allowing, for example, rain for a period of time or holding off rain for a period of time; God establishing kingdoms and destroying kingdoms, that is, God's overseeing the affairs of men; and control over illnesses and using everyday, ordinary things such as food to accomplish extraordinary things, that is, God allowing signs and wonders to be done by prophets in His name. Ultimately, only God retains the power to save, punish, or destroy people or groups of people. He dispenses or delegates such authorities to mankind and nature, all to meet His purposes. When God placed Adam in the garden of Eden, He gave Adam authority over everything in the garden.

> *Then God said, "Let us make man in our image, in our likeness, and let them rule over the fish of the sea and the birds of the air, over the livestock, over all the earth, and over all the creatures that move along the ground." So God created man in his own image, in the image of God he created him; male and female he created them. God blessed them and said to them, "Be fruitful and increase in number; fill the earth and subdue it. Rule over the fish of the sea and the birds of the air and over every living creature that moves on the ground." Then God said, "I give you every seed-bearing plant on the face of the whole earth and every tree that has fruit with seed in it. They will be yours for food. And to all the beasts of the earth and all the birds of the air and all*

the creatures that move on the ground—everything that has the breath of life in it—I give every green plant for food." And it was so. (Genesis 1:26-30, NIV)

The following scripture tells us how Adam, for example, used the authority God gave him.

Now the Lord God had formed out of the ground all the beasts of the field and all the birds of the air. He brought them to the man to see what he would name them; and whatever the man called each living creature, that was its name. So the man gave names to all the livestock, the birds of the air and all the beasts of the field. (Genesis 2:19-20, NIV)

God also told Cain that "sin is crouching at your door, and it desires you, you must master it or rule over it" (Genesis 4:7). This demonstrates that God has given us all self-control, yet like Cain we fail to exercise self-control and the discipline required to do what is right.

The devil holds the power of death, according to Hebrews 2:14. Other types of authorities include family and the family structure, fathers and mothers, and kings and other forms of governments. The list is endless. We can say that the most conclusive of all these is the fact that God's will expressed in His word is never going to fail. God's word will always be fulfilled! God has embedded into His words the distinct ability to be fulfilled any time He speaks them. Thus any authority or power expressed in all manner of forms and shapes leads to the same goal, accomplishing the will and purposes of God.

Authority or Power and Jesus Before and After His Death

Jesus told His disciples not to reveal who He was to the public on many occasions, especially after He had revealed something about Himself to the disciples. It will help us understand the discussion on the authority of Christ if we look at Christ in the context of one sent by God, or as a submissive Son to His Father, as a savior and a judge, or as one whom evil spirits and demon-possessed people recognized and feared, or finally as one who came to fulfill the words spoken about Him by the prophets, in the psalms, and in the books of law.

About the authority of Christ I have more questions than answers. For example, was Jesus without power or authority before He died and was resurrected? What type of authority did Christ Jesus have before His death and after He was resurrected? Were there any differences in His authority before His death compared with after He was resurrected? Before the cross, Jesus performed wonders and signs that no other prophet before and after Him had. I believe the wonders and signs Jesus did demonstrated that He was not lacking in power or authority. Here are a few of the signs and wonders Jesus performed:

1) Jesus forgave sinners their sins, something that was well understood at the time as something only God could do

2) Jesus healed the sick, including a man who was born blind and an invalid who had been sick for thirty-eight years. And don't forget the lady who thought she could stop her bleeding if she just touched the garment of Jesus, the Christ. She had been bleeding for twelve or more years, and probably the behavior of secretly approaching people had been cultivated as a result of the culture. She lived in a culture that had been taught according to God's law that the bleeding made her unclean. As a result of her uncleanliness whomever she came in contact with was believed to become unclean. No wonder she thought she could just sneak in and touch Jesus's garment and sneak away unnoticed. Surely Jesus understood that. If so, why didn't Jesus just let her go, instead of recognizing her in front of all the people? According to her faith she was healed. But sneaking away was impossible because Jesus felt her touch of faith—a touch that caused the Son of God to stop and look for her, a touch of faith that earned her more than the cure to her ailment: a welcome and reinstatement into the community in front of everyone. If this woman had been bleeding for twelve years, then according to the law of the Jews she had been unclean for twelve years and therefore abandoned by her peers and the community as a whole. She probably did not do much in public and had been shunned by everyone for fear of contamination and becoming unclean per Leviticus 15:19. Just wondering at this point: could it be that from her experiences she feared that by touching Jesus, she would make Him unclean, in spite of her faith that by touching Jesus she might be healed? Is it possible that that was why she did not want to be identified? You see,

33

although that contact with her would have contaminated and made unclean ordinary people like us, her shortcomings and even her bleeding were not enough to make the Son of God who was about to take the sins of the world away unclean. Her inadequacies were not enough to tarnish the sinless one, Jesus. Jesus sought her out and reinstated her as part of the community that had shunned her for all those years. Through her faith, this woman who had been bleeding for twelve years was able to get Jesus to respond to her the way God responds to people of faith. When this woman in faith reached out to God for help, God's Son reached back to her in love and care the way only God could.

What is noteworthy here is that the bleeding woman moved by her faith took action. Can we imagine if she had thought what she thought and not taken the steps to touch Jesus's garment, that is, put into the action the work required to make her well? Her bleeding would never have stopped. She would still be bleeding and not have been healed when she was healed. By her action, which was prompted by her faith, she was healed. Her act of faith was pleasing to God, so the Son of God, who knew immediately what had happened, sought to recognize her and make her action known. Did the disciples understand what had just happened? Can we see the smile on Jesus's face as He welcomed the fearful woman who through her faith had halted the advancement of the Son of God? Her faith was probably the size of a mustard seed or even smaller. But it was a good starting point. In spite of her hesitation she acted. Her action was enough to prevent

Christ from moving another step farther until He had met such a person who through faith reached out to the Son of God. Paul in Hebrews wrote that it is impossible to please God without faith. I think Jesus didn't let go because the woman's act of faith was pleasing to God and He wasn't going to let that go unrecognized.

Peter rightly pointed out to Jesus that there were too many people surrounding Him, including the disciples. Therefore anyone could have touched Jesus, probably just for the sake of touching Him, or accidentally. But this was no ordinary touch. I am sure this was not the first time Jesus had been in a situation like this, where the crowd had swarmed all around Him. As such, Jesus was probably used to people bumping and touching Him as He traveled. We can understand why Peter would react by saying it could have been anyone who might have just touched Jesus. But this touch was different. It was the kind of touch that only God feels, that is, a touch that was prompted by faith. It was a touch that made God stop and respond.

3) Jesus raised the dead—even called the dead to come out of the grave—and on more than one occasion, he talked of the dead as sleeping.

4) Jesus fed more than four thousand people and more than five thousand people with food enough for two or three people's lunch. Before Jesus fed the people, He told His disciples, who had noted that the crowd needed to be fed. The crowd had been with Jesus in the desert for some time and had

possibly eaten all they brought from home. To the logical human mind feeding more than a thousand people in the desert where there were no grocery stores was an impossible task. And even if food was available, the disciples did not have the means to pay for the amount of food required to feed everyone present. John's record notes that Jesus already had in mind what He was going to do. Of course not knowing what Jesus had in mind the apostles proved their humanity by asking the logical question or making logical statements such as "Where do we get enough food to feed all these people?" Or "Two months' wages will not be enough to buy food for all these people." These might be logical and reasonable questions for humans, but where God is involved, nothing is impossible and logic can take the backseat.

We read the records about Jesus feeding the multitude, which is an easier picture to construct in our minds: Be it five thousand or four thousand men plus women and children, we are talking about feeding about ten thousand or more people if we take into account that there probably more women and children than men. Is it easier for us to imagine what it was like trying to find a place close to Jesus to sit? Or trying to imagine how Jesus multiplied the five or seven loaves of bread with the fish to feed this large number of people? How do these acts of feeding the multitude by Jesus strike us or affect us? Do these acts of feeding make us see Jesus as one who can take care of our physical needs or as the One who can meet more that our physical needs? In John's account of one of these incidents, John 6:14-15, he recorded that the people said of Jesus, "This is indeed the Prophet who is to come into the world!" John also recorded that the people intended to make Jesus their king after they saw what He had done. Let us take a moment and read the following scriptures—Matthew 14:15-21, 15:32-38; Mark 6:35-44, 8:1-9; Luke 9:11-17; John 6:5-15—and see what happened. As we read these accounts, please let's pay attention to the following actions of Jesus: 1) He gave thanks and 2) He started breaking or kept giving the loaves to the disciples to set before the people. How many times can anyone break a few loaves of bread to feed more than a hundred people so that everyone is well fed and have some left over? What about feeding a thousand, two thousand, or more? The fact that there were leftovers indicates to me that the portions were enough to feed an adult male human being. The idea here is that the people present at the feeding of the multitude experienced what their predecessors experienced in the desert when God fed them with manna. The people had enough to eat in the presence of the Son of God.

The reaction of people who witnessed Jesus feeding them with the few loaves tells it all. They wanted to make Jesus king! Some wondered if Jesus was the Messiah. Let's take a look at the actions of Jesus that I just listed. Why did Jesus give thanks over the food? Was He giving thanks for the same reasons that we give thanks over our food? Paul said, "Every food was created by God to be received with thanks" (1 Timothy 4:3-5).

Was this why Jesus was giving thanks? None of the readings say that Jesus ate as the multitudes ate, so if we assume that He didn't eat with the crowd, then why is He giving thanks over the food? Was He asking the Father permission to multiply the food? I think He gave thanks over the food as an act of submission to His Father as He had done since He started His ministry.

To the second action of Jesus, I would like us to pay significant attention. For this act, most of the English translations capture the essence of the account as recorded in the Greek. The Greek words ἔδωκεν *(edoken)* in Matthew 14, and διέδωκεν *(diedoken),* in John 6, were used to indicate to us how Jesus multiplied the bread, but all the other records used the Greek word ἐδίδου *(edidou)* to tell us how Jesus fed the people using these few loaves and even fewer fish.

The first two Greek words ἔδωκεν and διέδωκεν are in the aorist tense in the Greek, which in English is the past tense. The aorist tense describes an action as a snapshot; the action is considered as a whole, without many details. The aorist tense also describes the beginning of an action or the conclusion of an action. The other word, ἐδίδου, is in the imperfect tense, translated in English present or future tenses. It describes a progressive sort of action—that is, a prolonged or ongoing action. Thus ἔδωκεν translates to "he gave," and διέδωκεν translates to "he distributed" or "he divided." Here the idea is that he distributed or divided hand to hand. Similarly, ἐδίδου is translated as "he kept giving." Let us abbreviate the technical discussion on the Greek so it does not become tedious or mind numbing. At the same time I hope this short discussion of the Greek will stimulate enough gray cells for the brain to generate a deeper understanding of what Jesus did when He fed the multitude.

When I envisioned the feeding of the multitude, I used to think that after Jesus gave thanks over the food, He multiplied it just like we saw in the story of Elijah and the widow or Elisha and the widow with the oil jars. With these two great prophets, Elijah's words caused the last dough of the widow to increase and it fed three people for three years, whereas it originally was good enough for only one meal for the widow and her son or maybe less. In the case of Elisha a widow of one of the prophets was in dire need. Her husband's creditors were threatening to enslave her sons. Based on Elisha's word the widow was able to multiply oil, which she sold to pay off the debtors. The only thing that stopped the oil from continuing to flow was the lack of jars. You see, it is easier for me to see a heap of food being passed out by the apostles to the crowd than it is to imagine what actually took place.

How do we think the people who were seated in front of Jesus saw the whole thing taking place? Why did the people react to Jesus the way they did according to John's account? I imagine the people did not see the basket fill up instantaneously with bread and fish. They only saw the boy handing over his food to Jesus, followed by the instructions for them to sit on the grass. With everyone seated, Jesus started breaking each loaf and each fish. They like us might have wondered how far the few loaves and fish would go. Then they witnessed that the first loaf in Jesus's hand was enough for five people, all of whom had about the same-size portion. Then ten people, or twenty, or fifty, or a hundred people received their portions and Jesus was perhaps still breaking off from the first loaf He took from the basket. Soon the number of people with bread in their hands had become too much for anyone to have an accurate count from where they were seated. Yet Jesus still had in His hands the first loaf of bread He had taken from the basket. He finally gave both halves to one of the twelve apostles to give to the people. Jesus took the second loaf and kept breaking it and giving it to the apostles to give to the people. Finally the last loaf was in Jesus's hand and He was doing the same thing. What is amazing about all of this is that the questions of how did not change. The people were probably still asking how He could continue to break the same loaf so many times that it was impossible to keep track. At last one of the astute observes asked, "Is this the king, the Messiah who was to come?"

With the bread in His hands Jesus expressed His will over the bread, choosing to break it as many times as He desired—just like He expressed His will over the raging winds, just like when His feet touched the waters and the bouncy water molecules stood still for Him to walk on them. In the hands of Jesus, the loaves could not behave as they would in any ordinary person's hands. Similarly, our lives in Jesus's hands become more than ordinary lives. In Jesus's hands, our lives take on an eternal tone. Thus as the people witnessed what Jesus had done, they desired Him for their king on their terms, not on God's terms, so Jesus rejected their advancement, preferring to spend time in prayer talking to His Father. Indeed the people had experienced no ordinary day!

Jesus in feeding the multitude with those few loaves did not exhibit fanfare. He did not do it for show-off reasons. He could have caused the food to multiply in the basket and heap up, but instead He broke a piece of bread at a time and gave it to the apostles to give to each individual in the crowd. He kept breaking a piece at a time until everyone was fed, and had some leftovers to be collected. Jesus not only was the source of the food as He broke the bread, but personalized each piece He broke, knowing exactly whom each piece of bread was going to feed.

Compare this with the temptation by Satan, when Satan implored Jesus to turn stones into bread. Jesus refused to focus on Himself. Instead His reaction to the temptation focused on God, His Father, and His desire to glorify the Father. Notice how everything Satan tried to get Jesus to do was focused on getting Jesus, the Christ, to gratify Himself. Also notice how Christ turned the focus right back to God. Jesus was about doing and fulfilling the Father's will in spite of the fact that He had the power to do as He pleased.

5. Solomon said in Ecclesiastes 8 that no man has the authority to restrain the wind, yet on more than one occasion, we read that Jesus told the wind to calm down and stop misbehaving, and the wind responded to his command and stopped. This was to the amazement of the witnesses who recorded the information. Those with Jesus worshipped him as a result of these signs or wonders.

6. When confronted by the enemy with challenges, as Jesus was confronted in Matthew 4 in presumably a weak moment, how do we react? Notice the restraints Jesus exercised during the temptation and during the demand for signs by the Jewish leaders, as well as on many other occasions where we would have expected Jesus to flash His powers. Also notice the complete trust Jesus had in the Father, especially when He was responding to Satan's temptations. Look at the restraint shown by Jesus during the temptation by Satan. Satan saw a vulnerable Jesus, the Son of God, after forty days without food and thought it was time to bring the house down? Shouldn't Jesus's restraint teach us something about the freedom we choose to exercise before God in doing His will?

    Jesus said, "If you love me you will obey my commandments." Question: How many of us have been able to keep all the commandments of Jesus perfectly? For example, how many of us have been able to keep the commandment to love one another like Jesus loves us? I know that I haven't. I also know that I keep trying but am still not perfect. The point is that none of us by our own accord can please God outside of faith. Faith is the vehicle by which we express our love for Christ and thus keep His commandments perfect or imperfect. Through faith we hang on to "every word that proceeds out of the mouth of God" (Matthew 4:4). Why, because God's word can sustain us and by it we will live!

Jesus with His life on earth demonstrated to us what God's expectations are. Jesus loved the Father and did what the Father had commanded Him or what He saw the Father do. In stating that if we love Him we will keep or obey His commandments, He maintained the same standard that He kept before the Father for us to keep. It helps to note that Jesus also said His commands are not burdensome.

Jesus Christ as He exercised both His power in various authoritative capacities restricted His liberties to what the Father had commanded Him. Certainly being the beloved Son, He could have done as He wished or pleased. Instead He showed an unequaled selflessness stimulated by an unequaled love for His Father and all humanity. Jesus was compelled by His love for His Father and for man, especially those who hear and respond accordingly to His gospel message of reconciliation to God because of His sacrifices on the cross. Jesus didn't have to tell the Father how good He was compared with, say, terrible Peter. Rather He prayed for Peter to be sustained when Satan sought to tear Peter down. He is currently serving as the intermediary on our behalf before the Father because of our insufficiencies. In 1

Corinthians 4:1-2, Paul establishes the fact that together with his fellow workers, they, the apostles, are ministers of Christ and stewards of the mysteries of God. I will say this holds true for all faithful men and women who carry the banner of Christ. He went on to say that it is required that a steward be found trustworthy or faithful. If we can learn anything from Christ restricting Himself to His Father's will, then being faithful to the Christ and His commandments should not be a matter of words and meaningless arguments but rather a matter of love for our master and the desire to keep His business moving forward.

Also, consider the baptism of Jesus: Why did Jesus respond to John the way He did in Matthew's account? Why did John consent to Jesus's explanation and not push further from baptizing Jesus, whom John had earlier mentioned as being mightier than he, John? Can we agree that John agreed with Jesus too quickly? Can we say that perhaps John understood what Jesus had just told him? I paraphrase here, "It is necessary that we, Jesus and John, fulfill all righteousness." In other words, Jesus said to John that it was necessary for the Father's will as it was written about by the prophets and other holy men to be fulfilled. In His strong desire to follow His Father's will and fulfill every word of His Father, Jesus saw it was necessary for even the things that we might see as insignificant to be fulfilled. Can we see why Jesus said that not even the minutest stroke or letter of the Father's word would go unfulfilled?

In Luke's record Jesus referred to John as Elijah based on Malachi's prophecy that John would come in the spirit of Elijah and restore the people to God. The prophecy continues that John will restore broken relationships between parents and their children. He will also pave the way for Jesus Christ. Also in Matthew's records we read that Jerusalem and all the districts around the Jordan were coming to John and being baptized by him. It was during one of these days that John saw Jesus coming to him to be baptized. If I were Jesus, I might have excluded myself from John's baptism, knowing that I was sinless and had a solid relationship with my Father above and no problems with my earthly parents. Yet Jesus, knowing the significance of John's ministry, set the example of submission to God's will. He availed Himself to be baptized by John, thus fulfilling another part of John's mission, which was to reveal the Messiah to the nation of Israel. And when John had difficulties with the situation, Jesus was ready with an answer to help him understand. Thus John yielded to God's will. I am not sure Jesus would have sinned if He had not come to be baptized by John, but what is clear was that God's will had to be accomplished. And Jesus, the example God sent to save us and teach us how to walk humbly before God, would not let fulfilling another will of the Father go astray. Why did God the Father affirm Jesus in the process? The Father was well pleased with Jesus's actions and proclaimed that in front of all the people. Indeed, it is only fitting that the One who expressed or manifested God's will during the Creation when God spoke the universe and everything in it into existence would not be willing for an iota or the smallest pen stroke of prophecy from the Father to be unfulfilled!

The Transfiguration

In Matthew's account of the gospel of Christ, in chapter 17, where Jesus was transfigured (changed in His physical form) a huge milestone was established. We read about the accounts and the events leading to the transfiguration in the fifteenth, sixteenth, and seventeenth chapters. After Jesus had just finished feeding four thousand men plus the women and children present, the Jewish leaders came to Him asking for a sign from heaven. It was as if what Jesus had just done had gone unnoticed. Even if a few days had passed, I would imagine that the people were still talking about what a marvelous act and sign that was. Feeding more than four thousand people with only seven loaves and a few fish! It is no wonder Jesus refused to respond to the demand for a sign. Right after this interaction Jesus asked His disciples who the public thought He was. Peter as usual jumped the gun and made a great confession that Jesus was the Christ, the Son of the living God, which Jesus confirmed. As if to further strengthen the confirmation to the confession Peter had just made, Jesus took Peter, James, and John to the top of a mountain, where He was transfigured before the three apostles. According to John's description of the incident, Jesus was changed into such a form that His garment was whiter than anyone has ever seen on earth.

As the three apostles looked on, they saw Elijah and Moses, two transforming figures in the history of Israel, appear with Jesus.

These two men appeared and started talking to Jesus. God gave the people of Israel the law through Moses, and Elijah was a prophet who restored Israel to God at a time when they had strayed from God. At this marvelous sight Peter again volunteered an opinion to build three tabernacles for Jesus, Moses, and Elijah. I am not sure I understand what Peter's intentions were here, but it does sound to me like Peter was no doubt amazed by the presence of Moses and Elijah joining Christ. I think Peter in his mind was probably equating the status of Jesus with Moses and Elijah, given that these two men in their lifetimes on earth were great prophets and did amazing things in Israel. Yes, God used Moses to bring the Israelites out of Egypt. No one can see God and live, so God allowed Moses to see His back and Moses ate in God's presence. He was no insignificant personality. Moses gave the laws that the Israelites lived by. Elijah was a man on fire for God! He prayed for there to be no rain for three years and God stopped the rain for three years. He prayed that God would send fire from heaven, and fire came down to consume a sacrifice drenched in several gallons of water dumped over it. He changed the hearts of the people and turned their hearts toward God. He was taken away to heaven at the sight of his apprentice Elisha. So with this brief history lesson we see that these men were very important personalities in the history of Israel. We know this partly because of the historical records and partly because of the prevailing opinions expressed about these men during Jesus's generation. In the light of these historical facts, it is easy to see why Peter's opinion about these two important men was extremely high. One can appreciate Peter's effort to place Jesus on the same pedestal.

However, God the Father had a totally different opinion about His Son, Jesus. God's Son was in a different class of His own. Paul said in the book of Hebrews that Jesus inherited a name that was much superior to any other. His name is that of the Father's. He is the Son of God. Thus as Peter was intending to make three tabernacles for the three present, God the Father stepped in and declared, "This is My beloved Son, in whom I am well pleased; listen to Him!"

When we look at this declaration, it is similar to all the other instances in the gospels when God the Father made such declarations. In this particular instance however, God the Father added "listen to Him." In all the other instances these three little words were not added. Yes, Jesus was different. He is the Son of God! Why did the Father choose to mention that we should listen to Christ His Son? Looking at this in light of Peter's actions I believe the impression God left on these apostles was one clear message, which was that Jesus is the one God desired for us to hear and obey. Moses did his job, Elijah did his, but Jesus's work was the zenith of all their work. They all pointed the way to Him. Additionally, the significance of leaving Jesus behind and taking Moses and Elijah away in the clouds is that the prevailing thought and traditions of the time where Moses's era continued and Elijah was adored. These prevailing thoughts and traditions were to be replaced with Jesus and His teachings. The law, the prophets, and the psalms pointed the way to Jesus. Before Jesus they were the established authority. They reflected, told, taught, and represented to the people what God's will was. God removed them all and sent Jesus to replace all of that!

There are many more actions of Jesus that we could point to show that He was not lacking in authority or power before His death. I can keep going on with example after example. What about how the people perceived Jesus? The scriptures say that the people noted that Jesus taught as one with authority and not like one of the regular rabbis. How about the centurion who came to Jesus to request healing for his servant? Certainly he understood authority. He showed that in his efforts to dissuade Jesus from entering his own home to heal the servant and cited his own authority and how that worked. He understood what authority is and what gets things done. He associated authority with Jesus. In fact, he respected Jesus's authority so much that he felt inadequate to have Jesus come under his roof. We can understand the centurion's behavior by looking at the Roman culture at the time. How about the bleeding woman? She also, I contend, understood that Jesus had the power to heal her. Jesus was not without power or authority before His death.

Jesus on several occasions restrained His disciples from revealing to the public who He was. This changed after he was resurrected from the dead. We see this when He charged the apostles to go and make disciples all over the world. The resurrection alone is a demonstration of power, for Jesus said he would lay His life down and pick it up and no one could take His life away from Him. This is exactly what happened with the resurrection. In the book of Ephesians, Paul says God demonstrated His great power by raising Jesus from the dead.

We see in all the examples listed above that Jesus exercised both power and authority before and after His death. Before His death even though Jesus had the power and could do as He wished, He chose to submit to the Father and to glorify God the Father in everything He did. Jesus said of His work, "For I have come down from heaven, not to do my own will but the will of him who sent me" (John 6:38). "Jesus said to them, 'My food is to do the will of him who sent me and to accomplish his work'" (John 4:34, ESV). This is important because Paul said in Philippians 2 that Jesus was equal to God but that He chose to empty Himself even to the point of death. So, in terms of authority and power before and after Jesus's death, did anything change? In John 13, John records that Jesus before He washed the feet of His apostles knew that it was time to depart to the Father and that the Father had given all things into His hands. This was before He was killed and resurrected from the dead. After His resurrection, according to Matthew's account in chapter 28, Jesus tells the apostles that (I paraphrase here) He has all authority in His possession. We have already noted that Jesus exercised unrestrained power at will though His focus was to fulfill the mission He was sent and glorify the one who sent Him. I will maintain that Jesus after His resurrection was as powerful as He was before His death. What changed was that whereas Jesus knew that everything had been put under His feet before His death, after His resurrection, He made it known that He had all authority in His possession. Knowing of something and having that something in one's possession are two different things. Also whereas Jesus demonstrated His power and authority as one sent before His death, after His death, He made it known that He had been put in charge and so what He said ruled the day. Hence the Hebrews writer puts it as follows: "[B]ut Christ is faithful over God's house as a son. And we are his house if indeed we hold fast our confidence and our boasting in our hope. Therefore, as the Holy Spirit says, 'Today, if you hear his voice, do not harden your hearts'" (Hebrews 3:6-8, ESV). Jesus is Lord and King; what He says is final.

Let us now look at the different sections of verse 18 of Matthew 28.

1) *Jesus was given the authority*—We might ask, Who gave all the authority to Jesus, or who had all the power and authority to give to Jesus after He was resurrected? During His ministry before He was crucified, Jesus exercised authority in different forms albeit as one who came to serve and save, not to be served and to judge. We list a few examples: He told the Pharisees He had the authority to forgive sin, though He did not tell them the source. He did miracles. He gave authority to His disciples to cast out unclean spirits. He taught the people not like any of the regular rabbis but rather as one with authority. He also told Pilate that he, Pilate, could have no power over Him if it were not given to him from above. Jesus did and said all of these as one sent by God. For even though Jesus was in the same form as God the Father, He humbled Himself and took on the form of a human, according to Paul in the book of Philippians. The Hebrews writer said He was made lower than the angels. Jesus said His work was based on the commandments He received from the Father. So Jesus clearly subjected Himself under the Father, who had all the authority.

Earlier on we established that God is the One who installs and dethrones kings and kingdoms. We have also established that God's power is not limited, though He limits Himself and functions within the authorities He sets up. Thus we have also established that God the maker of all authority has all authority. When Jesus said He had been given all authority, He did not say all power. We have seen that Jesus was not limited in the power He chose to exercise during His life on earth. However, He chose to work within the framework of His Father's will. So was the authority Jesus is said to have been given new? If so, then where might it have come from? There is no reason to believe that the authority Jesus was talking about was new, since nothing on the planet had changed. Even the New Covenant that Jesus ushered in through His blood that was shed on the cross was not new, I might say. In his letter to the Ephesians, Paul taught that God had planned for the New Covenant before the foundation of the universe. In other words, even though implementation of the New Covenant did not happen until Christ came to earth, God had set it up that He was going to save man through the gospel of Christ, and draw all who obey the gospel into the kingdom of His Son. Yes, sin has increased and we continue to devise ways to be even more sinful. God's plan to save man did not change, has not changed, and will not change. Christ ushered in the next phase of God's plan with the Great Commission, which is spreading the gospel. We might argue that things have changed drastically since Adam. That might be true, yet the basics have not. For example, the medium by which information is delivered might have changed, but people still have to hear, process, and understand to use the same or similar information just like Adam. My point here is that God set up how powers and authorities would work before we came into being. This might be a good reason why Solomon could say that there is nothing new under the sun. Additionally the laws governing the basic behavior of nature have not changed since Adam. God made them and they have been behaving the same way. For example, rain wets the soil and the sun dries it up. This little truth has been so since Adam.

Note what Paul says in the following scriptures:

Every person is to be in subjection to the governing authorities. For there is no authority except from God, and those which exist are established by God. (Romans 13:1) and

But each in his own order: Christ the first fruits, after that those who are Christ's at His coming, then comes the end, when He hands over the kingdom to the God and Father, when He has abolished all rule and all authority and power. For He must reign until He has put all His enemies under His feet. The last enemy that will be abolished is death. For He has put all things in subjection under His feet. But when He says, "All things are put in subjection," it is evident that He is excepted who put all things in subjection to Him. When all things are subjected to Him, then the Son Himself also will be subjected to the One who subjected all things to Him, so that God may be all in all. (1 Corinthians 15:23-28, NASU)

God the Father is the One who sets up and dismantles any form of authority.

Let's reflect on these passages and think about what Paul is saying. No authority can exist unless God puts it in place. Do we believe Jesus knew that? God established all the authorities we know of in the past, present, and future. Jesus submitted Himself to the will of the Father while He walked on the earth to the point of dying on the cross even though He was equal to God the Father. Can we imagine that Jesus would all of a sudden create a new set of authority different from that which the Father already set up without the Father knowing? I don't think so! Paul said in 1 Corinthians 15 that all things are subjected to Jesus's control by the only One who had such power. God the Father subjected everything under Jesus except for the Father Himself. That is, the Father is not under the rule of the Son. Thus if God the Father subjected everything under Jesus Christ, then He gave Jesus all the authority Jesus is talking about. This makes the kingship of Jesus, the Christ just like that of the Father's. The importance of this is that the will of Jesus is in agreement with the exact will of the Father. Therefore obeying what Jesus has commanded is obeying the Father's will. Additionally when Jesus said He was going to build His church, the Father was in agreement with Him. The Father had that planned already.

I am not sure we can completely answer the question of when God the Father gave all the authority to Jesus Christ. Certainly from Matthew's account we don't get any indication when this took place. Nor do we get this information from the other Gospel accounts except for John's account in John

13:3: "that the Father had given all things into his hands, and that he had come from God and was going back to God."

Though Jesus knew all things had been put under His feet, the passage does not mean that He had it in His hand before His death. After the resurrection, His statement meant He had the authority in His hands. As has already been noted, many times before His resurrection Jesus told His disciples not to reveal Him to the public. It certainly makes sense that after He had been honored and glorified by God the Father Jesus desired to make public the honor His Father had bestowed on Him. In Philippians 2:9-11, the apostle Paul said it best: "For this reason also, God highly exalted Him, and bestowed on Him the name which is above every name, so that at the name of Jesus every knee will bow, of those who are in heaven and on earth and under the earth, and that every tongue will confess that Jesus Christ is Lord, to the glory of God the Father."

In the first chapter of the book of Hebrews Paul paints a picture that looks to me like the coronation of the Christ as King, the King of Kings. Chapter 2 follows with a strong admonition to heed to Christ and not make light of the salvation that we have been given through Christ Jesus by ignoring it. Here is an outline of chapter 1:

God is speaking to us through His Son Jesus.
The Son is God's exact image. He holds the universe with the power of His word and sits at God's right hand after He purged our sins.

He has inherited an excellent name and is not one of the angels;
He is superior.

God declared Him as His Son and required the angels to worship
Him.
The Son is called God, He has a throne, and the scepter of
righteousness is the scepter of His kingdom.

He has been anointed by God with the oil of gladness.

He was there at the beginning of creation and will outlast the
creation once it has been eliminated and His enemies have been
condemned.

What Paul did here was put together the prophecies about the Christ to instruct us that the Christ did not put the kingship on Himself. The words foretold by the angels proved to be unchangeable, and God Himself bore witness by allowing signs, wonders, and miracles to be done. Christ would be illegitimate as a king if He had done this by Himself. He would have contrasted what Paul said in Romans 13:1 and had to anoint Himself king, which would have been inconsistent with how things were done. Thus as Samuel anointed Saul and David kings over Israel, so also Jesus had to be anointed king, and God did just that according to Hebrews 1. As no one is honored until his or her work is done, so also was Jesus honored once His work was completed.

2) *Jesus has all authority*—Today when we think about people
   with power, we think of the rich and famous, politicians,
   law enforcers, and the like. As powerful as these people
   might seem to us, their power is limited to the groups of
   people over whom they have influence or the law they
   govern by or enforce. For example the president of the
   United States is a very powerful man, yet his word cannot
   supersede the laws, in this case the US Constitution. He
   has to govern within the rights afforded to him by the US
   Constitution or face challenges in courts of law if he tries
   to rule beyond its limitations. On the other hand, rulers
   such as the pharaohs, King Nebuchadnezzar, the kings of
   the Medes and Persia, Alexander the Great, and the Roman
   Caesars were rulers whose words were law. For instance,
   if we study the interaction between Moses and Pharaoh,
   we realize quickly that Pharaoh's will or what Pharaoh
   desired was not up for negotiation. What he said was
   final, at least until Moses came along in the name of the
   Almighty. Take King Nebuchadnezzar as another example:
   when his wishes were not met, be it an interpretation of a
   dream or worshipping of idols he had set up, the sentence
   was death—and a swift one too. The point I'm trying to
   bring out here is that these rulers had what looked like
   total power that no one in his or her right mind would dare
   challenge. Those who dared to challenge them or who even
   smelled like a threat met their death swiftly. Jesus is more
   powerful than any of these kings and rulers, and it will
   serve us right to recognize that. Let us put His position in
   perspective when we approach to serve Him in any capacity

in His kingdom. It will help us to adopt His attitude of being humble, gentle, and lowly in heart when we come to walk with Him and just do as He commands. Jesus set a great example for us to follow by not doing only His will but focusing His efforts on doing the will of the Father who sent Him. If we have come into relationship with Him, it will serve us well to follow in His footsteps and do only what He has commanded.

Romans 13:1 as we saw above makes it clear that God establishes all rules that exist. This includes Jesus having all authority as well. Also when King Nebuchadnezzar had his first dream and was seeking its meaning, the dream and its interpretation were revealed to the prophet Daniel in a vision after he had prayed and asked God for help in interpreting it. As Daniel was praising God for making the king's dream known to him, he included the following statement: "It is He who changes the times and the epochs; He removes kings and establishes kings; He gives wisdom to wise men and knowledge to men of understanding" (Daniel 2:21). Nebuchadnezzar had these dreams after his kingdom had been established and was growing. The interpretation of the king's first dream affirmed that God has firmly established His kingdom. Also according to Daniel the interpretation of the king's dream revealed that God had shown to the king God's distant plans. In his first dream God revealed to the king a kingdom much superior to be established in the future. According to Daniel, God had revealed to the king a secret about a future king whose kingship and kingdom was going to be far superior to that of Nebuchadnezzar's or any that existed before or will exist after his. In this sense, King Nebuchadnezzar was one of the few privileged ones to whom God revealed what His plan for humanity was. To this effect King Nebuchadnezzar should have been mindful of God's graciousness and realized the purpose of his life. In the highest position on earth at the time, Nebuchadnezzar's destiny was to lead his people humbly before God and show them how to walk with God. Yet like most of us he failed to give God the glory or live up to God's expectations. King Nebuchadnezzar failed to walk humbly before God and became prideful and thought to himself that all his great accomplishments were solely because of his might. Jesus also knew why He came to earth, but unlike King Nebuchadnezzar He lived up to God's expectation and fulfilled His destiny, glorifying God throughout His life on earth. Jesus submitted to God like no other human ever had or ever would.

Nebuchadnezzar's dreams and their interpretations did not seem to have had much influence on him and how he ruled his kingdom. He continued to do whatever he wanted. He did not credit God for making him the great king he had become. In his second dream, the king hears the following sentence: "This sentence is by the decree of the angelic watchers and the decision is a command of the holy ones, in order that the living may know that the Most High is ruler over the realm of mankind, and bestows it on whom He wishes and sets over it the lowliest of men" (Daniel 4:17).

The interpretation of this dream troubled Daniel because he understood that the king was about to be disciplined by the one who gave him the kingship. This was unheard of. One might ask why. Well, for one thing Daniel had to inform the king what was going to happen to him, the king. But I also think that Daniel cared for the king's well-being and wished the king would do what was right before God. The king had not used his authority to glorify God. Instead the king thought of himself as the source of his own successes and had refused to acknowledge God role in making him into a great king. He did not recognize that God was the source of his power. Rather as he looked over his kingdom with pride from his rooftop, he said, "Is this not Babylon the great, which I myself have built as a royal residence by the might of my power and for the glory of my majesty?" (Daniel 4:30).

You see, King Nebuchadnezzar, in spite of all the wonders and blessings he had received and seen displayed in Daniel and his associates by God, never attributed his successes to God. He saw his successes as the results of his own efforts. So God, who has all power and is able to discipline even the most powerful king on earth at that time and any time, set out to humble the king. King Nebuchadnezzar was humbled by being made to behave like an animal for a period of time. He behaved as such until the designated time when the his punishment was completed. At the end of his sentence the king said,

I, Nebuchadnezzar, raised my eyes towards heaven and my reason returned to me, and I blessed the Most High and praised and honored Him who lives forever; For His dominion is an everlasting dominion, and His kingdom endures from generation to generation. All the inhabitants of the earth are accounted as nothing, but He does according to His will in the host of heaven and among the inhabitants of the earth; and no one can ward off His hand or say to Him, what have you done? (Daniel 4:34-35)

This is an incredible acknowledgment from King Nebuchadnezzar about the Almighty God. This great king finally recognized the God who made him king. He had come to appreciate the one source, the only power that could make or break him.

The only one who possessed such power and was capable of giving it to anyone has been established to be God, the Almighty One. He is therefore the only one who can give that sort of authority to Jesus Christ. All the authority in both heaven and on earth means just that! Jesus now is the King of Kings and rules not in the manner of any king the world has seen or witnessed in history or in our age. He rules just like His Father ruled while He serves as our mediator and pacifier for our sins, having Himself experienced humanity. Note also that earlier we saw that Jesus had power and could affect nature. However, in terms of authority, Jesus subjected His will to the Father's will.

At this juncture, it should be clear to us all why this part of the commission statement is of extreme importance. Jesus is saying here that He is the king in the manner of His Father who has had all the authority. Paul said in Colossians 2 that Jesus is the head of all rules and as King Nebuchadnezzar said, authority. God made Him so. Paul also said in 1 Corinthians that there would come a time when Jesus would hand over everything to the Father.

Although most of the famous kings in history had what looked like absolute authority, they could not control things like how the birds in the air went about their business. Jesus can alter anything He desires, including changing a murderer like Paul and affecting Paul's life permanently. This is the kind of kingship under which all Christians faithful and unfaithful alike are working, have worked for, and will continue to work for until He comes.

I asked earlier why this verse is important. Let me ask the same question in a different way: why is it important that Jesus inform the apostles at this time that He has all authority in heaven and on earth? First, just think about it for a minute: A kingdom cannot exist without its king. Only a king can establish a kingdom, and only a king can have absolute authority or a form of it. In other words Jesus is informing His disciples that He has been crowned King, the king God revealed to King Nebuchadnezzar. Naturally a king must have a kingdom, hence the rest of the commission. Second, as the apostles began to evangelize the world, if they were to be asked what their source of authority was, they could not point to God the Father like Jesus did, directly at least. But now with this new knowledge, they and anyone after them who followed their teachings would be able to point to Jesus as the source of their authority. In the book of Acts we see situations where the apostles or disciples were challenged by the Jewish leaders. As one might expect, the disciples pointed to Jesus as their source. Another point of significance that needs to be observed here is that the type of authority that Jesus is talking about is the authority that only God the Father had. It includes reigning over every realm that is. This makes the kingdom of God superior to any other kingdoms, be it in the past, present, or future. God's kingdom is superior, because the king is superior and it is the king who builds the kingdom. Finally, in John 16 Jesus informed the disciples that the Holy Spirit, the Comforter He will send to remind the apostles of everything He has taught them, will not do anything by His own authority. That is, the Holy Spirit will do nothing by His own initiative. Instead He will take from what is the King's and give to the King's people, the apostles in this case. Does this tell us anything about how the Godhead submits to one another? How about the way we submit to God and use the freedom we have been granted? Do we care about finding and staying within the bounds of the authority of the King rather than pushing the limits to please ourselves or others? Knowing who the King is and what His commands are sets the standards, and following them and refusing to deviate from them makes us faithful servants and stewards.

Before His death, Jesus knew it was time to depart to the Father and that the Father had given all things into His hands. He also said that "My Father is greater than I," a clear sign of submission to the Father. Paul in 1 Corinthians 15 said that God is the one who put everything under Christ and that God the Father is not under Christ. In putting all things under Christ, God also made Christ the first in all things and all dominions. This makes Jesus a very powerful king and doubtless one with all authority as He said Himself in this section of the Great Commission. Yet as we look at Jesus giving the Great Commission we might ask, Since Jesus died for the whole world and His sacrifice was to save all of mankind, why did He give the Great Commission? Couldn't He have just issued a blanket pardon that says everyone is saved? I imagine He could have, but God sets up authorities for a purpose. I imagine also that the purpose is to show that God is true to who He is and that He will be impartial and show no preferences. In fact these concepts of power, authority, and law as discussed here are all part of God's structure for keeping all of His creations in proper order so that there is an orderly fashion to how life is lived. For example, water flows downhill and on and on. Besides, the idea of a blanket pardon makes the sacrifice unimportant. If He were going to issue a blanket pardon, why give man the ability to make choices? If one cannot make choices, then one cannot be blamed. We sin because we have the capacity to sin; without choice that capacity will not be there. But as Paul discusses in Roman 7, we have the capacity to choose to serve God and do His will or to yield to the other law, which is in the flesh and is constantly at war with our desire to please God. That is, instead of doing good we find ourselves doing wrong. We are constantly torn between doing good and bad, or between pleasing God and pleasing ourselves and sin.

Thus like everything else in life, we have to make a choice. We have to make a choice to respond to the gospel, which has the power to save those who believe it, Romans 1:16, or choose not to respond favorably to the message of salvation. The fact is that through His gospel, Christ has given authority to His disciples to go and save the world. Those who hear and believe are saved by the power of the gospel. In other words, God has placed the power to redeem mankind from our sins and reconcile us to Himself in the gospel of Christ. And that is the word of God! So the power to save is not in the hands of the people sent to deliver the good news. Yes, they matter, but they cannot use the power to save as a tool to discriminate. Rather, anyone who hears the gospel and believes the message is saved. By the same token, it is not in the hands of another man to declare when a sinner has become good enough to be saved; rather, as Paul says in Romans 10, one has to hear the good news and believe it after he or she has been told about it. The decision to submit to the gospel and be saved is the sinner's and his or hers alone. That is, it is each individual's responsibility to decide to submit to the gospel and be saved or refuse to do so.

We might also observe that to exercise power one must possess that power. So for example, when God created the universe, He exercised His power at will. He called into existence at will whatever He wanted to come into existence. Also when Jesus broke the bread to feed the multitude, it is curious to me that He broke all the loaves that were presented to Him. He could have used just one loaf. Think about it for a minute: If Jesus broke one loaf to feed a hundred, couldn't He have fed a thousand with the same loaf? How about feeding the four or five thousand-plus with just one loaf? I contend He could have done whatever He willed with one loaf just as He did with the five or seven loaves! Jesus had the power to extend the feeding power of the loaves as He saw fit. As set up by God, though, authority requires more than one entity—that is, an entity that discharges or implements the power behind the authority, such as a person in position of authority who enforces the power of that authority, and the one who responds to the requirements and receives the effects and protections within the authority. The power to save is in the gospel, and Jesus enforces that saving power. All humanity is required to respond to the gospel and benefit from the saving protections of the gospel. We can choose to respond to or reject the gospel as preached by the apostles.

For example, the law says not to speed. If I go 40 mph in a 25-mph zone, the police officer in his or her position of authority who spotted me breaking the law might cite me and give me a ticket to enforce the law. On the other hand, if I do what the law demands and drive according to the speed limit, I can enjoy my drive without fear of the police car at the corner. Similarly, the authority over sin is held by the Devil, who has the power to enforce death. The wages of sin is death, according to Paul in Romans 3:23 and 26. Thus when we travel the way of sin, we encounter nothing but death since sin separates us from God. God's desire and will is for us not to sin. He told Cain to rule over sin, but Cain, like all of us, failed. Right from the garden we saw that God laid down the law that breaking His commandments meant death, and thus it was. Behind any authority are usually the principles or law(s) that ensure a uniform discharge of powers granted by the law to the person in the position of authority. Similarly, the authority in the Great Commission enables the disciples of Christ to save souls when they preach or teach the gospel message to all nations. The hearers of the gospel message may respond as the people did in Jerusalem by asking, "What shall we do?" which is believing and taking positive action based on that belief. Or they may scorn the message like we see on many occasions in the book of Acts. By believing, we choose to let God's will apply to our lives and the power of His forgiveness and reconciliation to reach us. Mark's account of the Great Commission says, "Whoever believes and is baptized will be saved, but whoever does not believe will be condemned" (Mark 16:17, ESV). Paul further says, "Now I would remind you, brothers, of the gospel I preached to you, which you received, in which you stand, and by which you are being saved, if you hold fast to the word I preached to you—unless you believed in vain" (1 Corinthians 15:1, ESV).

We note here that Jesus has all authority, including the authority of the Great Commission. Also, before Jesus, the law of Moses, the prophets, and the psalms were the primary sources of authority that informed the people of God about God's will. As Jesus has all authority, He becomes the primary source behind the New Testament and the sole authority when it comes to matters of God and man. No other authorities, including the law of Moses, the prophets, and the psalms matter anymore. Jesus is it! The previous sources are now sources for education, reference, and instructions, according to Paul in Romans 15. Their role is not the same as they were in the time of Jesus or before that.

3) *Territories or jurisdictions covered under this authority are heaven and earth*—Jesus said he has been given all the authority in heaven and on earth. One would say that very well covers the territory or domain of the King. We know from history that kings conquered lands and territories to expand their domains. Having all the authority arrayed in heaven and on earth leaves no other territory for conquest. Since heaven and earth are already under His control, what really is left for Christ to conquer? The territory for conquest then is not for land or domain but for the minds and hearts of all mankind in all nations for God, not with swords, or military armory or trickery leading to pain and destruction but with the gospel of Christ. We conquer the hearts of all people in all nations with the good news that Jesus died for the sins of all mankind. Each gentle word of the gospel teaches people of the Savior's death, burial,

and resurrection, offering God's hand of forgiveness and reconciliation and gently tugging the heartstrings of the sinner and the yielding soul, bidding the sinner to yield, yield to the call. It bids to the sinner to yield and enter the grace and riches of the all-loving Father's call. The Savior has triumphed over death, and as a result of that sacrifice God is forgiving the sins of all mankind and reconciling anyone who obeys the gospel to Himself.

Jesus had trained some twelve common men for three years—not especially talented men or upper-class people in the community, or outstanding citizens, just common folks, whose professional descriptions include fishing, tax collecting, and thievery. These were the men entrusted with the task of laying down the foundation or first principles for establishing the kingdom of God. Their tasks for laying the foundation for starting and building the kingdom were simple, really. They would lay the foundation by preaching the gospel and teaching everything Jesus had commanded with the help of the Holy Spirit. Let's pay attention to what Jesus told the apostles after He had instituted the Lord's Supper in both Luke and Matthew's accounts.

Luke 22:28-29:
"You are those who have stood by me in my trials. And I confer on you a kingdom, just as my Father conferred one on me" (NIV).
"You are those who have stood by Me in My trials; and just as My Father has granted Me a kingdom, I grant you" (NASU).

*"But ye are they that have continued with me in my temptations;
and I appoint unto you a kingdom, even as my Father appointed
unto me" (ASV).*

Matthew 26:29:
*"I tell you, I will not drink of this fruit of the vine from now on until
that day when I drink it anew with you in my Father's kingdom"
(NIV).*

Are these two passages in agreement or do they contradict each other? Jesus according to His birth, name, and prophecy was the anointed one. He was the Messiah, the Christ, which means the Anointed One. David was anointed king of Israel by Samuel when Saul was still alive. The scriptures do not give us time lines about how far along Saul was in His reign as king of Israel, nor do the scriptures tell us how old David was when he entered into service as a military member in Saul's army or as Saul's personal servant. However, a simple figuring will tell us that David had to wait anywhere from ten to fifteen years, perhaps more, before he was installed as the king of Israel. Thus for that length of time, David like Saul was God's anointed person to rule Israel, but he was in a waiting position. When he became Saul's enemy, David refused to kill Saul when he had the chance. David's reason was that Saul was God's anointed. Hence David patiently waited his turn until Saul passed away in war and he was installed as the king of God's people. In a similar manner, Jesus Christ, though he was born as God's anointed to rule over God's people, for a time walked on earth doing His

Father's will and submitting to the Father. Thus Luke's passage makes sense that God had conferred, or granted, or appointed unto Him His Father's kingdom. In other words, God the Father has appointed God the Son king over the Father's kingdom. Jesus conferred, or appointed, or granted the apostles as testators of the same kingdom His Father had conferred on Him.

Thus Paul said to the Colossians, "giving thanks to the Father who has qualified us to share in the inheritance of the saints in Light. For He rescued us from the domain of darkness, and transferred us to the kingdom of His beloved Son. In whom we have redemption, the forgiveness of sins" (Colossians 1:12-14, NASU).

Although David had to wait to assume kingship of Israel after Saul's death, Jesus had to wait to complete His mission on earth to assume the throne of His Father. This is the spiritual kingdom of God. God is forgiving sins because of the sacrifice of Christ on the cross and rescuing those who accept the message of forgiveness and leave behind their lives of sin to be transferred into this kingdom, the kingdom of His Beloved Son.

To sum up, we note that God the Father has all the power over all realms that exist. He is the only one who establishes and removes kings. "For there is no authority except from God, and those which exist are established by God" (Romans 13:1). God the Father is the only one who could give all authority to Christ, and He gave Christ all the authority in heaven and on earth. This makes the kingship of Jesus Christ superior to any other kingship that has ever existed. In fact the kingship of Christ is like that of the Father. My question is, if we are subjects to such a king, will we treat His commands as trivia or will we live under His command as if our lives depended on them? This section of the Great Commission is important for a couple of reasons: 1) Christ is the all-powerful king—in fact the only king there is to serve. We serve under His banner, and in His name we advance His course. 2) Because of His superiority in kingship everything is subjected to Him, and His will must be accomplished and obeyed. The interesting thing to keep in mind here is that we cannot live in the King's courtyard and do what we want. In order to continue to enjoy the King's favor and be under His grace, we must continually seek to please Him; otherwise we fall out of His favor.

Everything we do as Christians should have Christ as the source of authority. He is the King, the Savior, the Son of God, the One who knows how to please the Father. As we end this part of the Great Commission and move on to the next phase in the discussion, let us keep the following question in mind: By what authority do we Christians do what we do? Or by what authority do we teach certain doctrines, or engage in certain actions, or encourage a certain lifestyle? In other words, let's ask the question, Is that scriptural? Let us also keep the following perspective: if the Holy Spirit who is part of the Godhead could not do anything out of His own initiative when revealing and reminding the apostles in matters relating to Christianity, how is it possible for any man to add to or subtract from what the Holy Spirit revealed to the apostles? This is not being legalistic or lacking compassion or whatnot. It is a good commonsense question, because Christianity is about eternal salvation of people, all people whom God loves and in whom He has invested His only son for our salvation. It is not about feelings, and it should never be about us being better than any other. It is about saving souls and doing the will of the almighty king, King Jesus. Christianity is about one who gave His life so others might live. It is about pleasing God and submitting fully to His will, and to the will of the King He has installed to ensure that sin never again comes between God and His children. Just think about it: Say the president gives an order to some generals and the generals faithfully carry it out. But sometime later, a lieutenant comes along and changes the order for whatever reason. As fellow soldiers when that order reaches us, will we not ask who ordered this? Will we not ask the lieutenant, By what authority are you doing this? How much more it matters when it determines where one will end up in eternity. It is a great question to ask: by what scriptural authority are we teaching or doing this? As Christians we should not only ask this question in every aspect of our lives, but ask questions such as these with the attitude of servants, or bond servants whose only objectives are to know our master's will in order to please the master. Let us demand scriptural sources from the New Testament.

PART 2

Matthew 28:19-20

Their Charge, Our Charge

A: Make Disciples—Matthew 28:19

The next statement in the commission is the one we dwell on most when we talk about the Great Commission. We dwell on it because it is what we are about as Christians. Yet failing to see the immense value of the first part leaves out an essential part of the Great Commission. It leaves us lacking in education about the authority that empowers us.

The following is the New American Standard Bible (NASB) translation: "Go therefore and make disciples of all the nations, baptizing them in the name of the Father, and the Son and the Holy Spirit" (Matthew 28:19).

Here is the literal translation of the Greek: "Going therefore you make disciples of all the nations baptizing them into the name of the Father, and of the Son, and of the Holy Spirit."

Let's break this passage into two parts and examine each part separately. We'll use the literal translation for our analysis. Before we proceed, it is worth noting a few things about the Greek tense aorist, the tense for the word translated as "go" in the NASB, for example. The aorist tense is used in the sense of taking a snapshot of an event or action as a whole—that is, the entire action (not much about the detail is considered), the beginning of an action, or the conclusion of an action. So for example an aorist tense will place emphasis on an event or action as a whole, or at the beginning or the end of the event or action.

A. "Going therefore you make disciples of all the nations."

Is there really a difference between the literal translation "going therefore you make disciples" and saying the translation "Go therefore and make disciples" as rendered in the NASB, for example? Two things need to be pointed out here. First, the tense of the term translated as "go" or "going" is the aorist tense. Either translation might emphasize the beginning or the end of the event or action, or even the entire action. The participial nature of the Greek term thus makes "going" a better translation than "go." Second, the voice is passive, so "go" in the English sounds more active than the passive voice used in the Greek. The translation "going" is much more passive. Given these two notes, translating the term as "go" places the force of the command on "go" rather than "make disciples" or "you make disciples," which is also in the aorist tense but in the active voice and in the imperative mood; thus "make disciple" carries the force of the command. Additionally, the Greek term translated as "go" has the sense of moving from place to place. Thus, as we go about our daily lives, we take hold of the opportunities that come our ways and reach out to the world that does not know our King. We do so with the King's message of forgiveness, repentance, and reconciliation, the gospel, to change people and win minds and hearts for the King.

The Greek term translated to "make disciples" is where the force of the command is. As mentioned earlier, this term is in the aorist tense and also in the imperative mood. Given the nature of the aorist tense, then, can we say that making disciples is something we begin without continuing, in which case we have a clear start and finish point whereby discipleship begins and stops? Or is it something we engage in until a soul is won for Christ and we continue teaching him or her until they mature in Christ and become perfected in Christ? Or is it something that the Christian does throughout out his or her life while on earth? I believe it's what we live for. The imperative mood is used to express one's wishes or commands. Thus Jesus was commanding the disciples to go make disciples, and He retained them by teaching them everything He had commanded, as we will see later in this discussion. This is what kingdom business is all about: making disciples and training them to advance the King's will or wishes with His message. Does this sound like what our churches or congregations are doing? Services to the general community are great and noble, but if we are not using these opportunities to capture the hearts and minds of the people for Christ, the church potentially fails in its primary reason for existing.

The nature of the commission requires us to go, for we could not possibly reach all nations if the apostles had only sat in Jerusalem, or in our case today if we stay in our pews. Although we have to go in order to make disciples, I think Jesus placed the emphasis on making disciples because 1) He died so that the sins of mankind would be erased or forgiven; and 2) people need to understand that God is forgiving sins and resetting our relationship with Him through Jesus and that those who accept the message about Jesus become kingdom subjects with no debt, except to love one another. Thus we see in Acts 2 that Peter, after the initial presentation of Christ to the people, persuaded them with many other arguments, encouraging them to "save themselves from this corrupt generation." We also see in Philip's encounter with the Ethiopian eunuch in Acts 8 that Philip explained to the eunuch that Jesus was the one he was reading about in Isaiah's prophecy. Many other such examples are presented in the book of Acts, and the kingdom's inhabitants have to be trained to know and follow the King's command, or they need to know how to please the King. That is, the hearts and minds of mankind have to be trained to lean favorably toward God.

In the book of 1 Samuel, we read the story about God's order to Saul to destroy the Amalekites. Saul was rebuked for disobeying God's order after he brought to Israel the king of the Amalekites, even though in Saul's mind he had accomplished the task by destroying everyone and everything except the king, along with a few animals the men had saved for themselves. What Saul failed to recognize was that by saving the king's life the kingdom was still alive; it had not been destroyed entirely. In sending the disciples, the message is about the King. The excitement is about the King's conquest of death: He died and now He lives. The intrigue is about God forgiving the sins of mankind, giving us a clean slate, because of the sacrifice of

Christ, the King. Use the news about the King to win the hearts and minds of people everywhere. The King is alive and so the kingdom lives. We could summarize the task here as educating people and winning their hearts and minds for Christ.

Emphasis on go *versus* make disciples

We have observed that the Greek grammatical structure of Matthew's record puts the emphasis on *make disciples* instead of *go*. We have also noted that we cannot make disciples unless we go. With these in mind, we note that *go* has brevity to it. That is, when we go, we are bound to come back with a sense of 'the job is done'. On the other hand, when we make disciples, as I believe the Great Commission asks us to do in the Greek, we make a sustained effort to nurture and develop the people who have become disciples of Christ through the teachings of Christ. Although sometimes we need to join campaigns to share the gospel on a short-term basis, I believe that our efforts to make disciples should always have a long-term plan of nurturing and developing. Too often we are eager to go and come back with reports of how successful we were in converting lots of souls. On subsequent visits to the same locations, we often see that the people we baptized into Christ have either fallen away or are not faithful to Christ. Personally, I believe new Christians often are not familiar with their new life. They don't know how to respond to situations, temptations, and trials that Satan throws their way. After fruitlessly trying to overcome those challenges they give up and are not able to continue. I can cite the times that I struggled with my own faith as a teenager studying the sciences, specifically biology and physics. Most science textbooks contain enough subliminal messages and challenges to topple any young Christian's faith. I was at a point where my faith was being challenged and greatly tested with issues such as instruction in evolution. I was also noticing how my peers were living socially and enjoying themselves while I was being taught not to live like them. As a teenager and a young Christian what worked for me were the relationships and the close friends and a familiar preacher who addressed my concerns.

When there is sustained effort and continuity in relationship and fellowship between the disciple maker and the souls won for Christ, the disciple makers or the old and faithful Christians become the loving hands and neck of Jesus by which the new disciples are tuned and yoked through proper instructions and examples of how to live the new life. That is, Christ the master tuner reaches the new disciple through the faithful Christian to patiently but firmly transform the new Christian into a vessel that God can use to glorify His name. Jesus spent three years teaching and showing the apostles how to live to please God. In our efforts to make disciples, we need to go to all people and present them with the gospel. That is where we start. We also need to continue to stay in contact after the soul has been won for Christ. This I believe exemplifies the spirit of making disciples. The gospel reached me through Bible correspondence. One thing I remember about my teacher, Mary Moudy, was that she corresponded with me, and still does. In my teen years she inquired about my family and asked how they were doing. Her kindness affected and encouraged me in many ways. I remember thinking in those years how I would like to meet her, if not on earth, then in heaven for sure, so I could let her know how grateful I was for her concern and how that kept me going.

We cannot possibly end this segment without studying and understanding what it means to be a disciple. Here are some of the questions I seek to address in the effort to understand our role as disciples of Christ. Who is a disciple? What does God expect of me as a disciple of Christ? Whose disciple am I, and what is my identity as a disciple of Christ? What is the purpose for a disciple to learn and follow the teachings or instructions of the teacher or in our case the King, Christ Jesus? What about discipline and the disciple, discipline to retain the message of the king or teacher, discipline in lifestyle, and so forth and so on? Does our discipleship ever end, and if so, when? Let's try to address some of these questions if not all of them.

Who is a disciple?

Introduction

Μαθητής is the Greek word translated as "disciple." The same word is translated as "a person in training, a learner." A good disciple is one who practices what has been learned—an apprentice, in a sense. I imagine that when the apostles heard the words from Jesus that they should go make disciples of all nations, they understood exactly what He meant to a point. I can only infer that from the way the apostles and most of the Jewish Christians behaved, they did not understand for example that when Jesus said "all nations," He meant Gentiles as well, that is, both Jewish and non-Jewish people. Just look at how Peter had to be persuaded to go minister to the Gentile Cornelius, and then look at how the church in Jerusalem confronted Peter when he came back to Jerusalem after ministering to him. Furthermore, after several years the Jewish Christians could not get in their heads that God through Jesus brought both Jews and Gentiles together as one in Christ. Some of the Jewish Christians wanted the Gentiles to become Jewish via circumcision. Paul had to confront those teaching circumcision. We can point to many actions of these early Jewish Christians that demonstrate to us that they did not understand what God was doing. What we have here is a perfect God who desires to work with imperfect humans to accomplish His perfect purposes. God is able to use us because He is able to smooth out our imperfections. This is why as moldable objects in God's hand we need to be malleable so He can mold us to His will. Being malleable means shedding our ideals, our preconceived notions, our cultural influences, and our personal expectations, yielding all that to God and submitting our will to God's will. That is, we need to come to the understanding that Christianity is a new culture or works that God has prepared for us to walk and live in. This we do by faith. The fact is, God's will is going to get done. We can either yield and be shaped nicely, or be broken because we are too rigid or be abandoned completely because we refuse to yield. Remember John the Baptizer told the people, "God can raise these stones to be children of Abraham" to do God's will. As my professor observes, what are today's Christians missing because we are stuck in certain mind-sets and ways and therefore failing to see God's purpose demonstrated in our lives and in the church?

The fact is these apostles had been with Jesus for three years. They had seen Him live, teach, heal, and interact with their communities. They had watched Him deal with religious leaders, sinners, Samaritans, and all kinds of people. They had seen how Jesus treated many different people with compassion, care, love, firmness, and mercy.

Since we, today's Christians, don't have the same experiences as the apostles and some of the first-century Christians, we have to learn all about Christ through what has been recorded by eyewitnesses and historians about what He taught, how He behaved, and how He interacted with His generation while He was on earth. These will help us know who Jesus was on earth, what He taught, and what He stood for so we can live as the first generation of the disciples of Christ did.

A disciple is not one who does things according to his or her own will; that is, a disciple does not dictate how things ought to be. Rather a disciple follows instructions and commands, usually from an instructor or a master. In our case as Christians, our master, who is Christ, appointed and trained the apostles to teach the newly made disciple all that He has commanded, and the new disciples are to observe everything that Jesus had commanded. For the most part, a newly made disciple of Christ knows very little or nothing at all about Christ. Paul described the new disciple as one who did not know God in the book of Ephesians. As we come to Christ, we need to be trained in the teachings and ways of Jesus Christ, to which end as new disciples we follow, obey, preserve, keep in custody, or keep strictly these teachings.

In my preteen years, I spent a lot of time in a carpentry shop. I was not one of the apprentices. I was there just as a friend of the carpenters. Often I would be given chores such as running errands for the shop owner and some of the senior apprentices. Occasionally when the boss was not around, the apprentices allowed me to work on some of their assignments. What I observed over time was that when instructions and directives were dished out to the apprentices, I was never included. The apprentices had to follow their instructions carefully to get their tasks done. If they did anything other than closely follow their instructions, they always ended up in trouble, and the product of their work always failed to meet requirements. I observed this on many occasions. When that happened, the apprentice responsible was given more time to learn from a more senior apprentice or an apprentice who had done his task successfully.

Three points here: First, as one who was not an apprentice, even though I showed up often at the workshop, I did not receive any instructions on how to become a carpenter. They were not concerned with whether I learned the trade or not. Their only interest in my presence at the shop was how easy it was to use me to meet their needs such as going to buy nails for them and such. The second point is that they made every effort to spark the interest of the new apprentices in order to train them to become capable carpenters. The apprentices who focused on the training and were able to listen carefully usually did the best job and progressed through the training quickly. They got more responsibilities and over time were made to work independently with very little or no supervision. Oftentimes, the apprentices who paid the closest attention and followed instructions closely produced work just like the master carpenter. The other thing that I observed was how the apprentices learned their jobs. Some listened well and followed their given instructions well. Some learned by example, by watching skilled workers perform. On a daily basis, all of the apprentices perfected their skill acquisition by performing the tasks they had been assigned.

In the first paragraph of this section I mentioned that a disciple is an apprentice in a sense. Associated with an apprentice is the idea that the apprentice will eventually become an expert or a master of the trade in the future. I am not sure that Christ expects us to become experts or masters, for there is only one master, Christ Himself. Rather, I think Christ expects us to become matured or perfect, as His Father is perfect, by following His teachings and the doctrines of the apostles whom He entrusted with laying the foundation for His kingdom closely when we become disciples. An important observation is that an apprentice is trained to acquire critical skills for a specific trade, but as disciples of Christ, we are being trained to become like Christ. The final "product" of our discipleship looks like the Son of God. Now, I don't think anyone can specialize on their own. Christ transforms us into a final product in His likeness by which we benefit, because we become pleasing to God the Father, and the fragrance or effect of our transformation affects the world. Our call to discipleship is not to acquire skills for a trade; it is to live, breathe, walk, think, talk, and in everything become like the master who has called us to walk in Him and do as His will dictates to us. Hence in everything we aim to glorify His Father as He did. We do this by subjecting ourselves to Christ and His authority only. This is why I said "an apprentice in a sense." As we have come to Christ to learn of Him and from Him, we cannot be passive to Christ and His cause. We need to be active listeners and doers, putting in practice everything we learn from Christ. We need to learn Christ well so we can live for Him and be able to pass Him on to the next generation of Christians so they also can learn to submit to Christ and be molded to look like Christ.

What is my identity as a disciple of Christ?

> *"[A]nd the disciples were first called Christians in Antioch" (Acts 11:26, NASU).*

I have often wondered what the disciples in Antioch did in their community that led to them being called Christians. Apart from the Acts 11:26 record being the first historical record of the disciples being called Christians, it is clear that their community saw something in the disciples in Antioch that related them to Christ. According to Luke's record there was a strong evangelism effort going on, led by two different disciple groups in the city. This strongly suggests to me that the disciples in Antioch had a strong identity perhaps in their lifestyles and certainly by the proclamation of the gospel in the city that was easily recognizable as Christ like by the non-Christian community. As disciples of Christ, the way we behave within our communities can go a long way toward advancing or hindering the cause of Christ. The way we behave can set us apart within our communities in a good light, like in Antioch, or in a negative way that in turn hampers our ability to make disciples.

What does it mean to us to be a disciple of Christ? I mentioned earlier that the final product of our discipleship is to be like Christ, so that when God looks at us, He sees the exact image or a copy of His only Son. The discipleship to which we have been called is not one of acquisition of knowledge and skill. These are only accessories; they are gifts to be used to train God's people and bring the Lord's church to maturity. I don't think that Christ is interested in how skillful a disciple becomes; rather, from the parable of the talents we see that Christ is more interested in what was accomplished, or better yet what was done with the skill or skills. Can any of us teach as authoritatively as Christ? Can any of us be more humble than Christ? Can any of us be more loving, merciful, or caring than the master Himself? If we could atone for our sins or pay for it, Christ and the cross would be nonessential, wouldn't they? However, we can't, so when we subject our will to become disciples of Christ, we need to yield all of our will and submit to God and be trained according to the will of the master, Christ Jesus.

The training we undergo is one that should transform us. When we yield our will to Christ, we accept His terms without negotiations. Look over the following passages: 2 Corinthians 5:17, 1 Corinthians 11:1, Ephesians 4:17-24, Matthew 11:28-30, Luke 9:23, John 15:5, and 1 Peter 3:21. These are just a few scriptures where Christ clearly says through His apostles what He requires of His disciples. I will summarize these passages here, however; it will be good to take a break and look over these passages before going on. As new creations in Christ Jesus we are to shed the old body and put on the new self created by God in righteousness and holiness in the truth. Let us imitate Paul as He imitated Christ. As new disciples, we are invited by Christ to share His yoke, which is light and easy. Also let us deny ourselves and grab hold of our cross and follow Christ daily. And let us sip the sustaining juice from the vine in which we have been implanted, all the while yielding our will to God while developing our conscience in a favorable manner toward God.

Paul used the words *old self* and *new self* to inform us of the transformed state the new disciple comes into as a result of becoming a disciple of Christ. It requires renewing our way of thinking and behaving. Our thinking and behavior as new disciples always favor God; that is, in all we do, our goal and perpetual thought and concern centers on glorifying God. Like Christ, we actively seek to please God and desire that He look on us favorably. A while back, I was reading a book on ancient Hebrew alphabets and how we got to the alphabets we have now. As the reading progressed, I came across a story about how a young ox gets trained on the yoke. The young ox is yoked with an older, stronger, more experienced ox that dictates their movements and work. As I read that story, Jesus's invitation to share His yoke crossed my mind. I had a new appreciation for that invitation. As one who knows how to please the Father, Jesus is inviting us to submit to His authority so He can bend us toward the Father and teach us how to please Him. When we share in His yoke, Jesus is able to lead us into all things that are well pleasing to the Father. To put it another way, as implanted branches, we rely heavily on the main vine, which is Christ Jesus, to survive. If we fail to nourish properly, we wither and cannot bear fruit. When we come to Christ Jesus ready to surrender our will, convictions, judgments and feelings, we come prepared to be yoked with the Master who is able to train us and conquer our affinity to please the world and ourselves. Jesus calls us to be like Him by yoking up with Him, and to be changed from sinners to righteous and holy people. Now that, my friends, is not a mere transition from one state to another; it is a radical transformation from one state—a sinful and sorry state, where we are enemies of God—to a state where we are declared righteous, holy, sanctified, justified, and reconciled to God. The only way that is achieved is if we submit to God's will and follow His instructions as faithful disciples, so He does all the molding.

Labels that are not of Christ

Jesus said we cannot plant a good tree and expect it to bear bad fruit; neither can we plant a bad tree and expect it to bear good fruit. My question then is, If we are branches on the vine, why are there conservative disciples or Christians and liberal disciples or Christians? Why the divide? Is Christ feeding us the same food and yet we are bearing different fruits? I can't imagine that the juice we are sipping on in Christ Jesus is feeding some disciples a liberal diet and others a conservative diet or whatnot. Why are we labeling and dividing ourselves as liberals, conservatives, and whatever else we choose to identify ourselves with when the one who bought us with His blood has not so labeled us? The only thing these labels do is promote division among the disciples and provide a foothold for Satan to further his work against God's people. Those of us who seek to distinguish ourselves with these labels often hold views that promote our self-interests, not the interests of Christ and His kingdom. Keep in mind that being the kind of disciples we are entails more than just learning from a master. We are owned by Christ Jesus, for He bought us with His own blood. We are part of Him in the sense that we have been implanted in Him, the main vine, and are added to His body as we become His followers. Is it not enough to just be a Christian, Christ-like, without adding any labels? Let's think about this for a minute. When any of us make the claim to be, or are labeled as, liberal or conservative or whatever, does that not show a lack of discipline to the message we were instructed in as disciples of Christ? Who mentored or taught the patriarchs such as Noah, Abraham, and the like?

Take Noah, for example. His great-grandfather was Enoch, his grandfather was Methuselah, and he was the only one saved with his family in his generation when God wiped out the rest of the world with rain. It took more than a hundred years before the word of God came to pass. I am not sure whether Noah was instructed in the ways of the Lord by his father or grandfather. By the time he was born, his great-grandfather Enoch, who was taken away by God, was already gone. He might have heard about the purity of his great-grandfather from his father and grandfather. What is impressive to me about Noah is how faithful and disciplined he was to God's word for all that time—more than a hundred years—even though he didn't see any action or signs from God about the rain. Yet he stuck with the message, probably in the face of ridicule and mockery. I don't imagine he had room for his own opinions. When we label ourselves liberal, conservative, or anything else, we pollute the message of Christ by injecting our own opinions and ideologies instead of the only ideology that matters, the ideology of Christ Jesus and His cross, which reconciles us to God. I believe we can simply be Christians without these labels and stay faithful and firm to the word of God.

How comfortable does the following thought make us: If we consider ourselves conservatives, for instance, would we still champion Jesus's cause if He were a liberal? And if we consider ourselves liberals, would we still champion Jesus's cause if He were a conservative? I must confess that I lean toward the conservative way of thinking, so the thought of Christ being a liberal might make me quite uncomfortable. Here I have admitted that if Christ were liberal, I would be uncomfortable with Him, but the greater question then is,

Will I still follow Him? I will have to answer no if my conservatism has no wiggle room or openness to His teaching that challenges my viewpoints. Therein lies the challenge of labeling ourselves. When we allow ourselves to be divided by human ideologies or teachings or positioning other than what Christ has commanded, it is and will be impossible to be faithful, disciplined disciples of Christ, not making our teachings consistent with that of Christ, especially our love for each other. I am glad to know that Christ does not lean toward my ideology or philosophy. What He requires of me is that I follow him, not the other way around. Here is something to reflect on as disciples of Christ: if our worldly leanings, stands, philosophies, ideologies, and whatnot have not been conquered by Christ and His teachings, then whose disciples are we, really?

Consider the following two situations that illustrate what positions a liberal or conservative might take respectively. Suppose in my mind I like everyone and believe in the goodness of every human on the planet. In my preaching and teaching I deemphasize the state of human sinfulness and instead emphasize God's grace, mercy, and love being all inclusive without pointing out even once what God requires of the sinner. I don't point out that God asks sinners to repent and change their lifestyle to conform to His will. On the other hand suppose that in my desire to teach strictly from the Bible, I treat my opinion against having a kitchen in the church building as if that opinion has scriptural standing. I know the scriptures say nothing about a physical building for worship, let alone a kitchen in the building. But I am of the opinion that the place where the saints meet should be considered a holy place; thus the building the church meets in is a holy place and there should be no room for food to contaminate it. On this issue I have no wiggle room for arguments and that is where it stays. There are many more positions some in our brotherhood have taken that are like these, but suppose we take these positions and leave no room for discussion.

In these two scenarios there is nothing wrong with loving and caring for people and desiring to see them saved. Similarly, there might be nothing wrong with having a place to meet and desiring to keep that place clean and tidy, or even looking upon it as a holy place to go and pray. On the surface these viewpoints might seem noble, but when we dig a little more deeply, we find that an all-inclusive position nullifies the value of the cross and thus God's own plan to save mankind, and makes the Great Commission statement irrelevant. If our sinful state is irrelevant, then why the cross and why did Christ die? In the second case, is it not the body of Christ of which we are members that is holy and not the place the body meets? Consequently, is it not the body and its members that make the place holy? So why do some hold positions that offer no compromise for the sake of Christ? We end up bruising and beating the body of Christ by putting down its members. Aren't the nails and piercing on the cross enough for the body of Christ?

Shouldn't the liberties we take in interpreting God's word be backed first by love and admiration for the God whose word we seek to interpret? Secondly, shouldn't we fear God when we seek to present His word to our fellow man and be careful about what we are telling them since our fellow man, the hearers might build their lives around our interpretations? Finally, in our effort to be all things to all people, let's keep in mind that Paul warned the Corinthians not to go beyond what is written and rather, according to Peter, speak where the scripture speaks and be silent where the scripture is silent. Isn't Christ the standard to which we conform? We all need to carefully examine where we are in following Christ to see if He is first in our lives. In the first couple of chapters of Colossians, Paul says that God has made Jesus the first in everything. As His disciples, do we make Christ first in our lives? In my mind, we cannot truly say we are Christ's disciples if we cannot completely yield to Him and submit to His will.

Let's just think about it for a minute. Once we say we are conservative or liberal or whatever Christians, what have we done? We have separated ourselves by that manner of labeling and caused distinctions to happen in Christ's body that were not there before. In essence, what are we when we become Christians? When we are baptized in the name of the Father and of the Son and of the Holy Spirit, from that moment on what have we become? Have we not become Christ's? Or because we have not described ourselves as bond servants, we have wiggle room to distinguish ourselves from those who call themselves such, and so we can take liberties that separate us from other servants of Christ? The thing is, if we truly yielded to Christ when we submitted to Him in baptism and as a result God has possessed us as His own, any business we are about is God's business, and we require no extra identification to firmly and resolutely fight for or defend God's cause. That is, who we have become are God's ambassadors and representatives. We don't say anything different from what God has said, and we don't need clever maneuvers to let people know what God has said. We become appealing to people when we in sincere love care for people the way

God has called us to do. We might not be perfect, but we trust that the God whose we have become is working through us. He can and will make us perfect. In other words, when we strive in earnest and walk in the works God has since long ago prepared for us, He will always glorify Himself in our lives just like He did in Christ's.

I understand that conservatives want to preserve the scriptures as God gave them to us. I am on that bandwagon. I don't think we humans need to change the Word of God or even take liberties that assume it's one-size-fits-all or that take it to whatever extent we might like to go. I also understand liberals' desire to extend a hand to all people, with the intent of making God more pleasant or attractive to everyone. Though these positions are not the same, they tend to lead to the same thing: man attempting to make God into something His word does not say of Him. Instead we should be submitting to God's will by following and doing what His words say without any ifs, ands, or buts, for we do not see farther than God does, nor can we perceive or display wisdom more brilliantly than God. I believe God's word is going to stand whether we are able to defend it or not, but I also think that God is able to appeal to all people without our help, for that is what the scriptures say. He is the One who led Philip to the Ethiopian eunuch and prevented Paul and Company from going to Bithynia. God did all that without human help.

Is it a good thing that as disciples of Christ, liberal Christians find it difficult to worship with conservative Christians or vice versa? When we bear labels other than the name of Christ, what does the world see when they look at us wearing them? By virtue of these labels the enemies of Christ have succeeded in dividing us and the unity Christ prayed for has not been realized. What do such labels tell the world? Did Christ die for a liberal cause or a conservative cause? We all agree that Christ died to save sinners. These labels do nothing but tell the world that we have not truly been changed to be like Christ, for they see the labels before they see Christ. The world is already divided by these same labels, so when the world sees us, they see no difference in us, and thus the effect of Christ diminishes with those labels. I think that as Christians there should be no doubt who we are and what we stand for when we are introduced or mentioned. That is, that our commitment to Christ is unwavering and that we follow Him without second-guessing what His choices will be when we are faced with difficulties and challenges. Paul admonished the Corinthians to be of the same mind and the Philippians to let the mind or attitude of Christ dwell in them. Do these admonishments apply to us, and can any of us truly say that with these labels we are seen as one people belonging to Christ? It is either that these labels are wrong—or one of them is wrong—or that they do not represent Christ at all and should be shed. Shedding them means that we can simply be Christians who are passionate for Christ and that there is no doubt about our commitment to follow and do His will as it has been handed down to us by the apostles. Satan is too crafty, but God is supreme and His word is final. Let us abide by God's word, earnestly desiring to please God and be watchful to not give God's enemy a foothold to divide us and grieve God. There is much that can be said about this, but I have already devoted more time to it than I intended.

My concern about liberalism or conservatism is not that we fail to be identified or better yet have a strong identity associating us with

Christ. Far from it. Rather my concern is that a stronger identification with Christ requires no extra labels. They have the potential to lead to division. Furthermore, extra labels in the eye of the Great Commission or from the Great Commission point of view exceeds our mandate, in my opinion. Just Christ and the name He has given us needs to be good enough to tell anyone who we are and what our stands are on social issues, political issues, and so forth.

Whether we are leaders in the church or just attend church whenever we can, we need to keep in mind that we are all being discipled. That is, all of us who have believed and committed ourselves to Christ are continually being taught and molded through His commandments and instructions. We are disciples of Christ, which means we follow His instructions. Nothing we do is of our own accord but rather to please the Master; we pay close attention to His instructions and do them. Paul compared the Christian to an athlete or a soldier. A good athlete or soldier follows instructions. An athlete listens to the coach, who is on the sidelines watching the game closely and watching what the athlete is doing or not doing that might cause the game to be won or lost. Even though the coach's primary concern is for his athletes, he watches the opponents so he can advise his athletes and craft strategies that will help them overcome their opponents. Can you imagine what will happen if the athlete chooses not to follow the directives of his coach? The athlete is bound to lose the game. But if the athlete pays attention to the coach's instructions and executes the game plan as directed by the coach, there is bound to be success. Likewise, Paul told Timothy that the soldier strives to please his commanding officer. The only way the soldier can please his commanding officer is by following his officer's command. If he fails to follow the officer's command, the soldier can find himself in a lot of trouble. At this point I would like to observe that there are no ordinary Christians. Can we call one who has been bought with divine blood and in whom the Holy Spirit dwells ordinary? More like sons of God! Let us stay with that.

Is Knowledge In Love's way

Has Knowledge gotten in the Love's Way? Another way to ask the same question above is whether the gift of knowledge that God has given His to children for the purposes of advancing the gospel has become a hindrance to the ministry of making disciples? Or have we prioritized knowledge over love for fellow brethren and the souls that are to be saved? Here is an example of what I mean: in Acts 20 when Paul met with the elders of the church of Ephesus and he reminded the elders about his conduct for three years living amongst them in Ephesus and teaching the church the things that were of spiritual benefit to them in their new found life. After that Paul warned the elders to pay close attention to what they had received from him in his teachings and warned them to be watchful against false teachers both from within and without. I his letter to the same church a few years later, Paul commends the same congregation of their well-known love for the all the saints as well as their faith. Paul continued in his letter to the Ephesus that he prays for them so God will expand their knowledge about God. It is in this same letter that Paul prayed that these Ephesian Christians will be rooted and grounded in love, and that they will come to appreciate together with all the saints "… the breadth and length and height and depth …" of the love Christ. By the time the apostle John recorded Revelations, something had changed about how the Lords church at Ephesus loved the saints. It seems the Ephesian Christians had become so well equipped in knowledge but have forgotten the love aspect that Paul instructed them.

We note in Revelations 2 that Christ complemented the Ephesians for their knowledge and how they had stood their ground against false teachers and exposed those who had strayed from what they had been taught. But Christ did not complement them on their continued to love Him or the saints. Note that Paul complemented these Christian for their love in his letter. Years later, Christ warns that they had lost that same love they were highly praised for earlier. What happened to these Christians? Paul prayed that they grow in both the knowledge of Christ and the love of Christ. For Paul had written to them that:

> For this reason I bow my knees before the Father, from whom every family in heaven and on earth is named, that according to the riches of his glory he may grant you to be strengthened with power through his Spirit in your inner being, so that Christ may dwell in your hearts through faith--that you, **being rooted and grounded in love**, may have strength to comprehend with all the saints what is the **breadth and length and height and depth, and to know the love of Christ that surpasses knowledge**, that you may be filled with all the fullness of God. Ephesians 3:14 – 19 ESV

How is it that they were praised for one and were warned about their lost love which according to Paul is superior to knowledge?

Paul told the Corinthians in chapter 13 that the gift of knowledge will pass away, but love will reign supreme. How is it that the Ephesians who were once praised based on their love for the saints but failed at the same task of owning nothing but love. I don't think it is because they didn't know how to love or never heard of importance of love. I believe it is because they were so in tune and focused on getting it right but left out the piece that holds everything together, LOVE. Let us also note that the point here is not because knowledge is less to be desired. No and a big emphatic one at that. Paul's prayer was that Christians be fully equipped with the knowledge of Christ. But he asked most importantly that they be grounded and rooted in love and to acquire a greater appreciation for the love of Christ. Jude the brother of James, the brother of Christ instructed that we "contend", "defend" or "fight" for the faith. How do we do that? Or how can one defend our faith without knowledge? We have to acquire knowledge which God freely gives. However, we need to fight more earnestly to pay each other the love we owe each other because of Christ. Think about it this way, The Lord died for brother J and brother S equally. He awaits either brother eagerly to welcome them home. Do we all have the same understanding or do we all love at the same level? The answer is obviously no. Yet when we make the attempt to love more and learn to resolve our differences like saints who love and care deeply for the well-being of each other, we are bound to do better than the folks in Acts 11 where the disciples were first called Christians if not the same. Unless we come to appreciate the love of Christ and live in that love and let that love dominate our lives in the way we deal with each other even those who are wrong doctrinally, we cannot successfully capture the world for Christ. If we are dominated by the love of Christ and it shows in our lives, then every most in our lives will be like a spiritual Kodak moment for Christ (where the banner of Christ is prominently raised and swung bravely because of our actions toward God and our fellow man), because the picture that is captures is one that glorifies God and honors His holy name. Instead of the negative images that the disputes and unwillingness to work with each other to resolve spiritually irrelevant issues such as eating in buildings meet.

Let us not allow God's enemies to distract us with minor issues. Let us strive to get our teachings right in accordance to what the apostles taught that and subject ourselves to everything that Christ commanded His apostle. Let us seek knowledge and stand firm like the Ephesians, but let us not fall short in loving like each other they did. Let us put love in its proper place so we can truly put Christ on display in the proper and honorable light that only belongs to Him, our king. Let us make every moment in terms of displaying Christ's love to the world a spiritual Kodak moment that truly testifies to the world that God's people are different because they know what they are saying and most importantly, because they love God first and they love each other deeply. Paul's charge to the Ephesian elders still stand so let us not lose sight of his instructions to them to maintain what he had taught them and be alert and watchful for false teachers. And also similar instructions to Timothy to watch what he taught, follow the pattern of teachings handed down to him, to rebuke and reproof … But let us also turn our attention on loving each other and contend for our faith in love and with passion. Let us study more to present ourselves approved in God's sight and so doing handle God's word ably. But let us love each other like God has loved us.

Disciples Adhere to the Master's Instructions

I have used the words *followed* and *follow instructions* a few times in this discussion, for good reason. The calling to be a Christian—Christ-like—is not something we can become of our own accord. It is not something we get to be because we want to; rather it is a complex situation that God has set up so that if we follow His will and do as He requires, He is able to make us like His Son with whom He has called us to come into fellowship and be co-heirs. God's purpose depends on us adhering to His will and doing as He has commanded us. God's purpose depends on us adhering to His will and doing as He has commanded us because He seeks to transform us from our sinful state to a righteous state, making us into a people He has set apart and uses to fulfill His will. Take Peter, for example. Peter was just a fisherman from Galilee when he encountered Christ. After three years of walking with Christ, Peter learned what it really meant to forgive one's brother regardless of how many times his brother sinned against him. Within that time span, Peter made the great confession that Jesus was the Son of God, Peter walked on water as well as learned the bitter lesson of denial and regret. Christ had transformed Peter from a common fisherman to the greatest fisher of men. He preached a sermon that convicted men and caused three thousand souls to respond to his message. What about Paul, and the other apostles? All of these men came in contact with Jesus and were transformed into vessels that God used to glorify His Name. How do we imagine that happened? These men could not have been used by God to meet His will if they had chosen to do something different rather than follow God's will and His instructions. God could not have used them if they had not yielded to His molding.

As a disciple and a preacher in training, Paul stressed the idea of following instructions to Timothy. In his letters to Timothy, Paul not only entrusted Timothy with the responsibility of preaching the message, but told him to pay close attention to his own teachings, and to follow the commandments he had received from Paul. Why is this important? Well, if we are disciples of Christ, then our nature is to listen to and do what Christ tells us. Christ has entrusted us as individual Christians with specific functions, but we all remain disciples. I mentioned earlier that we are not experts. I don't mean to say that we should not engross ourselves in the Master's will—far from it. In fact my desire is to know God's will so well that even in my sleep I could tell anyone who asks me about my faith. This was Peter's admonition, wasn't it? If we dwell a bit more on the sports analogy, then what I mean is that we are more like the athletes and not the talking heads who sit at one place and play the whole game with their lips. My point is that, in our various functions—for all of us have a mission to fulfill in the kingdom—we allow God to use us mightily to accomplish His will far beyond our imaginations. That is, we humble ourselves under God's guiding hands and don't rise beyond our mandate or commission.

According to the parable of the talents, every single disciple is entrusted with a mission. Some of us can do certain things better than others, yet we all remain disciples of Christ. Christ told the apostles that they have only one master, Him, the Christ. Also, in Luke 17:7-10, Jesus tells of the servant who returns after working the field all day. Even though that servant might be tired, he is still required, once he is home, to serve the master and meet the master's needs before he can think of taking care of his own needs. The master does not tell the servant to stop serving because he worked all day in the field; rather the servant acknowledges his or her responsibilities. The servant does not look for appreciation from the master. As I think of this story, I sometimes think that Jesus is overlooking the servant's effort. But the more closely I look at the story, the more I see Jesus Himself as the example, I realize that Jesus is teaching me not just humility, but also to focus on pleasing God well just as He, the Son of God, pleased God the Father well. No matter how hard I might think of having worked for God, my attitude remains the same: I am only a vessel in God's hand that God is using to glorify Himself, and it is a privilege to be called upon. Jesus submitted fully to God the entire time He was on earth, and He focused on doing the will of His Father and not on what He wanted or desired. In this story, if Jesus is the master and we are the servants or people called to be His disciples, then whether we be elders, deacons, preachers, teachers, and so on, the perspective we keep is that we have been found favorable to be used by the Master. And we fully respond to the calling as disciples under the Master's instructions.

Let me see if I can get this out in a different way. Regardless of the capacity in which we find ourselves serving in the kingdom of God, our attitude is greatly helped if we can only think of ourselves as disciples who are still being groomed to maturity. Our will should be far second to what Christ's will is for us. Christ's will trumps ours, and we are okay with that. Let us remember that however skillful we might be, we manifest the gifts of the Holy Spirit. We have been given these gifts to help lead the church to maturity, according to Paul's letter to the brethren in Ephesus.

Making Disciples

Μαθητεύσατε (matheeteusate)—This is the Greek word Jesus used in the Great Commission and is translated as "to make disciples, to train in discipleship." Making disciples requires a long-term commitment just like any training form would. It requires both the student and the trainer to devote lots of time, dedication, and transference of knowledge, a process that involves lots of repetition. On the other hand, the Greek word διδάσκω (didasko), meaning "to teach in a public assembly," is translated as "teaching" like public teaching, or teaching in the assembly, like one instance of teaching a Bible class on a Sunday morning. This is just one of the many occasions when a learner, or disciple, might receive directives or instructions.

In Acts 2 we make the following notes of events after Peter addressed the people. First, Peter told the people about Jesus's death, burial, and resurrection and how they had contributed to letting Jesus be killed. Second, after hearing Peter, those who were convicted asked what to do. Third, Peter informed them of their need to repent and be baptized for the remission of their sins. Fourth, those who were baptized "continually [devoted] themselves to the apostles' teachings." Looking at what happened in Acts 2, therefore, we note that making disciples means fulfilling all of the Great Commission.

We cannot break the Great Commission into separate parts and obey those we like and leave those we don't like. Let us remember that partial obedience or selective obedience is still disobedience.

As Christians, we are disciple makers. We know and learn that and how we make disciples through the historical records. Let's look at some of those written about who made disciples. In other words, we are going to look at disciples who were disciple makers. I contend that every disciple of Christ is a disciple maker, whether we make disciples directly or not. God has given each of us a role in the process. I mentioned Brother Munko when I talked about my baptism. His wife, Sister Munko, had a practice of serving water and sometimes boiled egg to each brother who preached or taught a class, be it within the four walls of the building we worshipped in or at a public preaching appearance during one of our evangelism outings. My point here is that our contribution to advance God's work is of high value to God's final goal of winning souls and training those souls. No one's contribution is insignificant to God as long as we offer it in faith and with sincerity. Remember that the widow's coin cast to God in faith and sincerity meant more to God than the rich man's thousands.

Let's proceed and take a look at how God used some of the people in the first-century church to make disciples. Specifically, I want us to look at Peter the elder, Paul the image of Christ, Barnabas, Priscilla and Aquila, and Paul's instructions on how elderly women are to mentor the younger sisters to manage their homes well.

It is easy to look at the Philips, the Barnabases, and the Stephens among us and leave the burden that the whole congregation is supposed to carry on the shoulders of a few men and women. It is true that some of these men and women are like Energizer batteries—they can keep going and going and going—yet like the same Energizer battery, these men can run out of juice if not recharged, thus leaving crucial work unattended to. These people need to be encouraged to keep going, and where need be, supported by the church. While the Philips and the Barnabases can and do step up out of their own accord to fulfill needs when they see them arise in the local congregation or in the kingdom in general, the rest of us need molding, preparing, training, and grooming to adequately respond to our calling. The rest of us need the Pauls, Peters, Barnabases, and Priscillas and Aquilases who are self-starters and motivators to encourage us to kick in our talents or polish them. Congregational preaching and teaching are instructed by Christ. The Holy Spirit reinforces this through Paul in the book of Hebrews. For all of us, this is the starting point. However, for the full potential of the church to be tapped, each member's gift or gifts given by the Holy Spirit need to be uncovered and put to use.

The truth of the matter is that Christ has empowered all of us, His disciples, with gifts through the Holy Spirit. Christ needs at least one out of every eight of all the talents to be at work, according to the parable of the talents. Or if we look at it in terms of people, then almost 67 percent of us need to be working in the vineyard, not 20 percent, who tend to be the Philips and Barnabases among us. Christ needs all hand on deck. The question then becomes, How do we tap these talents and put them to work? This question of uncovering talents or gifts and putting them to work in the church deserves more time and discussion than we are able to give it in the context of our current discussion. However, I would like to fit our discussion about this under three segments: duty, desire, and destiny. In duty we seek to answer the question, What are my responsibilities as a disciple of Christ? In desire we seek to address the question, How do I cultivate the zeal for discharging the responsibilities and encouraging each other to use our abilities in the Lord? And then finally in destiny we address the question, What is in it for me—that is, why do I need to undertake these duties? Here is how the story of talents in Matthew 25 breaks down:

All talents on board

In the parable of the talents, we observe that the servants Jesus identified as faithful servants had the following traits:

Duty
- » They were given talents or gift according to their ability.
- » They went to work immediately with their talents.
- » Their talents bore fruit.

Desire
- » They engaged their talents in productive and fruitful work immediately; that is, regardless of their opinion of their master, they sought to please him.
- » They had an attitude of urgency.
- » They worked to gain additional talents.

Destiny
- » They were given accounts of deeds done.

» They were given more responsibilities,
» Each of them received an invitation to share in their master's joy.
» They were called good and faithful servants.
» On the other hand the servant Jesus called unfaithful had the following traits:

Duty

» He was given at least one talent according to his abilities.
» He did not put the talents to work; instead he went and hid the talent in the ground.
» His talent did not bear fruit.

Desire

» He did not have a good attitude toward the master.
» Fear of his master did not motivate him like it did the others.
» He lacked interest in pleasing the master.
» His attitude was not good.

Destiny

» His talent was taken away.
» He was cast into a place where there was weeping and gnashing of teeth.

As Christians we need not think of our duties as a set of tasks that we do and then check as done. That didn't work with the Old Covenant. Rather the way we look at our duties or responsibilities in the kingdom is what Paul wrote in Ephesians 2:10; that is, we are God's handiwork created in Jesus Christ for good works God prepared for us ahead of time so we could walk or live in them. God already had this all planned out so that when we become Christians, we live a life filled with the practice of good works. These good works have nothing to do with our abilities but have everything to do with living a lifestyle that glorifies God in faith. Our desire is our eagerness to place the Lord first in our lives and do as He has commanded. And finally, our destiny as Christians is a singularly focused desire to please our Master no matter what

As mentioned earlier, as Christians we have been called to make disciples. We have been called to make disciples because the Great Commission says so. We have already noted that the force of the command is in *make disciples* rather than *go*. Making disciples is what we do as Christians because that is what God has already set for us to do. It is our primary responsibility. Performing this primary task requires more than any human can offer as an individual; therefore God set up the church in the body of Christ with diverse functionalities to make sure the body grows to maturity by having every part working. These diverse functions are performed by members of the body of Christ whom God has given various gifts. It is worth noting that in the parable of the talents everyone was given a gift or talent. It is important also to note and understand that nothing we do in the process of making disciples is work of our own accord, but rather it is work that God has long planned for us to do. That is, we become God's hands and feet to accomplish His purposes, not our own. God uses us to spread and share His message of salvation to sinners who need to hear the message of forgiveness of sins and reconciliation with God, who sanctifies and justifies all who accept the message of the cross.

Duty: *Disciples Plus Our Talents*

In our duties, Christ through the Holy Spirit has freely given us gifts to use in His church to grow, to train through teaching and examples that imitate Christ to shape us into his image, and to learn and live the new culture and life God has called us to live. As such we have teachers, preachers, encouragers, mentors, people who can give freely of their means, and people with many other gifts to help us work effectively in God's kingdom. As we use our gifts, some among us can become great and so effective that they amaze us. Yet ultimately, their greatness and skillfulness should focus on glorifying God for empowering His children in such manner. I must say that there are some teachers I can listen to for hours and not blink because they are that good. I look forward to hearing such brethren and learning from them and the insights that God has given them. But like Peter, we can look at ourselves and marvel at our ability to walk on water and take our eyes off the Lord who made it possible for us to do so, only to find ourselves sinking and drifting away from the Lord. This is why we need to keep in mind that no matter where we are in our walk of faith or what capacity we fill in the Lord's church, we are still disciples in training and still being molded. It is very important that we look at our gifts as accessories to be used to accomplish God's purposes. It is the people God is interested in, so even though Paul encouraged us to pursue our gifts and not be ignorant of them, he also told us that love is the greatest and that we owe that to each other. True, we are going to be accountable to God for how we use our gifts, but won't it be great to eagerly love God with all of our minds, hearts, strength, and souls and love each other in a similar fashion, tenderly caring for one another and encouraging each other to keep on with the fight?

Examples of our duties:

A) Paul, the image of Christ—Yes, Paul was an apostle, but look at him in the following light: he trained others to become teachers and preachers, he encouraged others to live faithfully for Christ, he was sincere about his faith and it showed. When he had to hold Peter accountable, for example, it was not out of superiority but for the good of the saints and to better Peter as a fellow apostle and servant of Christ. Paul noted that Peter stood condemned because of his actions, so if Paul had not been interested in Peter's well-being and had wanted to show superiority, he could have put Peter down with no love at all. Also Paul cared for the good of the saints, as we see in the way he dealt with Onesimus's situation. In his own words he could have retained Onesimus for his benefit, but he was more interested in Onesimus's master, Philemon, who happened to be a disciple of Christ, a Christian; thus Paul's focus and discipline were on advancing the cause of Christ. Paul's objective was to become all things to all people so he could save as many as possible for the Lord. Can we separate our feelings and hurts for the cause of Christ like Paul?

B) Peter the elder—Peter admonished fellow elders not to regard their duty in the Lord as a show of power over the saints by exerting themselves, but to be examples to the flock. It sounds like Peter had finally learned something that the Lord had been trying to teach him. Remember Jesus washing the disciples' feet in John 13? He told them after that to be examples to the other disciples. A friend not too long ago

111

gave me an object lesson on shepherding. The lesson was about two kinds of shepherding: the American kind, where the shepherds sit on horses and send the sheepdog after the sheep, and the Middle Eastern kind, where the shepherd walks just ahead of the sheep, all the while calling and encouraging them to follow. He smells like the sheep because he picks them up and carries them when they are hurting and can't walk. We can easily see why the sheep will know that shepherd's voice and respond to his call in the case of the second kind of shepherding. Our elders set a tone with their leadership when they are close to the rest of the members by the way they care for each member, love each member, pray for each member . . . and are not viewed as distant because of their role and lack of interaction with the saints.

C) Barnabas the encourager—Remember, Barnabas was the first to reach out to Paul after he was converted. This was at a time when there were wounds inflicted on the church by the death of Stephen and the threats of Paul, formerly known as Saul was fresh on the minds of the new Christians in Jerusalem. Barnabas recognized Paul's potential for the work in Antioch, went looking for him, and brought him to help with the work there. Also remember that Barnabas was willing to accept Mark and include him on the mission team versus Paul, who didn't see the need to bring along one who had left in the middle of a previous mission trip. We need such men and women who are capable and possess Barnabas's abilities to not only bring harmony but keep us together and teach us how to keep working with each other as well as identify talents in the Lord's body and nurture then into fruition.

D) Priscilla and Aquila the mentors—A distinctive story about these two is their straightening of Apollos, who was already on fire. The scripture said these two took Apollos in and taught him the message more correctly. From younger preachers who need to be encouraged and properly directed to stay true to the word, to new disciples who have just been baptized, we all need mentors and cheerleaders to set us straight, cheer us on when the going gets tough, and let us know when things do not seem right. This is important for the growth of Christ's body so we can halt false teachings caused by improper understanding of Christ's teachings before they take root, or before we wither away because of improper nutrition. Let us mentor each other, but most important, recognize those with such potential and encourage them to take on the role of mentoring to champion the cause of Christ.

E) Elderly women need to model and mentor young women to manage their homes well. This is what Paul instructed his young trained preachers to do in teaching our sisters. Think of it this way: when we come to Christ, just because we have been dipped into water does not mean we have changed overnight. Yes, God has awakened our conscience to become much more alert to what He desires of us, but we all need Christ to be taught to us and modeled to us, especially if we are coming from a background that has no God at all. In that spirit, new and young women in the Lord need the mentoring of older Christian women to train them to be of sound mind in their relationship with their husbands and children. This is what Paul instructed Titus to teach older women. Paul's reason for this instruction was so that the name of God would not be blasphemed by those who are not Christians. This kind of training will distinguish our young sisters from their peers who are not Christians and show a clear contrast in their behavior as people belonging to Christ. In other words, young Christian women learn from older Christian women who have learned from the Lord how to walk in Him, starting from their homes.

F) Fathers and mothers need to model Christ in the home consistently to show our children what it means to live for Him. When they reach adulthood, these new adults with their newfound freedom might be well prepared to continue living for Christ and thus help stop the unfaithfulness of children raised in Christian homes. Although it is not possible to determine how our children are going to respond to their upbringing, we cannot as parents in the Lord fail to initiate that lifestyle in them. In the famous proverb of Solomon about training children, the Hebrew word חנך (chanak) means "initiate," "train up." The way I think about this verse is as follows: All of us have probably heard that children do not come with a user manual. I concede that I would be one of the most miserable parents since I don't like reading user manuals. It's a good thing God did! Rather than instruction, Solomon's proverb tells us exactly what we need. We need to initiate or prompt the abilities, intuitions, and capabilities of our children who were given to us as complete human beings with the proper guidance in Christ through love and consistently point them to Christ Jesus in both speech and example. In a way, we help our children lay the foundation for the life they will lead as grown people. As the foundation of a building determines what type of house is built on it, the foundation we help our children lay determines the kind of lifestyle they build for themselves. As Jesus said, "Build the foundation on a rock and the house stands firm during harsh conditions or build the foundation on sand and the house falls apart when difficult times arise."

Marriage is a wonderful framework that God has given us to properly raise the children with whom we are blessed. In this framework, God has specific functions for each party involved. The Christian husband is charged with loving his wife as Christ loved the church and gave Himself for the church. The wife is charged with submission to the husband. Like most of my brothers in the Lord, I like the second part—that my wife should submit to me. But lately I have been wondering how well I have done the first part. I wonder if I have truly been loving my wife as Christ loved the church, to the point of dying for the church. Notice the sequence: 1) Christ loved the church first. 2) Christ sacrificed for the church second. 3) Submission to Christ by the church came after the love and sacrifice had long been established.

The fact is that since I started comparing my love for my wife to Christ's love for the church, I've realized that I might not be fit for her submission if I cannot love her as Christ loves His church. I have also found that as I strive to meet that bar set by Christ's love for His church, I work hard to take hold of every opportunity my wife gives me to show how much I love her. As I strive to meet Christ's standard, I noticed that it is easier for her to go along with some of my craziest ideas. My point here is that, before we husbands start screaming, "Submit to me because the Bible says so," we should take on the challenge instead to love our wives as Christ loves the church; then we will have no need to make that pronouncement for our wives to submit. That is, if we love them first and show our love by our sacrifices in time, patience, and care, our wives will respond to us as the church responds to Christ. The thing is, we want to do everything for Christ because He loves us; thus let us love our wives so and see what happens. For my sisters in the Lord, because you love Christ, think of submission to His will as your submission to your husbands. Christ is going to hold us all accountable. I am not by any means claiming to have perfected the command to love my wife as Christ loved the church. Rather I am only observing that I am taking hold of the little windows of opportunities God opens to me in my wife's life so I can practice loving her like Christ loves the church. However imperfect my gestures and attempts to love my wife, I find that it makes life less challenging with her and that she does not have much difficulty following my leadership.

G) What about the orphans, the widows, and the needy? Do they feel at home when they come to our worship services or do they feel uncomfortable? Some of our congregations have programs that feed and clothe the needy. Is that all the poor need? Before we forget, the poor are more receptive to God's word than the rich. And the rich have a record of rejecting Christ and deferring to their own interests instead of Christ's. As we endeavor to reach all people, let us not neglect those who look poor and less fit, but welcome them and help them come to know Christ.

H) What about race? Are we aware that Christians by the nature of our calling are a chosen race, a holy nation, a people owned by God? That is what the apostle Peter said. Do we wonder what color of people Peter was talking about? It couldn't be what we will be in eternity, for Paul said we do not know yet what type of body we are going to have in eternity. For a people who have been called and set apart with the hope of spending eternity with God and with each other, how have we let our race relationships promote or hinder the cause of Christ? I can understand that different languages can cause us to meet at different times and places, but really, is that the issue or have we let the world we live in influence us rather than leading the way and demonstrating to the world that truly there are no Greeks or Jews among us? That is, once we have come to Christ, the only thing that matters is Christ, and it does not matter where my brother is from or whether he or she is much lighter than vanilla ice cream and I am darker than dark chocolate. Not to mention the other shades,

117

by any means. Or have we forgotten that we are waiting to be transformed bodily and for now are gradually taking on the nature of Christ? When it comes to the issue of race, the sad news is that we preach more than we practice, and it needs to be the other way around. I went to a gospel meeting in New York City in 1995. I had been told that "brethren from all over the country [would] be present." My interpretation of that was that I was going to truly see America, a mixture of people that reflects the different groups in this country, especially because we are people of Christ. The event was organized by black brethren in the area, and though the event was being held near an area where white folks met, I could easily count the number of white brethren who were present, one of whom came with my group. I do understand the issue of autonomy of local churches and thus one local congregation is not compelled to participate in what another congregation is doing, but I don't believe that was what was on display at the time. Rather the history of America was on display, whereby whites did their thing and colored people did their thing. How are we going to get together in Heaven if we cannot shed these kinds of cultural influences? I imagine we think eternity is a long time so we can get over our divisions then. But what message do we send to the rest of the world? Is it any wonder that we cannot reach America? We need to live like people who have been set apart and walk like people whom God has called to demonstrate His will to the rest of the world. My perception before I saw the gathering could have been wrong and may in fact be wrong, but the impression I left the hall with after the event was not. On the way home my group discussed the meeting, including the demographics of the brethren. We observed that the influence of Christ over American Christians has not overcome their history. I was not a citizen at the time and neither were most of the brethren in the group. I have since become a citizen of this wonderful country. I believe we need to take a good look at what we teach and preach to ensure it is consistent with what the world sees in us. We cannot preach that race does not matter and live like it matters.

I) Other duties that are included:

» The church teaches and receives instructions by teaching new disciples as well as sparking interests of disciples to share what they learn and practice.

» Exposing the new Christian to situations and opportunities by way of frequent fellowshipping (Christians getting together) will make the new disciple grow.

» We need to use the fruit of the spirit so the world can see.

» Our benevolent outreach should offer Christ more than goods; that is, we can find more ways to impress Christ on people we help than just offering silver and gold.

» Our homes need to be a place of training and discipleship.

» We need to maintain and retain the newly baptized by impressing on them that we are their new family.

» We need to make the people matter by impressing on them that we are the reason Christ died. Christ made the bleeding woman and the Samaritan woman at the well feel they counted.

» We need to make disciples who can make disciples by training everyone for that purpose, even if it means that they can only serve water to the one preaching.

» We need to share our real-life experiences with each other and get to know each other.

To summarize:

1. Let us sincerely love and care for each saint as we actively practice owing each other nothing but love. Jesus said to the disciples as He was winding down His work on earth, "a new commandment I give to you, love one another" (John 13:34). Jesus impressed upon the disciples their obligation to love each other as He had loved them. The church cannot be said to have attained maturity if the members, Christians, lack love for each other and we tear each other apart. In particular we need to love each other as Christ loved His disciples while on earth. To translate this command of Jesus into modern vernacular, I am to love my fellow Christian brother and sister as Christ loves me and vice versa. One notices that the standard set is that of Christ, to love as Christ loves. Can we agree that we have a long way to go on this?

2. All saints need to be encouraged to find out what their role is or where they believe they can be most effective for Christ, and be encouraged and given the opportunity to practice in those areas. Let us actively seek and prompt each other for these good works.

3. All saints need to know that Christ needs their effort and is counting on it to develop the church.

4. All saints need to understand that Christ needs us to be on fire and stay on fire. Remember, Christ cannot stomach lukewarm members; they come right out.

5. Let's call into action the Priscillas and Aquilases, the Barnabases, and the like.

When Christ told us to take His yoke and learn from Him, He assured us that His yoke is easy and His burden is light. Why do we need to take on the yoke of Christ and learn from Him? The answers to this question are obvious. Jesus Christ knows the Father better anyone, and He knows how to train us to know and love the Father. Like the story I mentioned earlier from Benner's book about the experienced ox yoked with a young ox for training, so we also when we take on the yoke of Christ are trained, shaped, and molded for the purposes of the Father. After Paul had been yoked with Christ and been well trained, he told others to imitate him for he imitated Christ. After Peter had also learned well of Christ, he could be an example to his fellow elders and give them proper admonitions for the growth of the Lord's body. Hence those among us who have faithfully served the Lord and walked before Him faithfully need to yoke with young Christians. Those young in the faith, not age, need the gentle guidance and prodding that those older in the faith, such as an elder, have learned from Christ so the young can learn how to serve the Master faithfully.

The kingdom of God today needs Barnabases, Priscillas and Aquilases, and the like who will open their lives and homes for disciples to be nurtured and developed. The kingdom of God needs homes where Christ is being modeled and children are picking up from their parents how to walk and talk like Christ. Is it possible that our fellowship with each other is unlike what we read in Acts because they met in homes and we meet in buildings away from our homes? If that is the case, do we need to start meeting in homes so we get to know each other well? If not, then how do we attain that level of unity we read about in Acts? Let's put in perspective the fact that we will be spending eternity with each other. The kingdom of God needs men who have raised faithful children to model to new Christian fathers as well as faithful women of the caliber of Sarah, Ruth, Mary, and the like to model Christ to new Christian women and young women. These are not about church programs but about individuals stepping up to fill seriously needed ministries. The kingdom of God needs individuals to whom encouraging and mentoring come naturally. For sure there are Barnabases and Priscillas and Aquilases among us today.

What we are talking about is walking and working with each other as Christians so we pick up the Christ-like behaviors we see in and learn from each other; that is, we are examples to each other in Christ. Some things we will learn and pick up instinctively, others we will learn or pick up in discussions. Yet still others we will learn or pick up from specific instructions. Paul said we should not judge somebody else's servants. The new disciple is Christ's servant just like the Christian who has known Christ for more than fifty years or more. Christ will judge us all alike. What we need to do is help each other learn and develop via teaching and examples so we all continue in the graces of the king.

Desire: *God, the Disciple, and Our Talents*
We see in the parable of the talents that the faithful servants had a sense of urgency about them and a need to get to work. The prophet Jeremiah talked about his zeal to do God's work as fire burning in his bones so he could do nothing but tell people about what God had put on his heart. During one of our spiritual growth workshops at the congregation where I worship, one of our guest speakers, whom I cannot recall by name, told a story about a newborn Christian. The man was so excited about becoming a Christian that as he walked in the mall, he could not resist talking about his newfound faith to everyone he met. As this went on, the older Christians found the situation a bit embarrassing, so they tried to show this new Christian the "proper way" to behave and told him not to be too loud about his newfound faith. Needless to say this new Christian never did that again. In other words this on-fire Christian had so much cold water dumped on his zeal that his fire was quenched. I don't know about you, but I relate very well to the older Christians in that story. I do like to behave properly when I'm out at the mall, and sometimes I like to hide when I see someone I know making noise about Christ in public.

Paul said we should earnestly desire spiritual gifts. But then he zoomed in on the gifts that benefit all, including those who are not Christians. It is worthwhile to note that Paul didn't say some gifts are more important that others, only that the gifts that benefit all should have precedence over gifts that benefit only the ones who possess them. As the Philips and Barnabases among us appear to need no motivation, we need to encourage and support these brethren and help them whichever way we can to advance the cause of Christ, not stall or discourage them. Such members in the body see a need and pick up the mantle to get the job done on their own. However, there are Apollos among us also who need to be shaped and redirected and then let loose to discharge the duties of soul winning or disciple making. Also among us are those who might or might not know how to serve because they think they have nothing to offer. According to Christ all of us have been given a gift to use in the Lord's church. The point is, for most of us our desires need to be kindled. How do we do that? one might ask.

Paul in 1 Corinthians 12:6 told the Christians in Corinth that there are different kinds of gifts or works and that it is God who is active in all of those works or gifts. Other versions of the Bible say God *empowers* or *activates* or *works all these gifts in us.* One might ask, If God activates the gifts He gives us, why do I need to have a desire to work in His kingdom? Good question. God gives us gifts, but we choose to use or not use them just like the servant in the parable of the talents. Let's think about it this way: God is the one who has given us the gifts, and He is the only one who knows how best to use them. As such we cannot think of anyone better to ask than God to help us use the gifts He has given us. We are not incapable of using these gifts on our own outside of God's help. However, the Greek word that is translated as "activate," or "empower" is also translated as "efficient," "mighty in," or "fervent." Given the type of adversary we have and especially with the new status that God has given us as His children, does anyone think that we can be efficient or effective in using the gifts God has given us without stumbling? God in all His might has all these things worked out such that even our efforts will be great through Him and under His protecting eyes and nurturing hands. That is, God is more than willing to partner with us to achieve His purposes, but He has to be in the driver's seat! God gives us gifts and then invests Himself in seeing to it that we are effective in using them. What else could it mean that God activates?

To this effect, we need to invite Him in to sup with us. Remember, Jesus has already extended the invitation, for He said, "Behold, I stand at the door and knock. If anyone hears my voice and open the door, I will come in and sup with him and he with me" (Revelation 3:20, KJV).

God persistently seeks after us. All of us have knocked on a door at least once and know that it involves knocking and waiting and knocking and waiting some more before we hear footsteps coming toward the door or going away. Jesus has not told us to do anything that He has not done Himself. He said we should ask, knock, and seek or search. Here He is, knocking at our hearts' door, asking to come in. Is it too much for us then to ask Him to ignite or set on fire our desire to do His work? Why do we wonder that God wants us to ask, knock, and seek before we receive? In asking, knocking, and searching would it be wrong to devote just an hour or two a day, or a week, or a month in prayer by ourselves or with other saints in prayer, imploring God to embolden and energize us in His work? Or are we too busy to eagerly seek and find the already extended hand of God to take hold of in partnership with Him working through His gifts in us and making ourselves available for His mighty hands to go to work in us? Let's all saints everywhere adopt more prayer-filled lives so God will put the talents He has given us to work.

Earlier, my list of our duties included examples from Acts or the epistles to the early Christians on how they ought to live and build the body of Christ. I also added some personal observations about the things we preach versus what we practice. The scriptures remain the only source we use to reach the lost. The early Christians made disciples and trained the new disciples to know God. That primary task has not changed today. The challenges have changed, but the task itself remains the same: making disciples of all nations. For example, whereas the apostles walked to reach people with the gospel, we have the Internet and can reach people from our sofas. Whereas Herod was murdering the apostles and the Romans were confused about the discourse between the Jews and the Christians, today we have the American Civil Liberties Union and many other groups telling us we can't mention God anywhere in public. The early Christians made a conscious and consistent effort to pray fervently when they were going through those challenges, asking God for directions and boldness. Will that work for us today? I will say a big yes. We cannot pray the same prayers they prayed because of our different needs, but we need to adopt their attitude toward prayers. In some way our needs are not so different. For example, they needed boldness, and we need boldness as well. They preached in public, but the way our community is set up makes reaching the public difficult. We need to pray the prayers that address our needs and be earnest about it. Like the early disciples, the church today needs to earnestly implore God for help with our efforts at soul winning. If Jesus can tell Peter and

Co. where to cast their net to retrieve more fish after getting nothing all day, and if Jesus can empower the same Peter and Co. through the Holy Spirit so Peter's preaching in Acts 2 can win three thousand souls, if the same Holy Spirit prompted or forbade Paul and Co. from going someplace to preach the gospel, then God knows exactly what He is doing. God is the only one who can lead us to the souls who will readily accept His word. We sing the song "the blessings come down as the prayers go up" can we not live an active prayer life that invokes God continuous blessing on our work in Him? Let's note that Nothing is impossible for God.

What I'm saying here is that we can plan all we want, and budget all we can, but if both the church as a whole and the individual Christian fail to yield to God or if God is not intimately involved in our efforts to discharge the responsibilities He has given us, we are bound to see a wasted effort and frustration because of lack of results. Jesus said, "[A]nd behold I will be with you always" (Matthew 28:20). Let us humbly ask God to take the lead role by calling on Him through prayers, and let us do it more often and long.

We've all heard it said that Americans are not receptive to God's word anymore. I have heard this statement from brethren, some working very hard in the field to save souls in their local community. As a result some have chosen to focus only on foreign campaigns. When I hear that, I mostly wonder why that is. For example, when we make a statement like that, does that mean we have conceded a battlefield to Satan and his minions and that God's word cannot break through? Does it mean that God is preventing His word from being preached in America, or is it that the vessels He needs to use are not effective anymore? Is it just an excuse for us to avoid confrontation and preserve the harmony of the great society that we have here in this country? Is it because we are afraid of lawsuits? Or is it because we are afraid to pay taxes? We all know that Christianity is under attack by all kinds of people who without us wouldn't be disturbed much at all. Thus what will we lose if we disturb the waters a little with the gospel? Are we lacking boldness or do we not believe in the saving message we profess? Are we not different anymore, and doesn't America see in us what the people of Antioch saw in the early Christians? Though we are disgusted by what we see going on around us and complain about it, have we forgotten that we possess the solution to all the insanity? It seems to me that some of us want politicians to resolve these issues. But we are the ones who need to impress on the politicians' consciences that they are in the positions they are because God put them there and that they are not accountable not only to the voters but, most important, to God. At the same time we need to impress on the consciences of our communities that God will hold everyone accountable for our actions or deeds. The only way out is to believe the gospel of Christ. When we preserve the harmony in our societies and disturb nothing, we might have peace for a little while, but the church is not visible and Christ is not visible either. If the church is not visible in the community, the community loses Christ and cannot know of its lost state. When the church is not visible, the community has no way of knowing and seeing God's love and the kindness demonstrated on the billboards, His people. He desires to save the world through Christ, and that includes our communities.

I believe we can reach America with the gospel again and be on the consciences of not just politicians but all of America if God wills it to happen. We can find that out through prayers and submissions. We need to subject ourselves to serious prayers for boldness, ask for God's leadership, and ask that He strongly kindle our desires to spread the good tidings of salvation through Christ not just to America but to other, apparently impenetrable, places. We also need to seriously examine the state of our congregations in the community. Let us start strengthening and doing some serious repairs to our relationships within the brotherhood. Let us show true love to each other by striving to resolve our differences in love and deep care for one another. Furthermore, let us as people of God present a united front with no division or factions. Let's make concerted efforts to resort to prayer and study to resolve our differences in love. Always looking to Christ and His word for the solution to our differences and the ones we cannot resolve, we can "let go and let God."

These are just a few of the things we can start with. There is more that each local church needs to examine and address with concrete steps to get the kingdom of God on track with God's business.

Like Peter said of the leadership in Jerusalem, let today's leaders of the people of God rise up to the same task and "devote ourselves to prayer and ministry of the word." This is where we need the leadership of the elders to stop waiting on tables and lead in cultivating the habit of praying so God will bust open the full resources and potential of the church. As the elders lead the way, they encourage the church to develop the habit of praying, which might lead to each family picking up the habit of praying, opening the door for intimacy with

God. Who knows what God will allow to take place. I know of no better way to develop intimacy with God than to develop a habit of talking to Him frequently and opening up to Him. Yes, He knows us better than we might know ourselves, yet He respects our choices and decisions so much that the only way He will take over is if we invite Him to do so. God intentionally made us with the ability to make choices so we can experience the joy and fulfillment that comes with sharing and sharing in His love, the kind of love that prompted Him to overlook our sins and save us. It is a beautiful thing God has done. No wonder the angels were trying to find out what God was up to when they saw God at work.

Note that barren Hannah prayed for a son, a single son so she would feel like the other mothers, but God gave her six children after all was said and done! Another Hebrew word that I would like us to get familiar with is גָּדַל (*gidal* or *gidel*). This form of the word is translated as "to make great," "to magnify," "to lift up," or "to bring up." In other grammatical forms the same root word takes different translation such as "great" or "elder." This root word is used in 1 Samuel to describe the young man Samuel developing in the presence of God. The scripture says, "[A]nd the young man Samuel grew in the presence of the Lord." Here is the same root word but it is pronounced "gadel." The same root word is used in Joshua 4:14 to say that "God magnified Joshua in the eyes of the people." What does that have to do with having a desire to do God's work or using our gifts in God's church? Do we wonder why Jesus sought to glorify the Father in all He did? In the end the Holy Spirit revealed to the apostles that God has given Jesus a name that is above all names. God has made Jesus the first in all things. Jesus is number one in God's book! God Himself testifies that He is well pleased with Jesus. After getting Moses to accept the job of bringing the children of Israel out of Egypt, God said that Moses would be like God to Aaron, and boy, did Moses become synonymous with the term *God* in the eyes of all of Egypt because of the dread and terror God brought on Egypt through him! Also at Lystra in Acts 14, we read of Paul and Barnabas being seen as the Greek gods Hermes and Zeus, respectively, because of the healing of a man who previously could not walk. No one can question the intimacy of Jesus and God the Father. But in Moses, Joshua, Paul, and all the other people who allowed God to use them we see that they end up bigger than they could ever have been had they worked on their own. What I am getting at is that when we allow God to work through us in His kingdom, He magnifies us. He makes us greater than we can imagine. God uses us to make us great because He is great and He is almighty.

The outreach to the lost has changed as our world has changed. Again we need to call on God to help us make the difference. The local church needs to find creative ways to reach out to the local community—that is, the local church needs to be more visible today. How do we go about doing that? This is a good prayer to send up. Among the creative things I have seen in my local congregation is what we call Fall Festival. At this festival we invite the community into the building where we meet for worship and introduce the church through different activities as we all eat together. Another one was at the county fair. My family walked by a booth that was "serving" the gospel to those who stopped by. The group was not expressly teaching the gospel as taught by the apostles in the book of Acts. It was the creativity in the presentation that caught my attention. My girls were presented with a string and gold, red, white, black, and green beads. The gold bead represented the streets of gold in heaven, the black bead represented our sins that prevent us from getting to heaven, the red bead represented the blood of Christ for cleansing us from sin, the white bead represented the forgiveness of our sins, and finally the green bead represented God's expectation for us to bear fruit. As I listened to the presentation, I thought to myself, What a creative way to let people know about what God has done for us. Like I observed earlier the message was not all there, but one ought to appreciate the creativity of the presentation. In other places the challenge is not mentioning God in public so outreach might be different, but in places where it is being made impossible to preach about God in public, we need to use all the creativity God grants us, using those opportunities to make the gospel known to the world and our communities. Jesus said that we should be as humble as the dove and as wise or crafty as the serpent. The mission and the message have not changed and need not change; we just need to adopt our delivery methods to meet the challenges we face in our world today. God can open the door for us to do so.

Destiny: *Disciple, Accountability, and the Reward*
Why do we need to be active in the kingdom of God? When the disciples, the members of Christ's body, have no desire or zeal for God's work or to take up God's cause, the necessary implication is that the Lord's church is not visible in the community. The lack of zeal for God in God's people is like a depressed body that has given up on life or something close to that. Such a depressed body has members who lack energy and do very little for the body's upkeep. In

the parable of the talents we see that the servants had to account for the use of their talents. That and many other parables and teachings of Christ instruct us that God is going to judge the world at the return of Christ and all of us will account for our deeds, Christians or not. In the aforementioned parable, we read of the rewards to the faithful servants and the condemnation of the unfaithful servant who showed no interest in pleasing his master. He buried his potential in a hole in the ground. One might ask the obvious question, What is our destiny as disciples of Christ?

Jesus said each servant was given gifts according to his ability: five, two, and one respectively because that is what the master deemed suitable for those who worked for him. The unfaithful disciple became unfaithful when he refused to use the gift given to him. It was not the quantity that made him unfaithful. The two faithful servants took their responsibility seriously, and it bore fruit and multiplied. The unfaithful servant had apparently not heard that if we do one thing a thousand times, we become great at it, but if we do a thousand things one time, we are no good at any of them. I can't help but wonder how good the servant would have become if he had chosen to invest his gift. Is it possible that this servant would have made more than any of his fellow servants if he had invested his talent? By failing to use his talent, he failed to see what he could have contributed and what the value of his talent was. He was like the eighteen-year-old who wanted a car but received a Bible instead and refused to open it, thus failing to realize that a check for the car was buried in its pages.

God through Jesus has made us heirs with Jesus. Also according to Paul's letter to the Colossians we have been made partakers of the inheritance with the saints in the light. If therefore we are heirs and partakers of the inheritance with the saints, then we inherit both the work and the rewards if we stay disciplined and do whatever is to be done to take care of the inheritance. All of us in Christ have been called by God for His purpose. We cannot live like the third servant and fold our hands as if there is nothing for us to do, or bury our talents as if the talents God has given us have no potential. Paul said that in the end we will all appear before the judgment throne of God and account for our deeds. By being inactive in the Lord's body, we fail to allow God to be active in our lives and waste the potential He has given us to nourish His body. Besides, we will enjoy the reward in the inheritance better if we allow God to put our talents to work and use them effectively to enrich His kingdom.

Not Experts, Just Disciples

If we like sports, then we know of the guys and gals who appear on the television screen who just talk and are usually referred to as experts. Compared with the experts are the guys on the ground playing and dealing with the reality of the game. The expert can talk up the whole game without listening to any instructions from anyone. The player playing on the ground, however, has to do the real hard work of winning the game. In that effort, if he fails to heed calls and direction provided by the coach, who is observing the game and has all the tactics to lead his team to victory, he is destined to lose the game. Paul said to imitate him as he imitates Jesus Christ. I guess Paul wants to be like Jesus Christ, and so he does all he can to be like Christ. In saying this, Paul points to Christ as the one He submits to and so we should do likewise. Let's look at three illustrations by Christ, when Jesus had several occasions to instruct the disciples on who was the greatest among them. In Matthew 18:1-6 the disciples asked Jesus who was the greatest; in Matthew 20:20-28 it was a mother's request for her two sons to occupy important positions in the kingdom; and the final opportunity came in the form of a warning or caution to the disciples against what seemed to be the norm of the day among the rabbis in Matthew 23:11. In the first instance, Jesus set a child in the midst of the apostles and told them that the greatest among them needed to have an attitude like that of a child and be humble like a child. In both the second and third instances Jesus told the disciples that anyone who seeks to be the greatest should be their servant. Couple that with what Jesus said of Himself: that He came to serve and not to be served. Can we come up with anyone greater than Christ in the kingdom? He is the preeminence, after all, and also the head. Could anyone be more important than Him? And yet, He humbled Himself to serve our needs to the satisfaction of the Father. Let us replace the child Jesus set in the midst of the disciples by placing Jesus in the midst and have our own discussions about what effect that has on us. Can we be as humble as Christ, who knew everything?

When we become experts rather than disciples, is it possible for us to know better than our master, the King? In Matthew 23 Jesus told the disciples that they should not be called teachers, for only one was their teacher, that is, the Christ. Yes, we can know a lot and be well versed by the King's will and words. In fact, we can be so well versed in the King's word and will that should we be questioned or asked to demonstrate even in our sleep, we could state and demonstrate them without any hesitation. What needs to be impressed on us is that we need to be totally engulfed in the Savior's wishes and will so much that it is second nature to us. To this end we continue in His teachings and commands, knowing and doing no more than He has commanded us and given us the ability to do in faith. It is not a good thing for us to come off as people who know more than Christ, love more than Christ, have more compassion than Christ—that is, to have an attitude that we know more than Christ and thus exceed our mandate or commission. In fact, when we know more than Christ, we become in effect like the Father whom Christ said is the only one who knows the date He will return to the earth. Christ said that He didn't know the time and that only the Father does. In effect when we become experts, we no longer need to listen to Christ nor do we need His guidance anymore, because we can do it ourselves. The unmentioned claim is that we are that good.

Christ often told stories about servants to His listeners that involved responsibilities. For example, in Mathew 24:45, Jesus stated that blessed is the servant whom his left in charge of the master's household and the master returns to find him doing just that. In the parable of the talents, Christ indicates that every one of the servants received a gift from the master before he set out on his journey, some more than others. We also read that each of these servants of their own accord did something with their given talent. The results of the first two servants yielded profit or grew their talents. However, the third servant dug a hole and buried his talent. He did not multiply his talent at all; it's the one thing dirt can't grow. He made his talent dormant. It is important to note that all three servants took the initiative on how they were going to use their talents, and depending on how they used them, they grew or failed to grow. My point here is that as His disciples, Christ has given all of us a gift in one form or another that needs to be invested in the growth of His kingdom. You can't use my talents for me and I can't use yours to bear fruit for you. You and I can encourage each other to use our given talents for the growth of the Lord's church. Christ expects each of us to take initiatives on our own to affect the growth and maturity of His church. This doesn't mean we can't work together as a unit. In most cases we need to work as a whole body to advance the kingdom's work; other tasks might call for individuals leading and working on their own. All of these should have one purpose: the maturity of the Lord's church.

Let us keep in mind that whatever our role or work in the Lord's church, we have it because of the gifts Christ has given each member. That is, none of us occupies a role because of our own will or abilities; rather we occupy it because of what Christ has called us to be and do, to which end He has given us gifts to enable us to accomplish His will. To that end, He requires us to nourish and be nourished. That is, as disciples of Christ, no matter where we are in our spiritual journey, Christ expects us to follow His will, do His will, and teach and be taught His will. This is so that we continue to be firmly grounded and firmly planted in his word. In our various roles, some are more visible than others. As a result we humans have the tendency to make one role more important than others. In discussing issues relating to gifts given to the disciples, Paul made it clear in 1 Corinthians 12 that no one gift or role is better than the other. Instead God chooses who gets what gift just like the master in the parable of the talents. The purpose of all the gifts to each disciple in the body of Christ is to make the body function properly and grow to maturity. In Luke 17, Jesus taught that just because we did what was expected of us as servants, we cannot look for a pat on the back. We should concede that we are just servants who have done what we were asked to do. Jesus said we need to adopt the attitude "We are unworthy servants; we have only done what was our duty" (Luke 17:10, ESV).

Paul said of himself and Apollos that they were just planters and "waterers." They were only doing the jobs they were assigned, nothing more, nothing less. In his letters to Titus and Timothy, Paul encourages them to abide within the teachings and instructions they had received from him, which he received from Christ through the Holy Spirit. Let us take Jesus at His words and consider ourselves unworthy servants. I believe it will make it easier for us to esteem each other and value each other's efforts if we are looking at the Master, our Lord and Savior Jesus Christ, and paying very minor attention to the vessels He is using to accomplish His will. Let us encourage each other unto good works with all of our full potentials while considering that we are privileged to humbly serve before the Almighty One.

Regardless of the capacity in which we are serving the kingdom of God, we need to recognize that in our leadership or nonleadership roles we submit completely to the authority of Christ Jesus. We follow His commands, and as far as His Church is concerned, we originate nothing new except for what He has commanded. We submit in all of our actions, decisions, and will to the will of Christ, just as He submitted to the Father and fulfilled the will of the Father to the utmost detail. We are disciples, servants, trainees, learners, and so on, so we follow the Master and do as He says.

Make Disciples with What? Or, How Do We Make Disciples?

This might not seem an important question, but I believe it is one we need to think about. What were the disciples to use to make other disciples? Or how do we make disciples? In other words, how did the people who received the charge of the Great Commission go about making disciples? Did the apostles use programs or modernize themselves to be attractive to the community to win followers? Just how did people become Christians in the first century? How did the apostles reach out to their generation? Whatever means the apostles used, will they work for us today?

Jesus personally called the twelve apostles. He walked with them for three years and they followed Him everywhere He went. Other disciples also followed Jesus, largely because of the signs they saw that led to their believing in Jesus before Christ died on the cross. It is important that we be able to differentiate between the times before and after Christ's resurrection. For one thing not a single word has been said about how Jews or Gentiles in particular would become Christians. The Jews were still under the law of Moses. After His resurrection, however, Jesus charged the twelve He had trained with the Great Commission to make disciples of all nations. After the apostles were charged with the Great Commission, nothing happened until the Holy Spirit came upon the apostles and led Peter to preach the first sermon that set Christianity in motion. What did

Peter preach, and what was Christ expecting the apostles to make disciples with?

In both Mark and Luke's accounts we read the following:

> *"And he said unto them, Go ye into all the world, and* **preach the gospel** *to the whole creation" (Mark 16:15).*

> *"[A]nd he said unto them, Thus it is written, that* **the Christ should suffer, and rise again from the dead** *the third day; and that* **repentance and remission of sins should be preached in his name** *unto all the nations, beginning from Jerusalem" (Luke 24:46-47).*

According to these two accounts the gospel of Christ is the message. Before Christ came to earth and died for us, God had already determined what message He would use to reach the world. Thus in Luke's account we see Christ quoting what had been revealed by the prophets long ago. Again we see Christ keeping the Father's will. If we were to arrange the Great Commission account chronologically, we might conclude that Jesus had already told the apostles that He had all authority. In Luke 24, observe how Jesus used established authority to outline the mission for the apostles even though He was the new source of the authority behind the apostles. This is important to the Jewish mind, because the law, the prophets, and the psalms were well-defined, authentic, and well-established sources of authority. If what Jesus was instructing to be done contradicted that which is known in any of these sources, they could by no means take Him seriously. However, if what He was saying is consistent with scripture, then it is a serious matter that deserves their proper attention. Hence, though the apostles had known Jesus for three years, it was still important that Jesus referred them to what they knew before He established Himself as the sole authority.

Upon careful examination of the message Peter preached to the Jews starting from Acts 2 through Acts 10 where the first Gentiles were ministered to by the same apostle Peter, the theme that runs through the message is the following:

1. Jesus died on the cross at the hands of the Roman soldiers on account of the Jewish leaders.
2. Jesus's dead body was buried in a tomb.
3. Jesus was resurrected from the dead.

In Acts 8, Luke records that Philip from the very same scriptures that the Ethiopian eunuch was reading taught the eunuch the good news about Jesus. What other good news could there be if not for the one already being preached, which was that Jesus after He was mercilessly and brutally murdered by the people and their leaders was raised by God on the third day. He was raised by God never to see death again! That indeed ought to be the good news since mankind first encountered death because of sin.

Let's take a detailed look at this message so we can understand what it means to us. This will help us connect some very important things together. We know what Peter preached in Jerusalem, and we have a fairly good idea what Philip preached to the Samaritans and the Ethiopian eunuch. In Acts 13 we read of Paul's first missionary journey and some of what he preached. In preaching to the Jews in Antioch in Pisidia, Paul related to them their common history, and then he introduced Jesus to them and told them about the following:

1. The death of Jesus on the cross at the hands of the Roman soldiers made possible by the Jewish leaders
2. The burial of Jesus's dead body
3. The resurrection of Jesus

This looks very similar to the preaching of Peter. The same Holy Spirit that led Peter to preach the message of Christ's death, burial, and resurrection to the Jews was the same Holy Spirit that was leading Paul to preach the exact same message. It is important to note that Paul had not met Peter after Paul's conversion. We know this because Paul later in his writings to the Galatians said that at the start of his ministry he did not go to Jerusalem to determine what his message ought to be. He went to Jerusalem after several years of preaching and converting people, both Jews and Gentiles. When he went to Jerusalem, it was to get acquainted with the other apostles. In fact the message to people at Pisidia sounds almost like the message Peter preached to the gathered Jews in Acts 2. In Acts 17 also at both Thessalonica and Athens, Paul preached to a Jewish crowd and then to a group of Gentiles, respectively telling them about the Christ whom God had raised from the dead.

We might ask, So the message both Paul and Peter preached are the same—what does that have to do with one becoming a Christian? We learn from Paul the importance and significance of this message in his letter to the Corinthians and to the Romans. Paul tells us the importance of the initial message preached which is the death, burial, and resurrection of Jesus Christ in the first few verses in 1 Corinthians 15. He elaborates further in Romans 6 on the significance of this message. We quote these scriptures:

Moreover, brethren, I declare unto you the gospel which I preached unto you, which also ye have received, and wherein ye stand; By which also ye are saved, if ye keep in memory what I preached unto you, unless ye have believed in vain. For I delivered unto you first of all that which I also received, how that Christ died for our sins according to the scriptures; And that he was buried, and that he rose again the third day according to the scriptures. (1 Corinthians 15:1-4, KJV)

What then shall we say? Shall we continue to embrace sin that grace may abound? May that never be, how much longer shall we flourish in it we who are dead to sin? Are you ignorant that as many as were baptized into Christ Jesus into his death were baptized? We were buried therefore with him through baptism into_death that just as Christ was raised up from the dead by the glory of the Father, so even we in newness of life should walk. (Romans 6:1-4)

The following is the literal translation of the first four verses of the same passage above:
1 Corinthians 15:1-4

I make known now unto you, brothers, the gospel which I preached [or proclaimed] unto you, which also you received [or have in

143

your possession], in which also you stand; Through which also you are being saved, what word [message] I preached unto you if you hold firmly in your grasp [or, if you hold firmly in your grasp word (message) I preached unto you] unless in vain you believed [or, unless you believed in vain]. For I delivered unto you in most important [or in first order, first of all] that which also I received, that Christ died for sins of ours [Christ died for sins our] according to the Holy Scriptures, And that he was buried, and that he rose again day the third according to the Holy Scriptures.

This chapter is often referred to as the resurrection chapter. As Paul tackled many challenging issues with the Corinthian Christians, he addressed the resurrection, as these brethren seem to have issues about that. Having just finished talking about spiritual gifts in the previous chapter, he delves into the resurrection topic. Paul starts as follows (I am using a literal translation):

I make known now to you, brothers, the gospel which I preached [or proclaimed] to you, which also you received [or have in your possession], in which also you stand; Through which also you are saved, if you hold firmly in your grasp what word I preached unto you, unless in vain you have believed.

By the way Paul starts this chapter, we know that the message of the gospel has already been heard by the Corinthian Christians. Paul makes the following important notes in his introduction: 1)He proclaimed to them the gospel (he outlines what he refers to as the gospel in the ensuing verses); 2)These Christians stand in the gospel Paul preached to them; 3)The Corinthian Christians and Christians elsewhere are saved by the gospel if they hold on firmly to the word they heard, unless they had believed in vain.

These points are worthy of some attention. The gospel saves if these Christians believed the gospel preached to them and held firmly to what they heard. It makes salvation conditional, based on the gospel. This is the work of God that can be accepted only by faith. It makes sense if we think about it in the following way: if we reject the gospel, we cannot be saved by it, neither can the gospel save us if we believe now but later come to reject it. If we don't stand firmly in the gospel message, how can we expect it to save us?

As a matter of fact Mark puts it as follows: "Whoever believes and is baptized will be saved, but whoever does not believe will be condemned" (Mark 16:16, ESV).

Paul outlined what he said was the gospel he preached to the Corinthian Christians: "For I delivered unto you most importantly or in first order that which also I received, that Christ died for sins our according to the Holy Scriptures, And that, and that he rose again day the third according to the Holy Scriptures." Before we proceed, let's note something very important here.

Paul said, "For I delivered unto you most importantly or in first order that which also I received." What is Paul talking about here? Is he just talking about how the gospel is delivered to the sinner or is he talking about something more important? Is Paul talking about the order of presenting the message or is he saying this is the first thing sinners need to hear? Let's analyze the Greek text and then some of Paul's preaching in Acts. First the Greek text, the literal translation of the opening of verse 3 of 1 Corinthians 15 goes like this: "For I delivered unto you first of all that which I also received, how that Christ died for our sins according to the scriptures; And that he was buried, and that he rose again the third day according to the scriptures" (1 Corinthians 15:3, KJV).

1 Corinthians 15:3 as translated in most of the major Bible versions:

"For I delivered to you as of first importance what I also received, that Christ died for our sins according to the Scriptures" (NASU).

"For I delivered unto you first of all that which also I received: that Christ died for our sins according to the scriptures" (ASV).

"For I delivered to you first of all that which I also received: that Christ died for our sins according to the Scriptures" (NKJ).

"For I delivered to you as of first importance what I also received: that Christ died for our sins in accordance with the Scriptures" (ESV).

"For I delivered to you as of first importance what I also received, that Christ died for our sins according to the Scriptures" (NASB).

"For I delivered to you as of first importance what I also received, that Christ died for our sins in accordance with the scriptures" (RSV).

"For what I received I passed on to you as of first importance: that Christ died for our sins according to the Scriptures" (NIV).

I think what Paul is saying here is that the thrust of the gospel He preached to the Corinthians was the death, burial, and resurrection of Christ. The Greek word translated "of first importance" or "first and all" is sometimes rendered as "chief" or "principal." Paul is saying here that this is the principal message he received. It is the same message he passed on to the Corinth Christians. Paul said this message is of first importance or the most important among the messages he delivered to the Corinthians that led them to become Christians. As he was writing to them, he stressed the important of this initial message and held firm to it. Why was that? Paul said it was because the initial message was what saved them.

How are we making disciples, and with what message? If the message as Paul preached it was important, then it must have some importance and significance to us just as it did to Paul's hearers. We will look at the significance momentarily.

The Death of Christ

When Jesus told the story about the wicked vineyard caretakers, He ended the parable with the heir, the vineyard owner's son dead. He said nothing about the son coming back to life. In that story the focus was on the ungodly behavior of the caretakers and what the owner did to them. But let's pause and look at the parable again. The story is found in Matthew 21 and Luke 20. We can all agree that the son in this parable is Jesus Himself. Thus He is the one the wicked caretakers killed. As I thought about the parable, I realized that Jesus had not extended the parable to His resurrection. Hence the thought occurred to me: what if Jesus did not rise up from the dead? I must confess that I was a bit confused and afraid at that thought. We have the benefit of seeing the whole story, but the apostles, for example, lived with Jesus, and though Jesus knew His fate and knew the end of the story and had told His disciples on different occasions that He would be killed but would rise again on the third day, the disciples still had a difficult time seeing the big picture even to the point where some still doubted Jesus had risen even though he was standing in their midst.

It should have been no surprise to the disciples when He was betrayed and killed. I ask myself what the disciples should or could have done. Should they have celebrated that the Son of God was going to die? What exactly was the expected response from the disciples? According to the will of God, we saw in the events leading to the death of Christ Jesus wickedness at its finest, hatred and lies on their best display, and injustice in man. On display was our inability to exercise control over sin, just as Cain failed to heed God's warning. He did not master his emotions to take control of what eventually led to sin, killing his brother. Thus Friday ended with the Son of God dead. In fact He died before any of the people with whom He had been associated unfairly died. We could dwell on the evil that had happened to the Son of God, but to what point? After all, the

Son was dead. For a moment, it looked like death had done it again! Death had conquered yet again, and this time not just an ordinary member of mankind, but the One who raised others. Jesus called Lazarus from the dead; He told others that the dead man was just sleeping. It was still Friday, and at that point death was looking, strong, impregnable, and impenetrable. Death was looking like an insurmountable challenge that could not be overcome victoriously, and it looked like God's plans had been foiled yet again by death. His love for mankind had again hit a brick wall—a solid brick wall called Death. It was looking like all was lost. God took a big gamble for love, and in the process He lost big. It was looking like God had lost His Son and mankind perhaps forever. Friday was not looking good at all for God's camp. Can we imagine what God's enemies were saying? "It doesn't look good at all for God and those He loves."

Friday has seen a divine life taken by death, the old antagonist. The divine body of the Son of God lay lifeless. The Son of God had suffered the same fate as any of mankind would, for death had not shied away from the divine. Terrible day, that Friday! It seems like death had conquered the one who said, "He is the source of life," for Jesus had told His disciples He was the way, the truth, and the life. For the first time the Son of God, the very source of life, was without life. He was no longer breathing the air he had created. The Son of God was without any consciousness. He was dead, stone-cold dead. Grieved and disappointed some secret disciples were emboldened to ask for His lifeless body for burial. They didn't have much time to give Him a proper burial. Because of time constraints, all these disciples could do was to wrap up the lifeless body and toss it into a tomb that had never seen a dead body before. The tragedy here is that the source of life Himself was lying dead, stone-cold dead. His life had been squeezed out of Him just like a defenseless lamb by the same people He came to save.

We can sum up Friday as follows: God's Son was dead, and death's stronghold was intact and didn't look breached at all. Death's clamps were still functional and holding strong and tight. The man who raised others from death was dead: He called the name of the dead Lazarus, and Lazarus walked out of his grave alive. He reached out His hand to a dead girl and she sat up. This man did not fight against His own death. No, He didn't resist His killers at all. The one who healed a man born blind could not heal the fatal wounds from the nails that caused His death—or did they? Jesus told His disciples He would lay His life down, and nobody took it away from Him. That was before the cross. Now on the cross, He said, "Father, into your hands I commit my spirit." He gave up His life voluntarily. Yes, He gave it up voluntarily. His body was lifeless, and the only possibilities to look forward to were rust, rot, and decay. Death seemed to have defeated the Son of God, the author of life. Death had conquered and been victorious, or so it seemed. Could the God who created the heavens and the earth not prevent His Son from dying? This list can go on and on.

What does the death of Christ mean to us? Well, Paul in 1 Corinthians 15 stated a simple truth of nature—that is, that a seed must die before it can bear more like itself. Also in the first part of Romans 7, Paul talks about marriage and remarrying in the eyes of the law. In 1 Corinthians 15 the example Paul uses suggests to us the need for us to put to death the old self so that we can walk in the new way of life. Or as Paul puts it in Romans 7, we cannot marry Christ unless the old nature dies and the covenant we have with sin is broken. Unless we do that, we cannot unite with Christ.

The question is, Should Jesus have died? Especially given the kind of death He was subjected to, should the Son of God have died such an awful death? Couldn't God, the Creator of all things, have found another way to save us from our sins? I am sure I am not the first to ask these questions and won't be the last. Christ had to die because God loves mankind, and mankind's sin was the subject of God's wrath. Christ died for the following reasons:

God the Father willed it to be so. Remember Jesus's prayer in the garden asking the Father to pass the cup away from Him except if it be the Father's will.

The law required that sin be atoned by blood. To this effect Paul says in Hebrews that the blood of animals could not take away sins, so the sacrifices for sin atonement were made yearly. Jesus offered His own blood to atone for our sins.

The prophets had prophesied that the fate of the Messiah would end in death.
Jesus's blood was the blood for the new covenant and dedication of the new covenant.

For our sins to be taken away or separated from us we would need to participate in His death, burial, and resurrection through baptism. In Romans 6:3-4 Paul asked the Christians to whom he was addressing the Romans' letter whether they knew that their baptism into Christ meant baptism into His death He continued, "[W]e were buried therefore with Him through baptism into His death."

Our sins can be cut off when we in obedience heed His call to obedience.

We can die to our sins and be separated from sin, torn apart from sin, completely dissolving the union we have with sin by cutting our cord attached to sin, and be united with Christ in a new union.

Jesus died to make void the grips of death and to annul the power of the one who holds that power, who is Satan.

Jesus died to bring into fruition God's purposes. Through the death of Jesus Christ God brought together both Jews and Gentiles as one body and heirs with Jesus Christ. The death of Christ removed the law that prevented the unity between the two groups.

There are many more reasons that we can find, some unmistakably spelled out, others that require a little digging to find out. God in His infinite wisdom had all this worked out before Creation began. God is not a god who reacts after something has already happened. He has His plan all worked out and is working it to perfection in accordance to His will. We might ask whether man is capable of staying away from sin or is capable of being sinless. If we understand what God has made us through Jesus Christ, then we will strive to stay away from sin. Not because we are capable of being sin-free, but because through faith in Christ we have accepted that God has set us free from sin in Jesus. So we walk like people who have been freed from sin. That is, because Christ makes us whole through faith, as we strive in faith with all sincerity we are able to please God well. God considers that faith as righteous as Abraham's when Abraham in faith trusted God. In that sense, yes, man can be free from sin, because God says we are, not because of our own efforts.

The dates are October 12 and 13, 2010. I arrived home from work very tired on the evening of the twelfth. The news was already on, so I started paying a little attention to it. The news was about the breakthrough to the Chilean miners who had been trapped underground for sixty-nine days. I had followed the story since the time it first broke that thirty-three miners in Chile were trapped. The news as I recall at the time was saddening. However, I forgot about it as time went by. So it was pleasant to the ear when the news did not report any deaths but rather that rescuers were on their way to bring the miners up. A lot of hard work had gone into the rescue efforts, and finally there was a breakthrough to rescue the trapped miners from their perilous situation and bring them to safety. I watched the first miner rescued and brought up to the joy of the family and the whole nation of Chile and possibly the entire world that was watching the event. I shed tears of joy as I saw the rescued man freed to safety. I tried to wait for the next rescue, but man has to work and morning comes early, so I went to rest my weary bones. As I was getting ready for work the following morning, the morning of the thirteenth, I witnessed the rescue of the eleventh miner. I saw the rescuers pull up the eleventh man the same way they had pulled up the first one. What was surprising to me was the way I reacted to the eleventh rescued miner. My reaction to the eleventh rescue was the same as my reaction to the first rescue.

I rushed home after work, eager to see the rescue of the last miner. As the tube carrying the last miner approached the top, I called my girls to come and see. Even though we didn't know any of these men, we were happy that all of them were safe and free. My reaction was no different from the ones I had seen earlier. In all of these, I kept thinking about what Jesus said about when a sinner is rescued to safety. Jesus said, "[T]he angels in heaven rejoice when one sinner is saved." I thought to myself, What a perfect picture As sinners, we are like the trapped miners, except that no human equipment or technology can dig us out to safety or dig a path for us to be rescued. Thus God pulls us out from under the burden of sin and its rot that has trapped us and rendered us useless. The only thing we were good for was condemnation. The only safe tunnel out is Jesus, who, like the capsule used to transport the miners to safety, transfers us into His kingdom, making us part of His body. God transfers us to safety in Jesus Christ, the only secure place there is from sin to hide the saved sinner according to God's design. The death of Christ means that we die to our old selves and make a new choice to walk in the new life God has called us into.

The Burial of Christ

The burial of Christ is probably one of the bizarre realities about the cruelties that crowned the tragedy of His death. Pressed for time, confused and alarmed about the events that had just taken place, some prominent but secret disciples whose encounter with Jesus had been outside the public eye stepped up to ask Pilate for Jesus's dead body to bury it. As it happened, the Sabbath, the Jewish day of rest, was fast approaching and they were pressed for time. The disciples were so short on time that the only thing they could do was to wrap up the still body of the Savior and toss it into a new tomb where no dead body had ever been laid. God's Son was buried in such a way that not even a pauper would be buried.

God has chosen the burial of Christ for us to partake in the death of Christ. Thus the significance of the burial to us is baptism. The word *baptism* is only a transliteration. The proper translation of the Greek word is "to dip" or "to immerse." Among the significance aspects of baptism are these:

Baptism is a direct command from Jesus Christ according to the Great Commission. Baptism is the answer to the question, What shall we do to be saved? or simply, What shall we do after anyone has heard the message of the gospel as Philip told the Ethiopian eunuch? That is what Peter told his fellow Jews in Acts 2.

Baptism is one of the prime tasks in the Great Commission. It is what the apostles and disciples did whenever anyone asked what is next. It is the next task as outlined by Jesus in the Great Commission.

Baptism is the only means that God has set up for us to enter into the death of Christ or share in the death of Christ. This is where our sinful body is separated from us. It is the medium through which God has chosen to cut off our sinful nature.

Baptism is a physical act with spiritual implications. Baptism is done through faith in obedience to the will of God. We don't submit to baptism out of our own initiative for good work. We submit to baptism because Jesus commanded it and God the Father wills it.

Baptism marks the point in God's plan of salvation where the sinner enters into the death of Christ and undergoes spiritual transformation, cutting off our sinful nature, surrendering our will and ideals, and abandoning all of our selves. The rise from baptismal waters is where we start living less for self and grow into bond servants as committed servants of Christ.

The Resurrection of Christ

The Resurrection—God in His wisdom has done everything right and all in its time per Solomon, the wisest man and king who ever lived. He added that God has done this so that man will look at what God has done and fear Him. This is no minor observation by King Solomon. Jesus was buried in a new tomb that no one had ever been buried in. Why is that important? we might ask. Just think about it for a minute: a new tomb, no one had been buried in it before, and before Friday and sometime during Friday it was still sitting empty. In the late afternoon this new tomb saw its first dead body. It is important to observe here that no one else could have been buried in the same tomb until after the Sabbath because of Jewish traditions and customs. In the early morning on Sunday the first visitor's or visitors' report caused an uproar. The dead body was not in the new tomb. One could easily have said that someone came and removed or relocated the dead body. One small problem with that was that the tomb was being guarded by no other than Roman soldier. Besides, those who could have moved it were all so culturally conscious of their traditions that they had to wrap the dead body and just leave it in someone's tomb, hoping to come back after religious observances were over to bury it properly. Secondly, these people who could have stolen the body had to observe the Sabbath, the Jewish day of rest, from Friday night to Saturday night. The only real time that anyone could possibly have had contact with the body after placing it in the new tomb on Friday night was early Sunday morning. So then, if the first witness or witnesses at the tomb saw nothing but an empty tomb, then the tomb was nothing but empty. Empty because it had had only one dead body in it and that body was gone. The tomb being new with only one body in it ensures that that tomb can account for only that one body, so when that body was gone, it was gone. Because no other body had been buried in that tomb before then, the empty new tomb is conclusive evidence that Christ was not in the tomb. On the other hand if the tomb had seen even one burial before Christ's body was placed in it, we could not conclusively say that the tomb was empty. This would have presented difficulties for the witnesses, because they could not truly say the tomb was empty, and if the tomb was not empty, then we could not say conclusively that Christ arose truly. It could have been disputable. But God had it all worked out so there would be no dispute! The empty tomb meant that the tomb was empty! Besides the time crunch and religious practice, political and military circumstances made stealing the body and hiding it impossible.

B. "baptizing them into the name of the Father, and of the Son, and of the Holy Spirit." This is a command.

I: "Baptizing them . . .":

Even though verse 19 of Matthew 28 has been divided into two parts, the verse as a whole is a complete instruction. It expresses a single thought or command, which is to make disciples. Just look at it; we use the literal translation here: "going therefore you make disciples of all nation, baptizing them into the name of the Father and the Son and the Holy Spirit." If we separate verse 19 as I have done and labeled as A and B, we discover very quickly that the first part makes sense because it can stand on its own, but the second part hardly makes any sense—it is a fragment. The reason is that we expect something to come before "baptizing them . . . ." If we state only the first part without the second part, we have taken away from God's word and have not stated the whole truth about God's word. Likewise if we choose to obey the first part of the Great Commission statement and fail to keep the rest, we have failed the whole commission. One cannot selectively choose which part of the Great Commission we like best, and for that matter which part of God's word to act on and which part not to act on.

Additionally, if we say only the second part to anyone, the first question that ought to be asked is, Who is Christ referring to as *them* or who are to be baptized? That is, who are to be baptized in the name of the Father and the Son and the Holy Spirit? The obvious answer is, those who are being made disciples. From this part of the Great Commission statement, the making of disciples is not complete until the second part is fulfilled or kept as well as the rest of the command. The full instruction requires that all parts of the Great Commission be kept or fulfilled. As disciples of Christ, the King, we need to keep in mind that in every kingdom the king's words settle all disputes or arguments. The king's words mean action and are final. We fail in making disciples for Christ our king if we only educate people about Him without proceeding to baptize them. We have only partially kept this commission statement and as such have not faithfully and fully performed the task of making disciples.

Why does Jesus desire His disciples to be baptized? Let's keep in mind that this is a direct, face-to-face command from Jesus to the apostles. Jesus was giving this command to the apostles in person. Now let's ask, Why would anyone say that baptizing the disciples or baptism is not important when Christ clearly states that as His desire or a command for the disciples to be baptized? Observe that Matthew's account of the Great Commission does not say anything about belief, or hearing of the message or even confession, or the sinner's prayer, or anything of that sort. It seems to me that many who profess Christianity today stress faith and grace more than they stress baptizing the disciples, which Jesus clearly commands the disciple makers to do in the name of the Godhead. In studying the Great Commission up to this point, the only thing mentioned about disciples is to make disciples and baptize them in the name of the Father, of the Son, and of the Holy Spirit. We will see later that we are to teach the new disciples to obey or maintain all that Christ commanded the apostles and therefore the present-day Christian. Why is it that faith or belief, repentance—the things that we tend to emphasize when teaching potential disciples of Christ—are not mentioned by Matthew? Is it because they are not important, or did Matthew forget?

Far from it. I don't think Matthew forgot to record this, and neither do I think Jesus neglected to mention it. Matthew's account of the teachings of Jesus tells a lot about repentance, faith, and believing in Jesus. So let's look at Jesus's statement again: "[G]o therefore and make disciples of all nations." How do we make disciples then? Or how do we start to make disciples? We see in the book of Acts that those who were made disciples had the gospel about Jesus taught or explained to them. In both Mark and Luke's accounts of the Great Commission, Jesus told the disciples that they were to use the gospel about the risen Savior, which is what the prophets of old had prophesied would happen. So when Peter, for example, preached to the gathering in Jerusalem on the day of Pentecost, he told them about the risen Lord and persuaded them with other arguments. The reaction of some of the people after hearing what Peter said is described as "they were cut to the heart" or "they were pricked in the heart." As a result, they asked Peter what to do, having been convicted in their hearts. Peter replied, "Repent, and be baptized every one of you in the name of Jesus Christ for the remission of sins, and ye shall receive the gift of the Holy Ghost" (Acts 2:38, KJV).

Similarly, we see from Philip's preaching and performing miracles in Acts 8 both in Samaria and explaining the scriptures to the traveling Ethiopian eunuch reactions similar to those in Acts 2. "And the people with one accord gave heed unto those things which Philip spake, hearing and seeing the miracles which he did . . . But when they believed Philip preaching the things concerning the kingdom of God, and the name of Jesus Christ, they were baptized, both men and women" (Acts 8:6, 12, KJV). And "Then Philip opened his mouth, and began at the same scripture, and preached unto him Jesus. And as they went on their way, they came unto a certain water: and the eunuch said, See, here is water; what doth hinder me to be baptized? And Philip said, If thou believest with all thine heart, thou mayest. And he answered and said, I believe that Jesus Christ is the Son of God" (Acts 8:35-37, KJV).

There are many other examples recorded in Acts that we could add to the above citations, but these examples give us enough information to address what it means to begin and make disciples. We see that the initial steps toward making disciples involved the following: 1) the disciples *preached Jesus* to their targeted audience; 2)those who heard *the word* reacted to the word and asked what to do; 3)Peter ordered those asking what to do to *repent* and be *baptized* a) for the remission of their sins and b) to receive the gift of the Holy Spirit; 4)both the Samaritans and the Ethiopian eunuch *believed* and submitted to *baptism*; and finally 5)the Ethiopian eunuch *made known* or *confessed* to Philip what he believed from what Philip had presented to him since their encounter. Paul sums it up nicely: "So then faith cometh by hearing, and hearing by the word of God" (Romans 10:17, KJV).

So believing, repenting, and confession are all effective responses to the preaching of the gospel from people who heard the gospel preached to them.

In early parts of Acts, the Christian movement was taking shape under the supervision and help of the Holy Spirit, which was leading and guiding the apostles, who were laying the foundations and first principles of the kingdom of God. The apostles addressed concerns and issues that arose with the guidance and leadership of the Holy Spirit. In essence, the movement had not matured. It took time and instructions by the apostles who were being led by the Holy Spirit to put the proper structure of the Lord's church in place. In the letter to the Corinthians, Paul puts the state of the movement as follows: "For we know in part, and we prophesy in part. But when that which is perfect is come, then that which is in part shall be done away. When I was a child, I spake as a child, I understood as a child, I thought as a child: but when I became a man, I put away childish things" (1 Corinthians 13:9-12, KJV).

Now, however, we have the completed New Testament, which has recorded in it all that we need to make us faithful Christians if we follow both the examples and the doctrine in it carefully. Thus the gospel of Jesus is preached to the potential disciple. Upon hearing the gospel of Jesus there is an expected reaction to what has been heard in the form of acceptance or rejection. In the reaction, acceptance involves believing in the Lord Jesus, repenting of one's sins, confessing what one has come to believe from the preaching of the gospel of Jesus, and submitting to baptism for the remission of sins and reception of the gift of the Holy Spirit. Rejection of the gospel simply means rejection of the gospel and refusal to acknowledge the Lord Jesus.

If Matthew's account happened to be the only one from which we read about baptism, would that strike us as something important to every Christian? If so, why is that, and if not, why not? We find the answers in the Great Commission itself. Jesus commanded that any disciple made must be baptized! Baptism therefore is an essential part of keeping the Great Commission. Jesus is the King, and His word on the subject is final. As a matter of fact, His word on any subject is final, for He alone has all the authority. Additionally, He is the one whose blood was shed, and He commands that the disciples made are to be baptized. Who then is saying otherwise? Also we see in Matthew 16 and Acts 2 that Peter, whom Jesus gave the responsibility of opening the kingdom on the day of Pentecost, ordered those convicted by the gospel of Jesus to be baptized. Jesus commanded baptizing newly made disciples and Peter ordered it done. Who is saying anything different?

I asked the following question earlier: Why does Jesus desire for disciples to be baptized? To answer this question successfully, we need to look at and understand the message that the disciples preached—the gospel message itself. When Peter preached the gospel, his message led to ordering that the hearers who accepted the message and sought to know what to do be baptized. The Samaritans who responded to Philip's message were also baptized, and the Ethiopian eunuch out of his understanding of Philip's presentation to him asked to be also: "[A]nd the eunuch said, See, here is water; what doth hinder me to be baptized"? (Acts 8:36, KJV)

What was the message that Peter and Philip presented to their audiences at the beginning of their making of disciples?

Acts 2 tells us exactly what Peter preached. After explaining to the crowd what was happening using the scriptures, Peter said the following about Jesus:

> *Men of Israel, hear these words: Jesus of Nazareth, a Man attested by God to you by miracles, wonders, and signs which God did through Him in your midst, as you yourselves also know Him, being delivered by the determined purpose and foreknowledge of God, you have taken by lawless hands, have crucified, and put to death; whom God raised up, having loosed the pains of death, because it was not possible that He should be held by it. (Acts 2:22-24, NKJV)*

Peter continued his preaching, explaining to the people that Jesus was the one the prophets had been talking about.

According to Luke's record, Philip preached Christ to the Samaritans; that "Then Philip went down to the city of Samaria, and preached Christ unto them" (Acts 8:5, KJV).

The same Philip taught the Ethiopian eunuch from the scriptures below:

> *And Philip ran thither to him, and heard him read the prophet Esaias, and said, Understandest thou what thou readest? And he said, How can I, except some man should guide me? And he desired Philip that he would come up and sit with him. The place of the scripture which he read was this, He was led as a sheep to the slaughter; and like a lamb dumb before his shearer, so opened*

he not his mouth: In his humiliation his judgment was taken away:
and who shall declare his generation? for his life is taken from the
earth. And the eunuch answered Philip, and said, I pray thee, of
whom speaketh the prophet this? of himself, or of some other man?
Then Philip opened his mouth, and began at the same scripture,
and preached unto him Jesus. (Acts 8:30-35, KJV)

From the above scripture, we can safely infer that Philip presented to the eunuch the suffered Jesus just like Peter had done in Acts 2. As we continue to explore for answers to why Jesus desires for His disciples to be baptized, let us not forget that we have already addressed some of the answers to this question. However, let us establish a few things before we proceed.

The word baptism

The word *baptize* is a transliteration of the Greek word βαπτιζω (*baptidzo*). The lexical meaning for this Greek word includes English words such as "to dip," "to immerse," "to cleanse or purify by washing," "to administer the rite of ablution" (a washing of the body or parts of the body), "to dip repeatedly," "to immerge," "to submerge," "to cleanse by dipping or submerging," "to wash or to make clean with water." These are equivalent words or phrases in the English language to properly render meaning to the Greek word βαπτιζω (*baptidzo*). Thus the proper translation of this word to English ought to be *immersion* or a word or phrase that accurately reflects the Greek.

Baptism: work of faith or something else

Often the argument against baptism is that it is a "work," and that it makes salvation no longer a gift of God to be received by faith. The funny thing is, by receiving this gift from God, we take an action, or make a decision; why is that not work? I do agree that salvation is a gift from God, but not because it is or is not work. It is God's gift because we did nothing to prompt God to save us. We had nothing to say about it in any way. God initiated, planned, and set in motion every aspect of our salvation. Hence God offers to us His gift as He has prepared it and knows it best suits our needs. Let's look at the heroes of faith and what the Bible says about them and how they acquired their reputations as people of faith. Let's look at some of these heroes listed in Hebrews 11:

By faith Abel offered . . . a more excellent sacrifice than Cain.
By faith Enoch . . . has been well pleasing to God.
By faith Noah . . . moved with a godly fear, prepared an ark.
By faith Abraham . . . obeyed . . . and went out.
By faith he became a sojourner . . . dwelling in tents [still speaking of Abraham].
By faith Sarah . . . counted him faithful who had made the promise.
By faith Abraham . . . offered up Isaac.
By faith Isaac blessed Jacob and Esau.
By faith Jacob . . . blessed.
By faith Joseph . . . made mention . . . and gave commandment.
By faith Moses . . . was hid [By Moses' parents].
By faith Moses . . . refused to be called the son of Pharaoh's daughter . . . choosing to share ill treatment with the people of God.

By faith he forsook Egypt [speaking of Moses].

By faith he kept the Passover. [still speaking of Moses]

By faith they passed through the Red Sea [speaking of the Israelites].

By faith Rahab . . . , having received the spies

If work is defined in its simplest form as an effort made toward something, then from the list above all these heroes did some kind of work to demonstrate their faith. Put differently, we know of their faith only because of the effort they put behind their convictions that were developed from their faith. If we define work as a physics student might—as effort over a certain distance—then we still see that heroes like Abraham demonstrated that without exception. Then we can observe and agree with James, the Lord's brother, that faith in the absence of work is dead. How do we show our faith in the Lord in the absence of our actions?

As we read Hebrews 11, especially from verse 33 on. Notice how the book of Hebrews author lists the actions taken by the heroes he did not have time to include details of their actions prompted by their faith. Can we say that these people's actions were works? Works they were indeed, but they were works that glorified God or were aimed at pleasing God. Just look the list over again: What did God bear witness to Abel about? Didn't God testify to Abel's actions, Abel's sacrifice? Enoch also had good testimony in his favor before he was taken by God. Enoch was commended as pleasing God well. What about Noah heeding God's warning and building the ark that saved his family and condemned his generation for their sins and for rejecting God's word? Noah "moved with godly fear," according to the KJV translation. Is it possible that building the ark was works? I contend it was. But it was work in response to faith and obedience. Noah took God at His word without knowing the future outcome. That qualifies as faith, doesn't it? Let's go through the list and pay attention to what these people did—the way they chose to live their lives because of what they had heard from God or because of what they were firmly persuaded was God's will for them.

Like Noah, Abraham's generation might have thought him crazy to abandon the comforts of civilization to pursue what some might call folly. Yet through faith he encountered angels, and possibly a visit by God. He endured hardships, threats, and difficulties, including responding to God's request to sacrifice Isaac. The life Abraham led and the actions he took were all aimed at one thing: pleasing God well. Also, the Egyptians perished when they tried to pass through the Red Sea. Passage through the sea was not an ordinary thing to accomplish. It required faith. It required taking actions that pleased God even if the Israelites didn't know what the result would be like. Without the works of these heroes, it would be impossible for us to tell why they were considered heroes. The writer of Hebrews said in chapter 11, verse 6, "[N]ow apart from faith it is impossible to please God well: For it is necessary [or binding, proper, behooved, inevitable] for anyone who approaches God to believe that He is and those that seek out diligently after Him a rewarder He is."

So, like these heroes of faith, we walk and do according to our faith just as they walked and did according to their faith.

"[W]e walk by faith, not by sight" (2 Corinthians 5:7).

What is the Hebrews writer telling us about faith? That without faith or firm conviction or firm persuasion it is impossible to please God well, that faith is a must, or faith binds, or faith behooves—or yet still, that without faith it is inevitable that anyone who approaches or comes near to God can please Him. We must believe or must be firmly convicted that God is, and that God is the rewarder of those who diligently seek after Him. It is hard to go through this passage without realizing that associated with faith is effort, persistence, and devotion. Now, looking back at Abraham, was it just by faith that things happened or did he show his faith in God by following through and doing what God had asked of him? Wasn't this the argument James was making in James 2 when he said, "Yea, a man may say, Thou hast faith, and I have works: shew me thy faith without thy works, and I will shew thee my faith by my works . . . Was not Abraham our father justified by works, when he had offered Isaac his son upon the altar?" (James 2:18-21, KJV).

How do we show our faith if not through what we do according to God's word and will? We develop faith because God's word was spoken and we heard it. We become doers of God's will because we choose to demonstrate our faith through our actions. We can do whatever we want or like according to our will and that requires no faith at all, but doing what God has asked us to do requires faith! Why? we might ask. This is because we take God at His word and follow through in obedience. So then, by submitting to baptism, the disciple shows his or her faith in God through works of obedience to the command of Christ. Because the disciple acts in faith, the disciple is not doing anything out of his or her own accord; rather he or she is following a direct command from Christ just like following Christ's direct command to go make disciples of all nations. Isn't it just like Noah listening to God and building the ark? Or Moses following through with the orders to observe the Passover, which saved the lives of the firstborns in Israel before they left Egypt? Thus there is a difference in works that we come up with in our attempts to please God versus doing works that God has planned for us to walk in them.

Let's see if these actions make sense, or if we would have engaged in them. Let's imagine we wake up one morning and decide to build a large boat. As we sit down at the table to eat breakfast with our family, we inform them about our plans. We look at the faces of our children and they spell skepticism. We spend the rest of the time at breakfast convincing them that God has given us a warning about an unusual rain that is about to fall. Moreover, we have the dimensions for the boat He requires us to build to exact specifications. Note that Noah could have built any ark of any size and not followed God's directives. If Noah had done that, his works would hardly have qualified for works of faith. They would have been his own works and not pleasing to God. That is because by not following God's plan, and following his own plan for the ark, Noah would have rendered God's wisdom less superior than his. Needless to say, we have had a hard time convincing our children that this is God's word and we need to act on it. Eventually, the children reluctantly agree to help build the boat. As we start cutting down trees and hauling them to build the ark, our neighbors start asking what we're up to. Imagine that we have already heard the whispers going around town about old Noah building some crazy thing called an ark and claiming God has given him the instructions to do so.

Let us continue to imagine that it has been a few years now since we first mentioned the news to our family and started work on the ark. Thus far we have the skeleton of the ark, which the neighbors have seen us struggle to build—well, maybe not struggle, but it has not been easy building such a gigantic structure for the first time. The structure is looking like nothing anyone in our generation has seen. We have no idea whether what we are working on will work, for there is no evidence that we know of that shows that such a structure will last or even float on water. Imagine that all the skillful fishermen are telling us that what we are building is called crazy, and that the earth is too big for a few days of rain to destroy it. They point to the oceans and say that even the ocean has not consumed the land, so how can we be convinced that what we heard was God talking to us and not our own imaginations. The mocking of our attempts has gotten to the point where our boys think we should give up the project altogether since it has been almost a hundred years now and there are no signs of the prolonged rain we have been talking about. Imagine we have become a daily target for mockery by the weather forecasters. Imagine that just the other night, we were featured leading some animals in pairs into the ark. This was followed by a couple of interviews in which the experts suggested that we be taken to the hospital for a checkup since we look crazy, tired, and out of control.

Imagine that all these criticisms have penetrated our family's consciousness to the point where our boys and their wives walk around town trying not to be noticed. They avoid public places so they won't have to answer another foolish question about their father's quest. We too have become cautious about how we move

171

about. It looks like all our friends and relatives have come to the same conclusions as the experts, so they are no longer stopping by as they used to, except for grandfather Methuselah, whose name means "when he dies it shall be sent." Even though he did not fully understand what was going on, he was a devoted man to God and we've dwelled on his wisdom from time to time. He was always there when difficulties and challenges showed their ugly heads, and offered meaningful words of encouragement. Like everyone before him grandfather Methuselah finally passed on. Because he lived for so long, it was difficult to imagine life without him. Imagine that at his funeral we listened to all the stories told about him and told a few that he told us while sharing some of the wisdom he shared with us. Against our better judgment, we tried to take the opportunity to warn people about the coming rain only to be met with jeering.

Imagine that a hundred years have passed and we have the ark built, and that all the pairs of animals we know of have been led inside. Imagine we have prepared the ark for as long as possible with all the things we know will provide us comfort as well as take care of the family's needs. We finally decide it is time to leave the house and move into the ark. Our sons and their families move in as well to avoid being ridiculed. All of a sudden one afternoon we realize that you cannot open the door to go out. We think, "We'll try a bit later for we are tired; we'll pry it open after a little rest," not realizing that the door has been shut by God. We look out into the clouds, and what was sunny and bright a moment ago has darkened a bit. Yet we think nothing of it. Within a few moments we look again and the skies have become darker. It has begun to drizzle, and then it starts raining. Shortly after it starts to rain, the boys gather around to inquire what we think, to which we say, "Only time will tell."

The last few paragraphs were an attempt to reenact Noah's faithful actions, with us as Noah. Let's endeavor to go through the scriptures and place ourselves in these stories as much as possible and attempt to relive them and make decisions and take the actions these heroes of faith took. The above story sounds crazy, doesn't it? Out of the naked blue, Noah started building an ark and telling people to heed the warning of God about the coming rain. For more than a hundred years, no rain came, at least not the rain Noah was predicting. Yet Noah stuck to the message from God. Consider Abraham, another example. After seventy-five years of the life he had known living in a town where he probably knew each corner, he packed up, dragging his father, wife, and nephew along and claiming that God had called him, rejecting the life he had always known and abandoning his own people to follow God.

Along the way, his father died and he moved from place to place without a permanent home. Onlookers and people he came in contact with thought he was crazy. Others tried to take his wife and properties. Abraham was forced to lie to save his life. He separated from his nephew to avoid a family dispute because of the feud between his men and the servants of his nephew Lot. As if all these things were not crazy and challenging enough, God's promises seemed to take a long time to come to fruition, such as the promise of a son by Sarah, his wife. The son Isaac is finally born, only to be followed a few years later by a request from God that he be sacrificed—a sacrifice in which the promised son, the joy of

173

both mother and father, the only heir, was to be used as the lamb. If we were Abraham, how would we have fared? How do we tell Sarah about this crazy idea of sacrificing *her son* because God has requested it? How do we go about our lives the day after, knowing we killed our own son, our only son, all because God asked it of us? Finally, how do we tell Isaac, the promised son, that he is the subject of the sacrifice about to take place? Abraham's conversation at the dinner table about God's request to sacrifice Isaac seems much more difficult than his ancestor Noah's challenge. How would we have dealt with the following situation? "Isaac spoke to Abraham his father and said, 'My father!' And he said, 'Here I am, my son.' And he said, 'Behold, the fire and the wood, but where is the lamb for the burnt offering?'" (Genesis 22:7, NASU). Are we having a hard time? Abraham came up with the only plausible answer, which was this: "God will provide for Himself the lamb for the burnt offering, my son" (Genesis 22:8, NASU).

God indeed provide the lamb for the sacrifice! The scriptures say that Abraham was at the point of killing his son to fulfill God's request when the angel stopped him: "But the angel of the Lord called to him from heaven and said, 'Abraham, Abraham!' And he said, 'Here I am.' He said, 'Do not stretch out your hand against the lad, and do nothing to him; for now I know that you fear God, since you have not withheld your son, your only son, from Me'" (Genesis 22:11-13, NASU).

Doesn't the angel's word capture it all? Abraham was motivated by godly fear and reverence for God and went through thick and thin situations to the point of sacrificing his own son to please God.

Could we or would we have done that? Or would we have found all the excuses possible to not go through with such a request from God? I might have done the latter. What was Abraham doing here? Was he showing his faith in God through his works and actions?

We could not talk about or learn from these heroes of faith if we did not have records of their works of faith to read. How would we have known how they went about pleasing God well if it were not for what was written about the way they conducted themselves in their societies and set themselves apart because of what they believed God was telling them? Let's think about it. We would not have known about them if not for what they did to stand out in their generations, taking a stand favoring God rather than going with the norms of the day. The follow-up question then is whether it is possible to please God. No one in scripture or in recorded history has been mentioned or is known to have pleased God from their own efforts; however, we have a lot of people who took God at His word and acted on it through faith. Put differently, these faith heroes produced fruitful works that glorified God because of their faith. That is, out of their faith came works that others could see and talk about, including us. Their works were pleasing to God.

God bore witness to Abel's gift. Pretty good witness to have on one's side, isn't it? God is the kind of witness we would like to have on our side when in front of a judge. He is an unequaled witness. His integrity is spotless. His word is truth; in fact He speaks only truth. He cannot lie—I mean, He cannot! If Abel were in one of our courtrooms today as an accused person and God was one of His witness, God would be the kind of witness that when He enters the courtroom, the judge stops all proceedings, stands, and asks, "God, who are you here for today?" God points in Abel's direction, and immediately the judge declares Abel's case closed with a big NOT GUILTY stamp and another big AQUITTED stamp without any interrogation of the witness. If God happens to be called to the witness stand, His testimony will be unquestioned and unchallenged. Ever seen such a witness? That's our God! Wait a minute: the sacrifices of both Cain and Abel were presented before the heavenly court with God as both judge and witness!

Enoch obtained the witness that he pleased God well. Do we wonder what these witnesses saw and how they concluded that he pleased God well? Noah condemned his generation and became the heir of righteousness because of his faith in God and believing what he had not seen. We can exhaust the list of examples. Talk about moving mountains with faith the size of a mustard seed. I must say that getting God to give favorable testimony on our behalf is greater than moving mountains. Better yet, our actions prompted by faith in God's word alone give us great credibility in the eyes of God. Just look at Abel's actions due to his gift to God, Enoch's actions earned him an acknowledgment that he pleased God, and Noah by his actions condemned his generation by being the only one to act on God's word. If these aren't moving mountains, I wonder what else could be.

Another thing worth noting is that some of these men and women waited for a while—well, a long time in some cases. Let's look at a few of them, Noah preached for more than a hundred years, all the while being disciplined in waiting for God. For more than a hundred years preaching the same message, something like, "It's gonna rain! It's gonna rain!" to the same people just about. Some probably thought he was crazy, yet he kept on preaching. Does it not sound like diligence? Hebrews 11:6 says God is a rewarder of those who diligently seek Him. Has time worn out our message? Or have our societies and generation adjusted to, diluted, or even changed our message about Christ so that it is not consistent with God's word as taught by the apostles? What about Abraham? He was 75 years old when God called him and he died at well over the age of 180 without a permanent home on the land God had promised to give him. In fact other people still occupied the land when he died. Yet he held on to God's calling and promises without complaints or grumbling. What about Isaac, Jacob, and the others—even the prophets who saw God's promise in the distant future and sought to be part of it by faith and remained faithful in ministry to God and his word through the diligence of their work? Doesn't it make sense that the God who never quits on us in spite of the heavy doses of disappointments we serve Him on a regular basis with our sins and failures desires us to seek after Him with some determination and resolve? Doesn't it make sense that the more we seek after something and show determination and tenacity for wanting it, the more we appreciate the worthiness of it once we have it? There is something about persisting to get what you want that leads to resolve, purity, and greater appreciation after you have obtained it.

I asked us to insert ourselves into these stories so that for a moment we might live and struggle with the lives and decisions these men and women heroes of faith had to go through to fulfill God's will for their lives. Without force or pressure these heroes of faith of their own accord chose and made decisions that looked unreasonable to their generations. Often these decisions were out of the norm—irrational, we might say. These men and women lived a certain lifestyle different from what was around them, sometimes in the face of ridicule, not knowing by any means the results or the outcomes of the actions they were taking in favor of God. Listen to what the Hebrews writer says faith is: "Now faith is a thing hoped for, a steadiness of the mind of evidence of works or things_done or deeds not seen. For in this the elders or people of old obtained testimonies to their characters" (Hebrews 11:1-2). It is only by our works can people bear witness of our faith! There is more to be said about faith, but I will limit my comments to this extent.

Additionally, in relegating baptism to a pile of nonessentials for our salvation or even a secondary position, we deny the critical role it plays in our salvation. For example, when Peter commanded the newly made disciples to be baptized, he added that they were to be baptized in the name of Jesus Christ for the remission of sins and to receive the gift of the Holy Spirit. Thus, the question arises about what happens if one is not baptized. Does that mean there is no remission of sins and thus no reception of the Holy Spirit? What about the rest of the statement in this segment of the Great Commission—"into the name of the Father, and of the Son, and of the Holy Spirit"? This section of the statement reads "baptizing them into the name of the Father, and of the Son, and of the Holy Spirit." As we already noted, the disciples are to be baptized according to Christ. The complete command is that they are to be baptized into the name of the Godhead. How relevant is this and why does Jesus command it? Could what Paul said in Colossians 3:3 (KJV), "For ye are dead, and your life is hid with Christ in God," be one of the reasons why Jesus wants the disciples to be baptized? I think Colossians 3:3 answers the question somewhat. To fully answer this last question we need to take a closer look at the message preached by Peter, Philip, and the rest of the apostles and disciples, Paul included.

We have already identified the message preached by the apostles and early disciples to the world. Hence we quote Paul's summary of the message in 1 Corinthians 15.

> *Moreover, brethren, I declare unto you the gospel which I preached*
> *unto you, which also ye have received, and wherein ye stand; By*
> *which also ye are saved, if ye keep in memory what I preached*
> *unto you, unless ye have believed in vain. For I delivered unto you*
> *first of all that which I also received, how that Christ died for our*
> *sins according to the scriptures; And that he was buried, and that*
> *he rose again the third day according to the scriptures: And that*
> *he was seen of Cephas, then of the twelve: After that, he was seen*
> *of above five hundred brethren at once; of whom the greater part*
> *remain unto this present, but some are fallen asleep. After that, he*
> *was seen of James; then of all the apostles. And last of all he was*
> *seen of me also, as of one born out of due time. For I am the least*
> *of the apostles, that am not meet to be called an apostle, because I*
> *persecuted the church of God. But by the grace of God I am what*
> *I am: and his grace which was bestowed upon me was not in vain;*
> *but I laboured more abundantly than they all: yet not I, but the*
> *grace of God which was with me. Therefore whether it were I or*
> *they, so we preach, and so ye believed. Now if Christ be preached*

179

that he rose from the dead, how say some among you that there is no resurrection of the dead? But if there be no resurrection of the dead, then is Christ not risen: And if Christ be not risen, then is our preaching vain, and your faith is also vain. Yea, and we are found false witnesses of God; because we have testified of God that he raised up Christ: whom he raised not up, if so be that the dead rise not. For if the dead rise not, then is not Christ raised: And if Christ be not raised, your faith is vain; ye are yet in your sins. Then they also which are fallen asleep in Christ are perished. If in this life only we have hope in Christ, we are of all men most miserable. (1 Corinthians 15:1-19, KJV)

We repeat the literal translation of the first four verses of 1 Corinthians 15:1-4 below:

I make known now unto you, brothers, the gospel which I preached [or proclaimed] unto you, which also you received [or have in your possession], in which also you stand; Through which also you are being saved, what word [message] I preached unto you if you hold firmly in your grasp [or, if you hold firmly in your grasp word [message] I preached unto you] unless in vain you believed [or, unless you believed in vain]. For I delivered unto you in most important [or in first order, first of all] that which also I received, that Christ died for sins of our [Christ died for sins our] according to the Holy Scriptures, And that he was buried, and that he rose again day the third according to the Holy Scriptures.

Look at how Paul says he delivered the message to the Corinthians: Jesus died for our sins, He was buried, and He rose again on the third day. We have noted that this message is similar to what Peter preached in Acts 2:22-36. We might ask, so why is this significant to our salvation? Why did Paul say that the gospel saved the brethren in Corinth? The Bible always explains itself if only we will dig a little more deeply for answers. Let's look at a similar message to the Romans in Romans 6:1-4, which reads as follows:

What then shall we say? Shall we continue to embrace sin that grace may abound? May that never be, how much longer shall we flourish in it we who are dead to sin? Are you ignorant that as many as were baptized into Christ Jesus into his death were baptized? we were buried therefore with him through baptism into death that just as Christ was raised up from the dead by the glory of the Father, so even we in newness of life should walk.

Paul's second question at the beginning of Romans 6 is quite telling. The question was, Shall we continue to engage in sin that grace may continue to come our way? Paul's answer to this was, God forbid! Why is that Paul's answer? The obvious implication of this question and Paul's answer or reaction was that we cannot continue in sin and expect grace to abound. This seems consistent with what he told the Corinthian Christians about holding on to the gospel. If we reject the gospel or do not hold on to it, and if we continue in our sinful ways after we've come under God's grace, does that not amount to rejection of or trampling on God's forgiveness made possible because of the cross? Paul asked again, how much further do we who died to sin expect to stay in it? It is worth noting that when we die, the soul separates from the physical body; they tear apart permanently. So using this idea of death, let's rephrase Paul's last question again: how can we expect to stay in sin when we have been separated or torn away from it—unless we choose to deal in sin again? The implication here is that if we are under grace, we cannot reunite with sin. Reunification with our sinful nature causes grace to cease to flow our way from God. Coming under God's grace does not mean sin's potency is lost. We become slaves to sin when we engage in sin. If we come to God and go back and engage in sin again as if we have never been saved, we cannot expect God's grace to continue flowing our way. Sin separates us from God and unites us with sin, but the blood of Christ separates us from sin and unites us to God. This sets us free and free indeed from all guilt!

Paul's question was, How can we who are dead to sin continue to live in it? My question is, When and how did these Christians die to sin? Did they die for their sin by repenting or is there something else? In the following verses of the same passage Paul seems disappointed about the lack of understanding on behalf of these brethren, for he asks, "Are you ignorant or do you not understand that as many as were baptized into Christ_Jesus into death his were baptized? We are buried therefore with him through baptism into death, that just as was raised up Christ from the dead by the glory of the Father, so even we in newness of life should walk." Paul answers both of my questions above. Let's look at the passage. Paul is asking these brethren whether they failed to understand that those who were baptized into Christ Jesus were baptized into His death. The Greek preposition εἰς *(ees)* is translated here as "into" in verses 3 and 4. It has the force of entering into something or anything. Thus, as many as were baptized into Christ Jesus, that many were entered into Him and thus also entered into His death. Or if we reverse the previous statement, those who entered into Jesus's death entered into Jesus. Paul's reminder to these Christians is that baptism enables us to participate in the death of Christ and die to our sins, for "we are buried therefore with him through baptism into death, that just as was raised up Christ from the dead by the glory of the Father, so even we in newness of life should walk." The literal version of the Greek is a bit harder to read, but we get the point.

Let's look at verse 4 a bit more closely. "We are buried therefore with him through baptism into death, that just as was raised up Christ from the dead by the glory of the Father, so even we in newness of life should walk." So, what does baptism do for us? According to Paul, through baptism, we partake of the death, burial, and resurrection of Christ Jesus. Thus, as we walk out of the baptismal waters, we enter into a new lifestyle as people who are free from sin. No longer guilty! The old self who causes us to struggle to please God, the self who causes us to focus on ourselves, that self who has a very high affinity for sin, is cut off and rendered dead. Before we continue let's look briefly at sin and its effects on us.

Sin's effect on us:

What is sin? The Bible describes sin: "But he who doubts is condemned if he eats, because his eating is not from faith; and whatever is not from faith is sin" (Romans 14:23, NASU). "Therefore, to one who knows the right thing to do and does not do it, to him it is sin" (James 4:17, NASU). "All unrighteousness is sin, and there is a sin not leading to death" (1 John 5:17, NASU). "Everyone who practices sin also practices lawlessness; and sin is lawlessness" (1 John 3:4, NASU).

Though God has put in place authorities to punish wrongdoers here and now, in the end He is the ultimate judge who will judge and hold each of us accountable. He will judge us all for the sins we have done. This fact is not negotiable! He will judge all without any favors. However, in the here and now God is offering a way to gain His favor in Christ. God is offering to forgive and make us sinless in Christ Jesus. In Christ Jesus, God is redeeming that which once was His. He is redeeming us, humans, from sin. Sin separated us from God. As sinners we became and we remain objects of God's wrath for as long as we are sinners and refuse to heed to the gospel. The Father seeks to make us sons in Christ, which will restore the Father-son relationships He established with Adam. Let's pay attention to what Jesus said in Luke 15 and to what Isaiah said of God's love for His children in Isaiah 49:15. In Luke 15 Jesus gives us a preview of how God the Father has anticipated and still anticipates the homecoming of His children. The prophet Isaiah gives us a sense of God's love, the kind of love Jesus talked about in Luke 15. The Israelites were God's chosen people to bring about God's salvation plans. They rejected God and sought to do as they pleased and were marred in sin and sin's entanglements. In spite of that, God sought after them fervently through the prophets and in many other ways. Yet time and time again, they rejected God and found themselves in trouble. Eventually God separated them from under His rule for a while and allowed them to be subjects of different human kings. Like all sinners, the metaphor of the relationship God had with Israel and Judah was clear. Sin separates man from God. Isaiah 49:15-16 gives us the gist of how God feels about His people: "Can a woman forget her nursing child, that she should have no compassion on the son of her womb? Even these may forget, yet I will not forget you.

Behold, I have engraved you on the palms of my hands; your walls are continually before me" (Isaiah 49:15-16, ESV).

William Cowper penned the words for "Hark My Soul It Is the Lord." He included the first part of the above passage in the song as follows: "Can a woman's tender care cease towards the child she bore, yet she may forgetful be, yet will I remember thee." Let's look back to when Adam and Eve sinned with this passage in mind. Can we begin to imagine how God felt when sin stole Adam and Eve from His presence and separated the Father from His children? Let's also look back at when God regretfully decided to wipe man off the face of the planet because of sin. With Isaiah's passage in mind can we possibly imagine God's decision to erase everything except for Noah and his family? We might enjoy the temporary bliss of sin and thus reject God and indulge ourselves, yet God does not forget us. God's love for us is not passive. Despite our sin God actively pursues us and seeks after us as one who has lost something very dear to Him. Though we were separated from God because of sin, though we were lost and had wandered away from God, though sin possessed us and in its clutches we were slaves, still God could not stand looking at sins and what it had done to us. He never once forgot about us. God's love for us is too great for Him to forget us. God's love for us is greater than the love of a nursing mother toward her baby—much greater than the love of a loving and caring nursing mother who because of her love for her child cannot stand hearing her baby cry or leave her baby for a moment. Yet such a mother might possibly forget her child. Not so with God. He does not forget us.

God's love for us is the reason for Christ. God lost us to sin. We could not tame our appetite for sin, so sin gained control over us. The more sin grew it tentacles in our lives, the more our appetite became insatiable and we yearned for more sin and evil. Hence sin prevailed over us and we were slaves to sin with no hope until Christ came. Sin crippled us and made it impossible for God to look at us, but God ultimately triumphed and conquered sin and made a way through Christ for us to reunite with Him. Christ dealt an unrecoverable blow to sin and gave us a way out to God. God's appeal to the sinner for redemption and forgiveness is Christ. Redemption because God paid the ransom price in Christ to get us back. Redemption because Christ had to pay the price we could not pay. He had to shed His blood to atone and pay for our debt because of our sins. God had to pay a ransom to the one who owned us as slaves and fed sin to us. Christ is the vehicle through which God has chosen to redeem and forgive. God beforehand had outlined how the whole process was going to work. In Luke's account of the Great Commission statement, Jesus reminded the apostles that God had revealed His plans through the law, the prophets, and the psalms. God put the power to save in the gospel of Christ Jesus. The gospel enables the sinner to come into contact with the blood of Christ through baptism, a process by which we died to our sins and are separated from it. Through the gospel, God erases our sins by cutting off those sins. God frees us from sin and saves us if we stand faithfully in the gospel. Redemption because God has set aside a day of judgment, a day when He will visit His wrath on His enemies. He has held off His wrath until such a day. Redemption because no sinner will be able to escape from the wrath of God's that is coming since none of us of our own accord can please God. Neither do we have a good enough excuse to exempt us from God's wrath outside of Christ.

For the wrath of God is revealed from heaven against all ungodliness and unrighteousness of men who suppress the truth in unrighteousness, because that which is known about God is evident within them; for God made it evident to them. For since the creation of the world His invisible attributes, His eternal power and divine nature, have been clearly seen, being understood through what has been made, so that they are without excuse. For even though they knew God, they did not honor Him as God or give thanks, but they became futile in their speculations, and their foolish heart was darkened. Professing to be wise, they became fools, and exchanged the glory of the incorruptible God for an image in the form of corruptible man and of birds and four-footed animals and crawling creatures. (Romans 1:18-23, NASU)

Or do you think lightly of the riches of His kindness and tolerance and patience, not knowing that the kindness of God leads you to repentance? But because of your stubbornness and unrepentant heart you are storing up wrath for yourself in the day of wrath and revelation of the righteous judgment of God, who will render to each person according to his deeds: to those who by perseverance in doing good seek for glory and honor and immortality, eternal life; but to those who are selfishly ambitious and do not obey the truth, but obey unrighteousness, wrath and indignation. There will be tribulation and distress for every soul of man who does evil, of the Jew first and also of the Greek, but glory and honor and peace

to everyone who does good, to the Jew first and also to the Greek.
For there is no partiality with God. (Romans 2:4-11, NASU)

A sinner who has heard the gospel of Christ and has responded in obedience to the gospel message according to Paul is saved. Let us recall the answers both Peter and Philip gave to their audiences when they responded to the gospel. Peter asked his audience to repent and be baptized so their sins would be forgiven and God's seal and gift of the Holy Spirit would be given to them. Also, from the account in Acts 8 of Philip and the Ethiopian eunuch, it looks as if Philip was still talking when the eunuch spotted the water, for he asked Philip, "See, here is water! What prevents me from being baptized?" (Acts 8:36, ESV). The eunuch's question leads to the conclusion that Philip had spoken to him about the need for baptism. How else would the eunuch have known about being baptized? Furthermore, why would the eunuch ask such a question given that he didn't even understand the scripture he was reading, which was the starting point of Philip's instruction to him? As they stepped into the water, Philip asked if he believed the message about Christ Jesus with all of his heart, to which the eunuch answered, "I believe Jesus Christ is the Son of God" (Acts 8:37). The eunuch confessed and made known what he had come to understand and believe from what he had been taught by Philip. Additionally, Paul said receiving the gospel and standing in it, or holding firmly to it, saves us. (1 Corinthians 15:1-2) Let us do well to recall that Jesus Christ is the one who commanded that the disciples be baptized.

The only vehicle for escaping God's wrath is Jesus. Jesus is the refuge that God places us in when He rescues us. "For He rescued us from the domain of darkness, and transferred us to the kingdom of His beloved Son, in whom we have redemption, the forgiveness of sins" (Colossians 1:13-14, NASU).

Forgiveness because as we sin, we trample, disobey, and abuse God's love toward us and His care for us. Worst of all we reject Him and His will. With our sins we show no appreciation toward the loving Father. Forgiveness because God's love for us is so great that knowing He has set aside a day of judgment, He dipped into His own Himself, we might say, to pay the price for our sins. He offered a very precious part of Himself in Christ Jesus, the Savior, to erase all of our faults to make us whole again. He did not just pay the price and say "Adios." He offers us a standing invitation in the gospel of Christ. He offers us adoption into sonship if we will accept the invitation by believing the gospel and submitting to His will. Forgiveness because He wishes us to live free of sin's shackles and to live in eternity starting now, because death for us, His people, is temporary!

In Luke 15 Jesus described the sinner as a son who is lost, a son who lost his focus and missed his father's presence. In the garden of Eden Adam and Eve lost their focus, which led to their dismissal from God's presence. I imagine Adam and Eve missed God's regular visits to them in the garden and found themselves lost because they yielded to temptation and the physical appeal of what God had told them not to eat. In fact the temptation took their focus off God and directed it toward what appealed to them. We need to pay attention to how the scriptures describe the events leading to Eve plucking the fruit and eating it. They found what God had told them not to eat was "good for food . . . a delight to the eyes . . . to be desired to make one wise, she took of its fruit and ate, and she also gave some to her husband who was with her, and he ate" (Genesis 3:6, ESV). I imagine that they quickly realized that the instant gratification and satisfaction did not last. I also imagine that they came to the realization that what they had gained—sin and its clutches—cannot be compared to what they enjoyed when God regularly attended to their needs and cared for them in the garden.

Eve was consumed with herself. Satan distracted Eve enough to get her to forget God just for a moment and to look at how the fruit appealed to her. Me, me, me! Adam did not do any better either. Their distraction from God led to sin and rejection of Him. The danger of sin is not that we cannot do what we want or desire. The danger is that it leads us to reject God and leave Him with no option but to reject us.

Adam and Eve found themselves lost in their own desires. Blindfolded by their desires, they focused on what looked good and pleasing to them instead of fixing their gaze on God. That minor distraction sent them wandering into the lost land of sin and they could not find their way back to God. In other words, sin owned them. This separated them from God and they became slaves to sin. Their immediate descendant Cain could not master sin after being warned by God to watch out for it. Instead, he proceeded to kill his brother and became a slave to sin. I believe Jesus described sinners as lost because they cannot on their own find their way back to God. God, the loving Father who longs for His lost children, has been looking forward to the day of reunion with them. Those who are lost are lost because they cannot find their way back home. Their sense of direction is off relative to home and their current location. Those who are lost do not know how to get back home from where they are. If that were not the case, it would not be said that one is lost. To this effect, then, Jesus said, "I am the way, the truth and the life, no one comes to the Father but by me" (John 14:6).

He offered not just hope but also a way back home. He offered hope and redemption to the lost, the sinner. The lost person has to take the right path to get back home safely. Jesus said He is that WAY that leads to the Father. Jesus offers the truth, and the one who is lost needs to know the truth to help him or her to get back home. Jesus is that TRUTH that leads to the Father. Jesus offers life, and one who is lost needs sustenance and preservation. Jesus offers that LIFE. Jesus paid the ransom for all mankind with His blood to purchase the sinner. He paid the ransom for the lost. He injects life into the found sinner through regeneration, which Paul describes to Titus: "[H]e saved us, not because of works done by us in righteousness, but according to his own mercy, by the washing of regeneration and renewal of the Holy Spirit" (Titus 3:5, ESV).

The lost sinner did nothing to be found. God the loving Father did all the necessary work to redeem His lost children. Out of His own mercy and love He redeems us. As sin robbed God of mankind, God paid the ransom in Jesus Christ. Sin owned mankind. Man was a slave to sin until Christ made the ransom payment on the cross. Through Christ, then, we are set free from sin and sin releases us if we yield our will to Christ. Christ paid the ransom. We have the choice to believe Him and submit to His gospel, or we can disbelieve and continue to submit to sin. God is working His plan to perfection. We might not understand everything He commands, but we can trust Him. All He expects is submission to His will.

Back to works of faith. If by submitting to the gospel message through baptism the sinner does works, are they works of the sinner's own desires or works following God's will? If submitting to baptism is work, it could not be work designed by the sinner to please God, or work according to the sinner's own accord, or will for the following two reasons: 1) baptism in the context in the Great Commission, and 2) the Greek grammatical structure of the phrase *baptizing them.* These two reasons are why if baptism is work, it is not work per the responding sinner's accord.

First, putting baptism in the context of the Great Commission, let's look at the second part of the commission again: "Go therefore and make disciples of all the nations, baptizing them in the name of the Father, and the Son and the Holy Spirit, teaching them to observe all that I commanded you; and lo, I am with you always, even to the end of the age" (Matthew 28:19-20, NASB). "Make disciples . . . , baptizing them . . . , teaching them to observe . . ." Who is *them*? According to the context, *them* refers to the people of all the nations who have received the gospel and have chosen to become disciples of Christ, right? If not, who else could *them* be? "They" are to be baptized by the apostles, disciples, and anyone following the Great Commission charge. "They" are the subjects to be baptized followed by continued teaching to obey everything Christ has commanded as part of the disciple making. How else does "baptizing them . . . , teaching them" fit the context? The point I am trying to make here is this: if submitting to baptism is work, then who is doing the work, the one baptizing or the one being baptized? The repented sinner who has come to respond to the gospel submits to baptism by being dipped into the waters, being dipped by the one or ones who are making the disciples. The tone is passive for the repented sinner but active to the one making the disciple. The dipping into the water is done to the repented sinner, and everything else that happens to the repented sinner while submerged happens without any efforts on his or her part. When he or she is dipped in the water, how the sinful nature is crucified on the cross, or how the sinner is separated from his or her sins through participation in the death of Christ is not something we see with the naked eye. In other words, the repented sinner is passive in the process of baptism.

All we know is, the sinner's sins are cut off according to Romans 6:

> *We were buried therefore with him through baptism into death that just as Christ was raised up from the dead by the glory of the Father, so even we in newness of life should walk. For if we have been planted together in the likeness of his death, so also resurrection we shall be: knowing this that old our man has been crucified, so that it might be rendered the body of sin useless, we are no longer to be in subjection to sin. For he who is dead has been accepted as righteous [or justified, made right, stand approved, stand accepted, vindicated, avouched to be good and true] from sin. Now if we died with Christ, we believe that also we shall live with him, having known that Christ has been raised from the dead no longer dies death no longer has lordship [or mastery, dominion] over him.*

I have used here the literal translations from Romans 6:4-14.

By faith we accept God's word through Paul that the sinner's sins are no longer with them when they come out of the waters of baptism. By faith we accept that we get out of the water in the same manner that Christ arose from death into newness of life. We no longer walk in the sinful past, but are new creations; we live for God.

Secondly, the Greek text, the original text, Βαπτίζοντες αὐτοὺς *(baptidzontes hautous)* is translated "baptizing them." The Greek word Βαπτίζοντες is a participle in the present tense, active voice, and in the nominative case. The nominative case in the Greek is treated as the subject in the English. In the English sentence structure of subject-verb-object, it looks like this phrase falls short of the structure even though as it stands, *baptizing them* can be independent. The question is, Where is the subject? The nature of the participle is such that the subject in *baptizing them* is embedded in the participle. Here the embedded subject is the ones receiving the Great Commission, that is, the apostles and disciples and Christians today who follow this charge. Who is the object of the sentence? This might seem trivial, but please indulge me for a few more minutes. The Greek term αὐτοὺς *(hautous),* translated "them," is in the case called the accusative case, which is translated as the object in English. In the subject-verb-object structure, the subject applies the acts on the object as the verb dictates. Thus, in *baptizing them* we see that the subject is embedded in the participle *baptizing,* which also describes the action verb. The object of the sentence has also been established as *them* as translated from the Greek. Hence *baptizing them* could read *you baptize them,* which fits the complete sentence structure of the English subject-verb-object.

So then, we can say that in the phrase *baptizing them,* the subject in the sentence is performing the act of baptizing on the object, which we have identified as *them.* From the context, we know that what we are referring to as *them* are the repented sinners who have heard the gospel and chosen to respond to the message. The sinner is the object receiving the action of baptizing. We note that the repented sinner is not receiving the action because the subject imposed the action of baptism on him or her by mutual consent, or by force from the subject, or by any kind of influence by any of the parties involved. We don't need to listen closely to realize that *baptizing them* is a direct command from Christ Jesus. If we read the Great Commission again and pay attention, we notice the following duties: "make disciples of all the nation, baptizing them . . . , teaching." We note that as part of their responsibilities in the Great Commission, all who are discharging the duties in the Great Commission are to make disciples, baptize them, and teach them to obey or keep strictly all that Christ has commanded. Jesus told His disciples that if they love Him, they will obey His commandments; thus by "baptizing them" we are only obeying Christ's command. Both the baptizer and the baptized submit to God's will by following this command, which is done in faith. The fact is, baptism is not about the removal of the physical dirt off our bodies; thus, whatever happens in the baptismal waters can and should be appreciated only through faith.

Now, in case we're still having issues with who the embedded subject is, let's spend a few minutes and figure that out. By this time we know that Jesus is talking to His disciples. More specifically, Matthew mentions in Matthew 28:16 that the eleven disciples—indicating the eleven apostles left from the twelve Jesus had chosen earlier—met with Jesus on a designated mountain in Galilee. This is when Jesus spoke, or gave the charge of, the Great Commission. These men received the Great Commission and discharged the duties therein. Using this information, let's reconstruct the second part of the Great Commission in our attempt to expose the embedded object in the participle *baptizing*. The literal translation reads as follows: "Going therefore you make disciples of all the nations, baptizing them into the name of the Father, and of the Son, and of the Holy Spirit." In the Greek μαθητεύσατε *(matheeteusate)* this imperative is in the second person plural and is translated "you make disciples." Jesus is telling these men "you make disciples." Now, let's reconstruct Matthew 28:19-20: "Going therefore you make disciples of all the nations, you baptize them in the name of the name of the Father, and of the Son and of the Holy Spirit, you teach them to keep strictly everything that I have commanded you." This reconstruction carries the same meaning as the words spoken by Jesus. Thus, at this point in our discussion, the embedded subject in *baptizing them* will be the eleven Jesus was addressing. We have seen how Philip, a disciple who together with Stephen was selected to serve at the tables in Acts 6, and Paul, a later convert and "smallest of the apostles," as he describes himself, discharged the duties and the responsibilities in the Great Commission. We have already seen that both Philip and Paul preached the same gospel message that Peter preached to his audience in Acts 2. In addition in Acts 8 after God scattered the church using Paul as His instrument, Luke said, "[T]hose who had been scattered went about preaching the word" (Acts 8:4, NASU). These people, one of whom is Philip, went about preaching the same message Peter had preached on the day of Pentecost, thus keep the duties required by the Great Commission. Simply put, the embedded subject in *baptizing them* is one who discharges the responsibilities in the Great Commission and sets forth to go make disciples.

	You	(e.g., an apostle, any disciple evangelizing)	→	Subject
baptizing them →	baptize	(action)	→	Verb
	Them	(repented sinners who obey the gospel)	→	Object

The person submitting to baptism is passive in the process. Here is why: Of course he or she walks into the water for the baptism to take place, but whatever happens during the baptism, from the physical immersion into the water to whatever happens spiritually, it happens to the person submerged without him or her influencing the process or having any effect on the action and its outcome. Let me use the following passages from Ephesians 6:10-18 and Galatians 3:27 to clarify what I am trying to say. In these two passages, we observe the language Paul uses. In Ephesians, Paul tells them to "Put on . . . so you . . . stand firm . . . , take up . . . and resist." The armored dress of a Christian is what Paul is admonishing us to put on in the first passage. Paul is asking us to put on the full armor of God. This is something we can do. On the other hand, in the passage from Galatians 3:27, Paul says literally that "as many as for into Christ have been baptized Christ you have been clothed," expressed in proper English as "for as many of you as have been baptized into Christ you have been clothed with Christ." In this second passage we note that we put on Christ in baptism. In this passage we are informed that as we are baptized, we are clothed with Christ. The tone is passive with regard to the person being submerged in water, for the act of baptism is clothed with Christ in the process. We don't get to clothe ourselves with Christ. That is, we cannot of our own accord pick up Christ and clothe ourselves with Him like we can fasten ourselves with the truth as in Ephesians 6. This is important, because in this section of the Great Commission, the disciple who is proclaiming the good news is to baptize per Jesus's command the person who has received the message and has chosen to submit to Christ. The repented sinner is a recipient of the act of baptism. If there is any work being done, it is being done by the one proclaiming the gospel. Furthermore, if there is any work to be done, we do those works after we have become disciples of Christ. We cannot begin doing works of faith when we have not first responded to God's call and accepted the Lordship of Christ. First we have to answer the call and then submit.

The Circumcision of Christ

What happens when a person dies? First we notice that a person who is alive is vibrant and full of life. His or her physical body can engage in all kinds of life-filled activities such as moving from one place to another, eating, talking, and other physical activities. The living body has life in it. We say that one is dead or a person has died when these vital life functions are no longer viable in them. We can all agree that those in difficult situations such as coma or on life support have life functions still taking place in them, so they cannot be said to be dead. Thus, a dead person is a human body that has physically become lifeless and has no capacity to show any signs of life no matter how minimal. That is, the soul has separated from the physical body, making the body lifeless. So when one dies, separation happens. Let's hold this thought as we look at circumcision.

In Genesis 17:10-14 we read about God's covenant with Abraham after He had just changed his name from Abram. The covenant was that Abraham and all his descendants and any male bought with Abraham's money must be circumcised. That is, every male must have their foreskins cut off, including any male eight days old born in Abraham's house. This was the perpetual covenant between God and Abraham and all his descendants. The consequence of failing to obey this simple covenant or agreement, God said, breaks the covenant and the culprit must be "cut off from his people." Abraham passed this on to his children, who also passed it on down the generations. This is still observed by most faithful Jews today. In the process of circumcision, the foreskin is separated from the main body of the male. Let's hold on to this thought as well. At the same time let us recall that we have learned from Paul in Romans 6 and 1 Corinthians 15 that we participate in the death of Christ through baptism, a process that leaves us dead to sin and alive in Christ.

In Colossians 2 Paul presents an intricate relationship that God has set up for us in Christ that is quite amazing. This is what I want us to look at this point. Starting from verse 9 and following we read that in Christ the whole Godhead dwells in bodily form, that we are made complete in Christ who is the head of all principalities and powers, and that in Christ we experience a type of circumcision that is not done with hands called the circumcision of Christ, which is the removal or cutting off of the body of sins of the flesh. We are buried with Christ in baptism and are raised through faith through God's handiwork just as He raised Christ from the dead.

Let us try to understand these statements found in Colossians 2:9-12. It will help to look at verse 13, where Paul describes the state we had come from to be united with Christ. Verse 13 essentially says that we were dead in our sins and uncircumcised of the sins of the flesh. That is to say, our sinful nature was attached to us before God cut it off with the circumcision of Christ. This necessarily implies that as long as we have not experienced the circumcision of Christ, our sinful nature is attached to us, in the same manner that the foreskin when it is not removed through circumcision is still attached to the individual male. If we can conjure a picture in our minds about how sin when attached to us weighs us down, it will be like the prisoner in chains whose hands and legs are tied such that his or her movements are controlled strictly by the weight of the chains. Imagine such a prisoner pardoned and freed from those chains. Imagine hearing the clanging sounds of the chains as they fall off. Such a picture is what comes to mind for me when I read about Paul talking about the circumcision of Christ. We might not hear the great clanging sounds of sins' bonds and chains dropping off as God cuts them, but we can see through faith that we are free because God through the apostle Paul says we are. The sins that have strapped us and kept us captive and filthy looking and condemned to death are finally off our backs and we are free. Like the surprised prisoner who receives an unexpected pardon that is effective immediately, we are freed from sin when we submit to the gospel in baptism. As the pronouncement of the pardon immediately sets the prisoner free, we are set free from sin at the point of baptism. At that point, we can be assured that our sins have been taken away and we are sin-free. We might ask how we know that our sins have been forgiven and that we are free from sin. We know by faith and because God's word says that is the case. Like Abraham those who come to God can take God at His word and act upon it through faith. Abraham believed what God had told him and acted on it and it was credited to him as righteousness. We also are called descendants of Abraham when we believe God like he did.

It is critical to understand what God has done because this helps us see the important role baptism plays in our salvation. Let's tie a few things together as we keep in mind what we have just discussed. We observe that on two or maybe three occasions when God was grieved about the state of man's sinfulness, His course of action was eradication. We see this in Noah's time, with Sodom and Gomorrah and to some extent replacing the people living in the land of Canaan with the people of Israel. Eradication still remains since God will eliminate the universe as we know it in the end, saving those who believe in Christ and punishing those who do not. For a moment let's take a look at Colossians 1:13-14. In this passage Paul says that "He has rescued us from the power of darkness and transferred us into the kingdom of His beloved Son. In whom we have redemption, the forgiveness of sins."

Notice the word *rescued*. In some translations *delivered* is the word used. Let us make no mistake, for condemnation is what still awaits the sinner who has rejected Jesus and His saving message. But those who respond to the gospel of Christ (in Romans 1:16 Paul said the gospel saves) as the Colossians received Christ are rescued and redeemed and their lives are hidden in Christ. The wages of sin is death as condemnation is still in store for the unrepentant sinner who rejects Christ Jesus. God planned all along to surgically remove sin from any sinner who chooses to obey God's plan through Jesus Christ, which is saving and making us sin-free. All of us have the option to be saved or to perish.

In the circumcision of Christ, God separates the sinners from their sins permanently for as long as they hold on to the gospel. This happens when the repented sinner is baptized according to Paul in Colossians 2. In participating in Christ's death through baptism, the mechanism that God has set up for the purpose of removal of sins, we become separated from sin, never to be associated with it again if we stand firmly in the gospel we received. That is what Paul said in 1 Corinthians 15:1-4. The gospel saves us if we stand firmly in it. Both circumcision and death have a permanent effect of removing sin from us permanently on the condition that we remain in the gospel that was preached to us. To this end Paul says that "I have been crucified with Christ nevertheless I live, yet not I but Christ liveth in me." Notice that our old self, which has a very high affinity for sin, is cut off through the circumcision of Christ. It is killed, put to death in baptism, and should not have any influence on us as we enter into Christianity and into a newness of life.

The above statements are not just great for slogans or bumper stickers—they mean something! On the cross, Matthew records that Jesus "yielded His ghost," that is, He gave up His spirit and His body became lifeless. We need to observe that Jesus could have not given up His spirit and died. But He had to die so His spirit would separate from His body. Likewise we have to participate in His death through baptism and be separated from our sins, separated so that we no longer live like we used to live. As such, Paul's further instructions to the Colossians, in Colossians 3:5, was that we put to death, kill, render impotent, or mortify everything that is earthly in us. Why? Because we are not subject to these earthly things anymore. Because we have died to the old self and sin cannot dictate our lives anymore. This necessarily means that what I used to be I am no longer. The old me, the old you, or the old us is dead and cut off, not covered or glossed over. It is no longer part of us, and we need to let it die so we can learn of Christ how to live like God's people and learn the new culture and life we have been called to. Paul said, "[T]he life that I now live in the flesh, I live by faith in the Son of God who loved me and gave Himself for me"! (Galatians 2:20)

Now, if God has cut off our sins, why do we still need to kill everything earthly in us or mortify the old self? Though the chains came off the pardoned prisoner and he was set free, the challenge and the urge that led him into trouble in the first place are still there. The only thing that can keep him from going back to prison is if he trains himself to fight those urges when they arise, and disciplines himself so that those urges do not control him as they did before. Similarly, as saved sinners we strive to stay pure and holy for God who has rescued us. The only way we can do that is to ensure that we have parted ways with our old ways. Paul again puts it best: "Every athlete exercises self-control in all things. They do it to receive a perishable wreath, but we an imperishable. So I do not run aimlessly; I do not box as one beating the air. But I discipline my body and keep it under control, lest after preaching to others I myself should be disqualified" (1 Corinthians 9:25-27).

The new life God has called us into is a lifestyle that involves love, forgiveness, selflessness, self-control, humility, discipline, and many other practices that do not come to us easily. These traits are not natural to us. Such life traits and attributes can be learned, practiced, and lived based on diverse motivations, but to love like Christ, forgive like Christ, be selfless like Christ, control ourselves like Christ, submit to God like Christ, and be disciplined like Christ in every aspect of our lives is something only Christ can train, lead, and mold us to become. Let's keep in mind that God's objective is for us to be perfect like He is. If we were to define what it means to be perfect like God and set that as a goal, how many of us would attain that goal on our own? Yet that is the goal God has set for us. That is why it makes sense that He would prepare works for us to walk in since He is the only one who understands how to be like Him. To the Christian, this new lifestyle is to be lived in faith because God desires us to live by faith. He has called us to walk in good works He has created for us since long ago because His Spirit lives in us. Additionally, without being taught everything that Christ has commanded, we will have no clue what this new lifestyle or culture of Christianity is about.

Some other scriptures to ponder on the subject of baptism:

"And now why tarriest thou? arise, and be baptized, and wash away thy sins, calling on his name" (Acts 22:16 ASV).

"[I]n whom ye were also circumcised with a circumcision not made with hands, in the putting off of the body of the flesh, in the circumcision of Christ; having been buried with him in baptism,

wherein ye were also raised with him through faith in the working of God, who raised him from the dead" (Colossians 2:11-12 ASV).

"[N]ot by works [done] in righteousness, which we did ourselves, but according to his mercy he saved us, through the washing of regeneration and renewing of the Holy Spirit" (Titus 3:5 ASV).

"Or are ye ignorant that all we who were baptized into Christ Jesus were baptized into his death? We were buried therefore with him through baptism unto death: that like as Christ was raised from the dead through the glory of the Father, so we also might walk in newness of life" (Romans 6:3-4, ASV).

Baptism-related issues
Issues with the thief on the cross
If the Son sets you free, you will be free indeed. Jesus said this to the Pharisees in John 8. Thus it is no surprise that He will set free a man bound by sin. He is the Son of God, His word is as good as His will! The writer of Hebrews noted that while a person writing his will is alive, he can always change his mind and redo his will. It is only after Jesus dies that the will He had written can take effect. Now *that* no one can change!

What do we know for sure about the thief on the cross? (Luke 23) The thief on the cross was one of two criminals crucified with Christ. This thief rebuked the other criminal for not fearing God. He understood the difference between them and Jesus Christ. He was repentant of his error-filled ways. It seems both thieves knew who Jesus was. The first thief addressed Jesus first. Both wanted to be freed. The first wanted to be freed, but not so he could live a different life; the other asked for mercy from the Son of God who could truly set him free from his sins.

What don't we know for sure about the thief on the cross?

We don't know the names of the thieves on the cross; in particular, we don't know the name of the thief who acknowledged his waywardness and appealed to Christ for "recognition" at the point of transitioning into death. Knowing this thief's name, the one who admitted his crime and guilt, might suggest to us where he was born or came from or who his parents were. For example, Jesus was called Jesus of Nazareth when Nathaniel was being introduced to him. We know of Simon of Cyrene, and also names like James the son of Alpheus and such. Still that will not be sufficient to tell us whether he received the baptism of repentance that John the Baptist was giving at the time.

As such we surely don't know whether the thief on the cross had received John's baptism. So what if we did know that this criminal facing justice on the cross had been baptized for repentance of sins by John? Would that have made any difference to Jesus? My opinion is that whether the thief was baptized by John would not have changed Jesus's inviting and securing his life on the cross in paradise for the following reasons: 1) Jesus forgave sinners of their sins and healed people of all kinds of infirmities while he was on earth. That is, Jesus showed that he had the power to change people who asked Him for help. 2) The thief asked Jesus to remember him when Jesus came into His kingdom. To that Jesus responded, "Today you will be with me in paradise." The thief was taken to paradise with Jesus. 3) The command to baptize all who hear the gospel and believe came after Jesus was resurrected from the dead and had walked on the earth for forty days.

The key here is that the thief on the cross was saved by Jesus, who was the only one on earth at the time who could save regardless of our states. Jesus had not instituted the command for baptism. It was still before Jesus's death and it was still pre-resurrection, and Peter had not opened the gates to the kingdom at the time; he had not received the key at the time of the cross. Besides, who can question Jesus on how and whom he chooses to save? The fact is, He saved pre-resurrection and He is saving after resurrection. How He does that is best left to Him. Remember He had said, "[I]f you love me you will obey my commandments" (John 14:15). Here Jesus was doing what He came to earth to do and we are acting like the older brother in the parable of the prodigal son! Who is to say when Jesus saves by baptism or without baptism? The clear distinction between the situation with the thief on the cross and Christians thereafter is that the thief had the physical presence of Jesus Christ, who was still alive and forgiving sins, and furthermore that Christ had not issued the command in the last chapters of Matthew and Mark. A point worth noticing is that even Paul who saw Jesus during his conversion was instructed to be baptized. No other disciple who came to Christ in Acts 2 and thereafter was in the presence of Christ. Hence if Christ changed His will when He was alive, who can say to Jesus, "You did A when you were alive but your will says B"?

Cornelius's Conversion—*The Significance of Peter's Point of View*

Was the conversion of Cornelius different from that of any other disciple or for that matter any other Gentile? Peter's point of view is significant to understanding and appreciating the conversion of Cornelius.1) Peter had the key to opening the church Jesus had mentioned He was going to build according to Matthew 16. 2) Peter was a Jew who probably had never thought much about God and Gentiles in the same thought, or imagined it possible for Gentiles to come close to God. This is particularly revealing when we look at Peter's initial response after hearing Cornelius tell him why he sent for Peter. As God's people, the Jews saw no need to have any kind of union with Gentiles, who were not God's people. In fact Gentiles were considered enemies of God as Paul made known to some of the Gentile Christians, often in regard to their former states. Also the reaction of the Jewish congregation in Jerusalem after they heard about Peter visiting Cornelius affirms the idea that Gentiles were not welcome, or at least that was the impression. 3) Peter had a unique role among the apostles. In a way we might say he was the spokesperson for them. Jesus chose Peter to usher in the church of Christ. Let us note that Jesus did not set Peter as the leader of the apostles. He only gave Peter a task to perform. Peter preached the gospel to the Jewish people, which led to the Jewish congregation in Acts 2. It is only appropriate to have the same Peter usher in the Gentile church in Caesarea. Peter had no influence on how God worked. Influenced by his culture, his people, and the prevailing attitude of God's people toward those not described as God's people, Peter tried to resist God as seen in his attitude toward the vision.

Peter's lack of understanding of God's purposes did not stop God's plan from moving ahead. God's purpose prevailed. He used Peter to bring both Jews and Gentiles to God in Christ Jesus. 4) Why was it important for God to communicate to Peter in a vision that what God has made holy no one should call unholy? Why was the revelation to only Peter and not to any of the other apostles? The sheet in the vision Peter saw contained animals deemed unholy by Jewish law. In the vision it was not the animals God was concerned about. God was teaching Peter a lesson about His ability to declare holy that which previously might have been considered unholy. At the same time, God was teaching Peter a lesson that Peter later understood when he heard what Cornelius had to say. "Peter began to speak: 'I really understand now that God does not consider some people to be better than others. He accepts anyone who worships him and does what is right. It is not important what nation they come from. God has spoken to the people of Israel. He sent them the Good News that peace has come through Jesus Christ, the Lord of all people'" (Acts 10:34-36, Easy to Read Bible, ERV).

Peter finally puts it together and understands what their, the apostles', mission was about. At this encounter and the events leading to this point in Acts, Peter finally perhaps had lights going off in his mind that the gospel is to be preached to all nations, exactly what Christ had commanded. The good news is not about Jews only, but about all people. It is about God making peace between two groups hostile to each other. It is about God uniting these two groups into one in Christ who is our peace. It is about God's love for all people and Christ dying for all people. This is what Paul reiterates later in the book of Ephesians and also what old man Simeon tells us in Luke 2

209

when he met the Savior in the form of a child. Old man Simeon said, "Lord, now you are letting your servant depart in peace, according to your word; for my eyes have seen your salvation that you have prepared in the presence of all peoples, a light for revelation to the Gentiles, and for glory to your people Israel" (Luke 2:29-32, ESV).

Though it seems Peter's understood what God had done, Paul informs us in the book of Galatians that Peter stood condemned because of his behavior toward the Gentile brethren, which caused even Barnabas to separate himself from the Gentiles. This was a lesson the young Jewish church did not fully understand or appreciate, and we see them struggle to adjust to the new reality that both Jews and Gentiles are God's people in Christ Jesus. It will be sad for us if we fail to rise above the issue of race and differences in the way God's people look—white, black, brown, tan . . . as we have the benefits of seeing the early disciples struggle with this issue, including Peter. What matters is that God has accepted us all, according to Peter, and He is not partial toward any people or group. God's acceptance of all of us into His fold ought to be good enough for us to accept each other. If we fail to accept each other, not only will we be rejecting people God has accepted, but we will also have against us the failure to learn from the mistakes of the early disciples in which case we will stand condemned like Peter. 5) Finally what Peter said after he had witnessed how God brought in the Gentiles. It is important to observe that Peter was only a vessel God used to accomplish His purposes. God poured His Spirit on the Gentiles just as He had done for the Jews. "While Peter was still saying these things, the Holy Spirit fell on all who heard the word. And the believers from among the circumcised who had come with Peter were amazed, because the gift of the Holy Spirit was poured out even on the Gentiles. For they were hearing them speaking in tongues and extolling God." In Acts 10:44-46 Peter said, "Can anyone withhold water for baptizing these people, who have <u>received the Holy Spirit just as we have</u>?" (Acts 10:47, ESV).

Peter saw that Cornelius and his group had received the Holy Spirit just as the Jew had received the Holy Spirit. Since that was the case, why did Peter, led by the Holy Spirit, instruct Cornelius and his group to be baptized? Was Peter trying to overrule God? To the second question I will say not so, for even if Peter did not understand fully, he had seen enough to convince him that God was at work. To the first question, I will say consistency. For though this group did not ask the question What shall we do? like in Acts 2, Peter was in the midst of these Gentiles because these Gentiles were seeking God and God already knew that. What they were missing was Peter to point them in the right path and instruct them about what they needed to do.

Notes: The falling of the Holy Spirit on the early disciples happened twice only in Acts: in Acts 2 and Acts 10. Both were in keeping with God's promise through the prophet Joel to pour His Spirit on all flesh. The first happened to a group of Jews, including the apostles, who were empowered at the same time to begin their work. The other was to let the Jews know that God considered the Gentiles holy and was reaching out to them. God poured out His Spirit on Cornelius and his friends as Peter was ministering to them. God poured His Spirit on both Jews and Gentiles to unite both groups as one in Christ Jesus who is our peace. Hence God poured His Holy

Spirit on the Gentiles in the same way He had done to the Jews. Is it any wonder that we did not see a conversion like Cornelius's in any of the other Gentiles elsewhere? God elevated the Gentile to the same status as the Jews, the Jews having been God's people. The Gentile who accepts the gospel of Christ and is baptized into Christ becomes just like the Jew who accepted the same message and is baptized into Christ. Peter realized that, so all He could do was command that these Gentiles be baptized just as the Jew was baptized. In the end how Cornelius became a Christian was not different from the way others came to Christ in Acts. Cornelius was unique in that he was the first Gentile to be converted to Christianity and God used Him to make known to the Jewish Christians that saving the Gentiles was just as important to Him as saving the Jews.

II: " . . . into the name of the Father, and of the Son and of the Holy Spirit"

"[B]aptizing them into the name of the Father and of the Son and of the Holy Spirit."—(Matthew 28:19, ASV) When we analyzed this section earlier, I mentioned that the Greek word translated as "into" in the ASV or "in" in other translations has a force of entering into something. Apart from the entities in the Godhead such as God the Father, God the Son, and God the Holy Spirit, no other entity or person can enter into the Godhead of their own accord. Paul instructed that God lives in unapproachable light, in 1 Timothy 6:16. From Moses and Isaiah to other encounters where a human saw God's form or appeared in what seems like God's presence, there is always the sense of reverence, dread, awe, and profound sense of worthlessness on the part of the person involved. I bring these out to note that no one can approach God let alone enter into the Godhead. Yet in Matthew's version of the Great Commission, Jesus instructs that the convicted disciple is to be baptized into the Godhead. This is profound and very different from what God's people have known. We cannot approach God of our own accord. When we are baptized, we are baptized into the Godhead, not of our own accord. We are baptized into the Godhead because Jesus said so. Paul sums it up as follows: "For you have died, and your life is hidden with Christ in God" (Colossians 3:3, ESV).

What is in a name?

Growing up, my mother used to tell us that those we associate with in large part define what or who we are. She would say, "Show me your friends, and I will tell you who you are." Names usually have meanings and associations. As a means for identification, names often have reasons behind them. Names and reputations are often synonymous with each other. For example we can describe a person by his or her reputation without mentioning his or her name and friends of that individual will know exactly who is being talked about. Similarly, when a name is mentioned in the physical absence of the person, all who know or recognize the name immediately react either negatively or positively to that name. A name may or may not have credibility. A name is respected and honored, and in God's case, revered. A name can be identified with the authority associated or a title. When a name is mentioned, we immediately identify the person whose name has been said with their title or position, what he or she means to us, his or her possessions, and whether he or she is good or bad. The position held by a person and his or her name sometimes becomes synonymous, such as Jesus called Christ or the

Savior. A name can show association or associations, inheritance, possession, lineage, nationality, identification, identity, and so much more.

The Bible uses God's names to tell us about God, such as God, the Lord who sees, the God almighty, the everlasting God, the Lord of hosts, I am, God is love, God is light, the God of salvation, the Lord is my shepherd, the Lord is peace, and many other names that describe God to help us understand and appreciate who He is. Thus from a scriptural standpoint, a name has value to it.

Why did Jesus want to have the newly made disciple baptized into the name of the Godhead? Was this just a mere formality He wanted to have His disciples go through or was there something more? We have mentioned the baptizer and the baptized above, but where and how does God fit into all of this? Is name all that important? Before we delve more deeply into this discussion, I want us to look back into history for a valuable perspective that will help us understand and appreciate what Jesus did with this part of the Great Commission.

In Proverbs 22:1 and Ecclesiastes 7:1 in the ESV version of the Bible we read that "A good name is to be chosen rather than great riches" and "A good name is better than precious ointment." These two scriptures give us an indication of the value people in King Solomon's time put on names. When it came to God's name, God included in the Ten Commandments that His people should not take His name in vain. To this effect the Hebrew would rather say "the Lord" than mention the true name of God, which in English is pronounced Jehovah. God's name was revered. Under *God, names of,* in *The Strongest Strong's Exhaustive Concordance of the Bible* under the "Nave's Topical Bible Reference" section we find the following narrative on the view of ancient people on name. I have made this narrative into a list for convenience.

1. A name is virtually the same as the person who bears it.
2. Giving to a person or thing is identical to owning the person or thing.
3. Changing a person's name could mean elevating the person's status, whereas getting rid of a person's name meant destruction of the person.
4. God's name and being are often used side by side such that believing in the name of Jesus is the same as believing in the person of Jesus Himself.
5. The name Jesus in the Greek is similar to the Hebrew Joshua, which means "salvation of Yahweh."

Let us to hold on to these thoughts for now while we develop other thoughts.

We learn from Romans 6 that through baptism we partake of the death of Christ. In the letter to the Colossians, Paul told the saints in Colossae, "For He rescued us from the domain of darkness, and transferred us to the kingdom of His beloved Son, in whom we have redemption, the forgiveness of sins" (Colossians 1:13-14, NASU) and "For you have died and your life is hidden with Christ in God" (Colossians 3:3, NASU).

Our effort here is to understand how and when the Colossian saints died and their lives were hidden in Christ. That is, how were these saints transferred into the kingdom of God's beloved Son and how did their lives get hidden with Christ in God? Is it possible that spiritually speaking, these saints and all the saints before and after have their lives trusted to Christ for safekeeping away from the reach of God's enemies? I would like to think that that is what Paul meant by 'their lives were hidden in Christ'. Also, is it possible to be in the kingdom of God's beloved Son without the forgiveness of our sins?

In Romans 7 Paul explains adultery in the eyes of the law, the law God gave to the Israelites. In the first three verses, Paul compares the association between the law and the Jews to a marriage with the Jewish people as the woman married to the law. Paul proceeds to explain that a woman who marries another man while her husband is still alive commits adultery. Paul further says the following:

> *Therefore, my brethren, you also were made to die to the Law through the body of Christ, so that you might be joined to another, to Him who was raised from the dead, in order that we might bear fruit for God. For while we were in the flesh, the sinful passions, which were aroused by the Law, were at work in the members of our body to bear fruit for death. But now we have been released from the Law, having died to that by which we were bound, so that we serve in newness of the Spirit and not in oldness of the letter. (Romans 7:4-6, NASU)*

Notice that Paul is not condemning the law as being bad; rather he is noting that the effect of the law caused those under it to not be able to keep it. That is, the law was good, for it revealed sin or exposed sin. By the same token the law created a situation where those under it craved to do what it prohibited. So in the final verses of the chapter Paul describes a situation where he desires to do what is right but finds himself doing the things he did not want to do—a situation created by the law as a result of exposing sin. So what is the alternative? This is where the analogy Paul opens the chapter with comes into play. Paul says that while the husband is alive, the woman is bound by the law to stay married to him. If she marries another man while the husband is still alive, she commits adultery, but if the husband should die or pass away, the woman is free under the law to marry another man. This fact has not changed. Jesus said, "What God has put together, let not man put asunder."

Paul starts verse 4 with *therefore,* signifying that he is about to use the points he had just established to further build his case. And his point was "[Y]ou also were made to die to the law through the body of Christ, so that you might be joined to another, to Him who was raised from the dead, in order that we might bear fruit for God." The law for marriage was first established by God when He presented Eve to Adam and said, "Therefore a man shall leave his father and his mother and hold fast to his wife, and they shall become one flesh" (Genesis 2:24, ESV).

God put this law in place as a result of the union between Adam and Eve. From one man God made two people, and then He declared that the two, man and his wife, became one flesh; thus the two became one. Even though Paul was stating truth in this scripture, his objective was not to teach marriage and the cause of adultery and remarriage, though this principle will apply in such cases. Neither was Paul saying that the law God gave to the Israelites was bad or sinful. Rather, without the law sin meant death. The law brought sin to light and as a result made clear two conflicting parties in us. One party, the inner man, also called the Spirit in Galatians 5, has a greater affinity to please God, whereas the other party, which is the flesh, has a greater affinity toward sin. Those under the law were bound to the law and constantly exposed to this struggle. Those not under the law did not have the benefit of understanding why their inner being had conflicts with their fleshly desires. Paul explains in Romans 2 that some, though not under the law, followed their consciences and kept the requirements of the law. Yet still some not under the law like those under the law yielded to the fleshly desires and sin. The fate of all who sinned, which is practically all of us, was death. So then what is the solution to making us whole? For those under the law, Christ's death on the cross removed the law plus cut away the sinful nature, the flesh that causes us to sin. For those not under the law, the sinful nature, the flesh that causes us to sin, is cut off while the law that separated us from those under the law was removed so the two could become one. With us partaking in the death of Christ, God reached to the core source that causes us to sin for both those under the law and those not under the law.

I believe Paul was using the truth about marriage to teach about the kind of union that those who hear the gospel message and receive the message have with Christ. Mark's account puts it, "Whoever believes and is baptized will be saved" (Mark 16:16). According to Paul this union is between Christ and the baptized sinners. By "baptized sinners" I mean one who has received the gospel just like the people did in Acts 2. Why is that? And how does this union happen? We have already seen from Paul's letters to the Romans and the Corinthians that we partake in the death of Christ through baptism and die to our sins in the process. We also see from Paul's letter to the Colossians that when we die to our sins in baptism, the sinful nature of the flesh that we have just learned is in constant battle with our spiritual nature is cut off, thus forgiving the baptized sinner all of their sins. This is not to say that we instantly become people who do not commit sin. In fact the struggle continues. Paul admonishes us to kill or mortify or make impotent that part of us that has been crucified on the cross. That is, we ought not live as people who have not been saved. In essence, the baptized sinner should have a greater affinity toward pleasing God, meaning that the spirit side of the battle Paul described in Romans 7 has a better chance of winning the conflict. So what happens when the forgiven sinner sins? Paul said the gospel the Corinthians received saves them if they stand in it. As the sinner is being perfected, there are many situations whereby the forgiven sinner will fall short and on occasion fall into sin. But as long as we are faithful in our effort to serve God, the dynamism of the blood of Christ guarantees that we will stay cleansed and forgiven. (Ephesians 1:7 and 1 John 1:5-10)

Thus those who were under the law and those who were not under the law both partake in the death of Christ and are separated from sin. The only way we know that we partake in the death of Christ is through baptism (Romans 6). Also according to Romans 7 we die to sin so that we will be joined to Christ Jesus who was raised from the dead. Now we note in Colossians 3:3 that Paul said of these Christians that they died and their lives have been hidden in Christ Jesus in God. Additionally, Paul told the Galatia Christians that through baptism they were clothed with Christ. If we put all these truths together, what we have is that through baptism those who receive the gospel message partake in the death of Christ. In the process their sins are cut off and they are united with Christ Jesus. Also in the process, their lives are hidden in Christ Jesus in God and they are clothed with Christ Jesus. If God had this all planned out ahead of time, and I believe He did, then it only makes sense that to immerse those who believe the message of the gospel in the name of the Godhead is no accident. That is, God does everything He does with purpose.

Furthermore, the Greek word eis *(eeis)* is translated as "to, into." According to *Thayer's Greek-English Lexicon of the New Testament* eis governs the accusative (the object case in English), which is the Greek case of the word onoma, translated as "name." Thayer's Lexicon further states that in this situation eis denotes "entrance into" or "direction." What this suggests to me is that in baptizing the hearers of the gospel message into the name of the Godhead, God brings these disciples under His authority, protection, and possession. God expresses His intent that those who have obeyed the gospel of Jesus Christ and the sin-forgiving message are top priority for Him and He personally is responsible for their well-being. Jesus clearly states this purpose for baptism by associating baptism with the name of the Godhead. Jesus says that the newly made disciples are to be baptized into the name of the Godhead, which places the saved into

Christ. Let's think about it. Christ covers us and lives in us as we live in Him! A marvelous thing God has made!

Let's summarize what we have discussed so far. When the gospel of Jesus Christ is presented to people, it generates response in the hearer. The hearers of the gospel can choose to accept or reject the message of the King. If we choose to accept the message by believing the message of the gospel, that should lead to repentance from sin. Like the Ethiopian eunuch we have to make known our faith to the one teaching us about Christ by professing openly what we have come to believe. Baptism is the next logical and scriptural order, because that is where the forgiveness of sins and the reception of the Holy Spirit take place. We have pointed out in this section of the Great Commission that baptism continues the instruction to make disciples of all nations. As a result it makes baptism a part and parcel of the command to make disciples of all nations. Jesus commands that all who are being made disciples be baptized. We fail to keep any aspect of the King's command if we fail to keep all His command, and that is not good. The role baptism plays in our salvations is much more significant than the idea that it is just works, and if it were works, it is the type of work by which our faith is demonstrated. If it is works, then it is works in response to God's commandments. The magnificence and brilliance of God is seen throughout His word. We need to study carefully and analyze with great care God's word with great awe and reverence to the God Almighty. Baptism is in this sense no different. It surely saves us, according to the apostle Peter, who opened the kingdom for both the Jews and the Gentiles.

The matter discussed here concerns eternal life, so let's diligently search the scriptures for answers to our questions and resolve them. The Bible is the only true road map to eternity with the Lord. Any other resource such as this material, no matter how accurate or inaccurate, should be taken only as a sign pointing in the right or wrong direction. It is never to take the place of the Bible. Most important, we will answer for our actions on the judgment day.

You see, making disciples does not stop once one accepts the gospel and submits to Christ in the obedience of baptism. We continue in the apostles' doctrines, growing from babes to maturity as our new natures that we take on through baptism are perfected through feeding on the milk of the word and the meat and potatoes of the word. Our discipleship continues until we graduate, from learning the elementary things of the faith to chewing on the most thought-provoking doctrines of the faith that cannot be digested by untrained minds.

The Parable of the Wedding for the King's Son
"For as many of you as were baptized into Christ did put on Christ" (Galatians 3:27, ASV) or "For all of you who were baptized into Christ have clothed yourselves with Christ" (Galatians 3:27, NASU).

To elaborate on this, let's look at the parable in Matthew 22 that Jesus told, comparing the kingdom of heaven to a king who gave a wedding feast for his son. In this parable none of the king's distinguished guests honored his invitation to come and enjoy his son's moment of a lifetime. These guests went their own way, doing their own things with utter disregard for their king and his son. The king sent his troops to go take care of those wicked people and then sent his servants to go into the streets and invite people both good and bad to be guests at his son's wedding feast. After the new guests arrived, the king came down to greet them and saw that one of them was not wearing a wedding garment. So the king asked him, "'Friend, how did you come in here without wedding clothes?' And the man was speechless" (Matthew 22:12, NASU).

In this parable the question I always ask myself is, Why was this particular guest without a garment? Did the king make available garments for these new guests? I would like to take a little liberty to respond to my own questions. First, because these new guests were called from the streets, it sounds to me like most of them would not be prepared for a wedding, let alone a wedding feast for the king's son. Second, there were both good and bad people among these impromptu guests, but the man without a garment was not identified as good or bad; it was just that he did not have a wedding garment. Third, because these guests were called off the streets, it is likely that those who could afford a garment might not have had the time to dress up properly before attending. It is also possible that a lot of these new guests might not be able to afford a wedding garment at all. Their coming from the street means there was a greater likelihood that none of them would be well dressed. Knowing this, the king, whose idea it was to bring these new guests in, might have made provision for, say, an outer garment to enable these guests to be fit for the occasion. Finally, the man without the garment was not dressed appropriately for the occasion.

Otherwise, if everyone was wearing their own clothes, why would the king single out this man for not having a wedding garment and sentence him to condemnation? The man's clothes might be tidy or not tidy, but like the others he was invited and the guards saw him walk through the king's gates. So why was he condemned for not having a wedding garment? Why was the king looking at the garments of his guest at all? Why did the lack of a wedding garment in this parable matter?

Looking at how swiftly and severely the king dealt with the situation, we are left with a strong impression that having the proper garment mattered to the king. The man without the wedding garment received as severe a punishment as the ones who dishonored the king's invitation and were called enemies of the king. This guy got the invitation and honored the invitation by showing up at the wedding feast. He could have been well dressed or had on filthy-looking street clothes. Either way he was condemned for not having on a wedding garment. I think it matters because he and the people who rejected the king's invitation seem to be the focus of the parable, or else Jesus would not have related it to the kingdom of heaven.

Given the liberties I mentioned earlier it would be safe to say that the guest without a wedding garment ignored the proper protocol when he entered the king's palace for the wedding. Thus he missed the opportunity to dress up before entering the banquet hall. Again the parable did not say anything about how well or poorly these guests were dressed, just that this particular guest did not have on a wedding garment. The other thought is that the man without the wedding garment sneaked into the banquet hall, depending on his human abilities, or thought this was a joke and disregarded the generosities of the king. That is, he lacked faith in the king's word that the invitation was good and did not trust that it was possible for him to be in the presence of the king. Thus this particular guest, though he responded and tried to honor the king's invitation, failed to follow the proper protocol.

As through baptism we put on Christ or are clothed with Christ, we shed our identity and take on that of Christ. Paul in Colossians 3 adds that we are dead and our life is hidden in Christ Jesus. The way I like to think of Galatians 3:27 is like this: we put on Christ in baptism, and from then on when God looks at us, He no longer sees Jim or Jack but rather copies of His beloved Son walking about and doing the things He desires us to do. Without Christ we stand alone as the hopeless and condemned sinners that we are, condemned to death just like the guest who did not have the proper wedding garment was condemned.

B: Teaching the disciples—Matthew 28:20

Introduction

"Teaching them to observe all that I commanded you; and lo, I am with you always, even to the end of the age" (Matthew 28:20).

Teaching them to observe (teerein is the infinitive of *tereo*—"to keep watch upon, guard," "watchful," "to watch over," "to mark attentively," "to heed," "to keep strictly," "to preserve, shield," "to keep in custody," "to maintain," "to keep in a condition") all things whatsoever I have commanded you (eneteilameen, the aorist of *entollomai*—"to enjoin, charge, command," "to direct"): and behold I am with ("together with," "on the same side as," "party with," "in aid of") you all the days until the completion ("end, consummation") of the age.

Over the first two verses of the discussion on the Great Commission, we discussed some important truths, facts, and concepts pertaining to salvation. We discussed authority, power, and law. We also discussed how God gave the authority to Jesus Christ, His Son, who is enthroned in heaven. Jesus has authorized His disciples with the power of the gospel to save souls. Those who accept the message of the gospel of Christ Jesus are saved by the gospel. We have also discussed baptism and challenged the idea that baptism is work, pointing out the difference between doing works prompted by faith and doing works that are not based on faith. We have also pointed out that baptism saves and that God through baptism enables us to partake in the death of Christ and many other significant issues. In this section, we will look at the body of believers and try to learn from them and possibly imitate what they did and practiced.

Let us assume we are one of the apostles, or one of the 120 faithful followers of Christ who were reported to be present in Acts 1 and participated in the replacement of Judas, the betrayer of the Lord. Let's consider the events from the ascension of Christ into heaven to the end of Acts 2. As one of these disciples or apostles, we have seen the Lord appear to us and others under different circumstances and at different times after His resurrection over a forty-day period. Now, just when we thought we had seen it all, we see yet another amazing site as Jesus finishes giving the Great Commission. Let's imagine that we are in the midst of the disciples, listening intensely to these final instructions. Without any warning we notice the Lord's body in an upward motion. At first we make nothing of it, perhaps thinking that the Lord might have jumped. We do not realize what is actually happening until we find ourselves looking at the bottom of the Lord's feet. Soon our upward gaze has been so intense that none of us realize how far our heads have been tilted backward and how long it has been since the Lord's body disappeared into the skies. In fact we are still gazing up when we hear some voices asking us how long we are going to keep looking up. It seems that with time Jesus had removed any doubts that were still lingering. Overwhelmed and filled with excitement but not knowing exactly how to process the Lord's ascension, we conclude that God has blessed us indeed to allow us to witness all these events in the past few days. Hence we stay in Jerusalem as the Lord commanded and Peter suggests that Judas needs to be replaced. At this all of the disciples faithful to the Lord came together, and in unison names are suggested and submitted to the Lord in prayer and He selects the one He desires to replaces Judas.

With Mathias in place and a few more days in waiting, another amazing thing happens. We are all gathered in a house near the temple on the day of Pentecost when all of a sudden there is a sound like that of a mighty wind filling the house, except that the nearby trees are holding still and the branches are not moving any faster than their usual back and forth. The only thing that has changed is the appearances of the apostles and perhaps the rest of the disciples, all of whom have what look like tongues of fire sitting on top of their heads without the normal consequence of being burned. As Luke's record indicates, "They were all in one place." We don't know whether *they* represents all of the 120 people who were present during the replacement of Judas or just the 12 apostles. In my humble opinion, whether or not the 120 or just the 12 were present is really not an issue. The significant point is that all the apostles whom the Lord personally selected and entrusted with the responsibilities of His church were present. I believe we can conceivably make that point from Luke's record in Acts 1.

As the house is filled with the Holy Spirit and tongues of fire settle on the heads of those present, we begin to speak in languages as the Holy Spirit allows. With this the multitude of Jews who had come to Jerusalem to commemorate the feast of Pentecost begin to gather around to inquire with amazement, for they are witnessing an amazing sight. They can individually understand the utterings in their respective languages. As humans will do with things we don't understand, some begin making comments such as "These men are drunk or crazy." Except that there is a small difference or minor detail: usually what drunks say is incoherent, unintelligible, and for the most part no one can understand them. In this case, however, the gathering audience can understand what is being said. What the apostles have been empowered by the Holy Spirit to do is something like this: Imagine I have never been to China, nor have I taken a course to learn the Chinese language, yet all of a sudden as I speak to my friends, those in my audience who understand the Chinese language hear me speaking Chinese with all the proper inflections without any stumbling. In such a case, though my audience is friendly, they might think that something is wrong with me and react like the crowd who gather to witness the manifestation of the Holy Spirit in Acts 2. Further, imagine that there are thirteen others in the audience who speak thirteen different languages, and all of them can understand what I am saying in their own dialect. The reactions of my friends might even be stronger since they don't understand what is going on with me. That was happening in Acts 2. The Holy Spirit had empowered the apostles with the ability to speak in such a way that those Jews present who probably not only spoke Hebrew but other native languages could understand what the apostles were saying in their own native languages. On that day if a Jew born in China had been present, he would have understood what the apostles were saying in Chinese. The apostles did not have a friendly audience.

Peter and the rest of the apostles stood up and began to explain to those present that what they were witnessing was not the delights of alcohol or the influence of it; rather they were witnessing the fulfillment of God's promise foretold by the prophets. As Peter continued his powerful sermon, he convinced the crowd that they were witnessing what God had chosen their generation to fulfill—what God had said through the prophets. He had allowed the Christ to be crucified on the cross, buried, and resurrected by the mighty power of God. As Peter continued to preach, those who gathered around asked, "What shall we do?" perhaps thinking they could right the wrong done to the Christ. In any case, Peter, after telling them to repent and be baptized, continued to persuade them until about three thousand of them were baptized. An amazing day that was. The promised Comforter was received and the gospel was preached and three thousand souls or more were won and converted to the Lord. As one of the apostles, imagine looking back to the day when Jesus gave the Great Commission and the events that had since unfolded in the past ten days, and realizing that God indeed was fulfilling His promise to the Fathers through the prophets and that we are the instruments He chose to make that fulfillment come to pass. What a humbling thought! As we realize the enormity of the responsibility, we feel the chill run down our spines as we finally begin to grasp what Jesus was trying to show us while on earth. The way we all envisioned the kingdom of Christ has been totally different from God's vision. This realization is even more humbling. All of a sudden the chill turns into excitement and energy. We are partaking in God's fulfilling His promise through the prophet. What an exciting time that must have been!

Now that the three thousand souls have been immersed in water into the name of Christ Jesus, what is next? This is probably a good time to pause and reflect on what just happened in Acts 2. Having been empowered by the Holy Spirit, the apostles preached the gospel of Christ and won souls using the gospel, and those who responded to the message were baptized into the name of Jesus Christ. I believe it is safe to say that not all who were present responded favorably to the gospel message preached by Peter. If that were not the case, Luke would have recorded that "all who were present" instead of "those who" received Peter's message. This is important because individuals who hear the gospel message will make up their own minds about whether or not they will accept it. In this light, God is going to hold the individual who heard the message and accepted it accountable just as He will hold the one who did not accept the message accountable. What had just happened in Acts 2 was the discharging of the tasks in the Great Commission. Disciples were made by the teaching of the gospel, baptizing them into Christ Jesus and thus the Godhead. (If we doubt this point, then how do we explain that it delighted God to have the full Godhead dwell in Christ in bodily form?) The closing of the chapter shows that "they," the new disciples, continued in the teaching of the apostles. We might ask, What are the "apostolic doctrines" or teachings? We will look into this shortly.

The keen observer might say, Well, this is all good, but those present were all Jews, or had a Jewish background in one form or another. The Great Commission said all nations. Yes, it is true in Acts 2 that Jews seem to be the only beneficiaries of the gospel message at that time. What about Gentiles, then? Although Acts 2 was for the Jews, God did not leave out the Gentiles. God's promise through the prophet was "He will pour His Spirit on all flesh." In Peter's report to his fellow Jewish believers in Acts 11 after he had ministered to Cornelius and his family and friends, he observed that the Holy Spirit (not the gift of the Holy Spirit, which was given to those who received the gospel, repented of their sins, and were baptized) fell on Cornelius and all present—all the Gentiles present in the house of Cornelius—just as He had fallen on the Jews in the beginning, that is, in Acts 2.

What is of great interest to me in the conversion of Cornelius and all those present who heard Peter speak is that "the Holy Spirit fell on all who heard the word" (Acts 10:44 ESV).

This indicates to me that at Cornelius's house only the Gentiles at this time received the Holy Spirit. After Peter explained to the Jewish brethren why he was at Cornelius's house, his interrogators, having been satisfied with his explanation, observed, "Then to the Gentiles also God has granted repentance that leads to life" (Acts 11:18 ESV).

Cornelius's conversion was the beginning of God bringing Gentiles into Christ. If we look at all the other Gentiles since then, none of those conversions physically saw the Holy Spirit at work in the way that those present saw with their eyes in the case of Cornelius or the first time it came on the apostles on the day of Pentecost. This difference is significant to keep in mind when talking about issues relating to conversions such as baptism, because we cannot cite a special case such as Cornelius's conversion as the reason baptism is a public symbol. When we look carefully at the events leading to the conversion of Cornelius, we must ask why the angel told Cornelius to send for Peter. Since God knew exactly what He was going to do, which was to save Cornelius, why didn't God just inform Cornelius through the angel that His faith had saved Him? Christ did that on many occasions when He walked on earth. If God had told Cornelius that his faith had saved him, then at the arrival of Peter the baptism of Cornelius and his group would truly have been a symbol of public acknowledgment. But this was not the case. Rather, as the angel was delivering the message to Cornelius, God was fine-tuning Peter's sensibilities and instructing him not to call unclean that which God had made clean. God prepared Peter so Peter could overcome his cultural influences and biases.

I don't know if Peter fully understood what had happened until God's mission to bring in the Gentiles was accomplished and he had to explain it to his fellow Jews. After arriving at Cornelius's home and being told the reason he was sent for, Peter said, "Truly I understand that God shows no partiality" (Acts 10:34, ESV).

Peter proceeded to preach the gospel to them, for there was no doubt that God had seen Cornelius's faith and just as God sent Philip to reach out to the Ethiopian eunuch, He sent Peter to reach out to Cornelius. Like the Jews in Acts 2, Peter would instruct Cornelius on what to do to be saved. The only thing different about Cornelius is that he was a Gentile. Previously, all who had been saved were Jews. To show Peter and the rest of the Jews that God's intention is to save all of mankind, God showed Peter and all the other Jews present that the Gentiles also had been granted a share in the repentance that leads to eternal life by letting the Holy Spirit fall on the Gentiles just like the Holy Spirit fell on the Jews. So God poured His Holy Spirit on the Gentiles, whom the Jews at the time had no respect for and considered unclean. God had poured His Holy Spirit on the Gentiles just as He did on the Jews with no difference at all. At this Peter could only conclude that what he had just witnessed was from God and had been led by God. So he followed through with the rest of the task in the Great Commission, which was to order that they be baptized. What is clear here is that just like in Acts 2, the Great Commission was followed as it was given. Thus the gospel was preached, and those who heard and believed the message were baptized just like the Great Commission statement commands. By staying with these new disciples for a few more days we can conclude that Peter continued to teach these new disciples the apostles' doctrine. It seems to me all of this took place at the home of Cornelius, which could not be a public setting. Thus their baptism could not be for public symbol.

Let us continue to imagine ourselves as one of the apostles. At this point, the gospel has been preached and heard far and wide all around Jerusalem and the neighboring cities and towns. The whole experience has been breathtaking and amazing. God is truly at work saving people from sin, and we are His hands and legs and mouth. As the body of believers has grown, we have heard Peter's report about the Gentiles receiving the gospel message. We have also heard that the gospel has reached the Samaritans, who in times past we did not care for but who now share in the spiritual blessing of God with us. The craziest of all this is that we have heard that the young man who has taken upon himself to purge Jerusalem of people in The Way, as some called the body of believers, has been won over and is preaching the good news. Of course the apostles are still in Jerusalem and God is accomplishing great things through them.

The body of believers has grown to such an extent that the apostles spend more time teaching and developing the saint, as well as seeing to it that all the proper structures are in place to take care of every believer's needs. Certainly, with the number of believers increasing, challenges are arising and God through the Holy Spirit is leading the apostles to resolve them.

To overcome the challenges facing the church in the early stages of the Christian movement the apostles had to dwell on God's direction. Let us think about this for a moment. God is the only one with the plan and its details for how this new movement is going to work. God is the only one who can thus provide the proper direction to the apostles in order for them to lead the way God desires. It makes sense then that Peter, led by the Holy Spirit in Acts 6, would be unwilling to spend time waiting on tables, but would focus the leadership's efforts on prayers and advancing the gospel. As they stayed in tune with God, they maintained an attitude of servitude toward God, who had the master plan and was directing the affairs of the movement. By staying in tune with God through prayer, the apostles maintained a position that enabled them to know God's will and hand it down to the newly made disciples.

The intricacy involved with the Godhead is amazing in all of this. The Father generates the plan. The Son puts the plan into action and tells the apostles that the Comforter who will be sent will not act on His own, but will take from what was the Son's, which in turn belongs to the Father. As the Son implemented the Father's plan, He taught the apostles and trained them to preach the gospel, since God had planned to save all mankind through the gospel. With the

Son's mission done, the Holy Spirit whom the Son called the Spirit of Truth was sent to remind and maintain everything that the Son had implemented to the finest details according to the Father's plan. Can we understand why Jesus said the Holy Spirit would not act according to His will? If part of the Godhead could not deviate from the Father's plan, how can a mere human deviate from the Father's plan and not suffer any consequences? The Holy Spirit took from the Son's, which is the Father's, and gave it to the apostles. As a result, the apostle could teach only what was given to them by the Holy Spirit. In Daniel 1 we learned that Nebuchadnezzar had the best young men among his conquests selected and trained in the culture and literature of Babylon for three years so they could serve him. Nebuchadnezzar was an inferior king compared with Christ. Should the people won for Christ not be raised and trained in the new lifestyle and culture that the Christian is to live? No one knows about the culture in heaven but the Godhead and those who live in heaven. And no one in heaven will know heaven better than the Son for whom everything was created. Certainly Christ will know; hence it makes sense to me that He would command that His disciples be taught all that He has commanded, for He would know what pleases the Father. Let us not lose faith when we are made fun of for adhering to apostolic doctrine, because in the end it is everything that Christ commanded, holding fast and not adding or taking from everything Christ had commanded. For us the apostolic doctrine ought to be the final authority. Let us now delve into the final section of the Great Commission.

Teaching them to observe whatsoever I have commanded you

Like the second part of the Great Commission discussed earlier, this section of the Great Commission statement cannot make much sense on its own unless we observe that those who are to be taught are those who have been made disciples. This instruction is simple as well; the new disciples are to be taught to observe whatsoever Jesus Christ has commanded the apostles, including the Great Commission that we have been discussing.

This part of the Great Commission is so specific and straightforward, it should not need any comments. However, I would like to make some notes. The *new disciples* are to be *taught to observe,* or *to fulfill,* or *to keep* whatever Jesus has commanded the apostles. I imagine that this would include commands such as the disciples loving one another, the Great Commission, treating others the way we want them to treat us, and all the teaching of Christ in the gospel accounts. The force of this command in the Great Commission cannot be overstated. Let's take another look at verse 18, which was discussed earlier. In verse 18, before Jesus outlined the duties in the Great Commission to the apostles, He told them that "all authority on earth and in heaven has been given to Him." We have already seen and established in earlier discussions that God the Father had all authority and gave it to Jesus Christ as God crowned and anointed Him King of Kings.

All authority means all authority—real, absolute authority, not the kind we associate with kings like Nebuchadnezzar. It leaves zero authority for anyone else. I made the point earlier that only kings might have absolute authority. Jesus in essence told the apostles and all who had gathered at the time (suppose more than the apostles were present) that He is king over heaven and earth. Taking into consideration the jurisdiction over which Jesus is to exercise all His authority, we observed that with the claim that all authority has been given to Him, Jesus leaves no room to anyone else for competition. Jesus claims absolution in the exercise of authority over heaven and earth. Narrowing this to the task on hand for the apostles, Jesus is telling the apostles that the source of any authority for their actions comes solely from Him. Let's think about it. Jesus has all authority, and He tells the apostles to teach the new disciples all, or everything, or whatsoever that He has commanded. Thus His word is final. Just as no one gives commands in a kingdom except the king and those to whom He has entrusted responsibilities, so it ought to be in Christ's kingdom. What the King commands must be obeyed; otherwise the penalty for disobedience can be and is most often severe.

This is a good time to discuss the significance of the authority of Christ. Why is the authority of Christ significant? It is critical to note the difference between power and authority. For example, God is all powerful. He has the power to do anything He chooses to do. That is His nature. We see in the Creation account that God called His creation into existence as He wished. He has all power and is all powerful. No one can take that away from Him. However, when God made Jesus the savior of mankind, He set up an authority to save man. Hence God limited Himself and His ability to save through the vehicle of salvation, the savior Jesus Christ. Similarly Jesus is all powerful, as we saw in the discussion on authority. We saw the Great Commission that while on earth, Jesus exercised power over nature, illnesses, and other things. But as a Son of God, He submitted to the Father and limited Himself to doing what the Father commanded Him. Thus when Jesus talked about authority, He was not talking about the power of God, and we should be able to see the difference. When Jesus talked about authority, He was talking about the powers that God has delegated into authorities. God has established these authorities—not only the earthly ones as Paul mentions in Romans 13:1 but also those in the realms beyond earth. These authorities execute their responsibilities by expressing the power God has delegated, like the Devil is delegated with the power of death and executes that responsibility over sinners. What is significant about Christ's authority?

To answer this last question we need to take in perspective what Gamaliel told the Jewish leaders in Acts 5. After attempting to dissuade the leaders and their attempts to put down the new teachings of the apostles Gamaliel added, "[F]or if this plan or this undertaking is of man, it will fail; but if it is of God, you will not be able to overthrow them. You might even be found opposing God!" (Acts 5:39 ESV).

This truth applies to the legitimacy of Christ's kingship if we take into consideration what we have already mentioned about the power of God and His will expressed in His words. If Jesus set this all up by Himself, it will be an authority set up beside God and thus illegitimate. But as we have seen in the opening chapter of Hebrews, God enthroned Christ and crowned Him as king. Thus before God the kingship of Christ is legitimate and acceptable. According to Paul in 1 Corinthians 15 God is the one who subjected all things under Christ and thus gave Him all the authority. Christ did not usurp the authorities He claims to have. God gave Christ His position and all that is associated with it. Christ's authority thus is legitimate and was established by God, who indeed establishes all rules and authorities as we have seen in both Paul's writings and Daniel's prophecies. Given that Christ's authority is acceptable before God and legitimate, we conclude that the authority behind the Great Commission was established by God the Father, or Christ, who has all authority. Thus the authority Jesus gave to the apostles was proper in the sight of God, as this was confirmed with the coming of the Holy Spirit. All of us who undertake the preaching of the gospel tap into that authority. The point here is that we cannot make disciples without the authority behind the Great Commission. That is to say, without the Savior we cannot be saved, and without the King who is the Savior, there can be no power behind the apostles. And as a result there can be no power behind the message of salvation that we preach as disciples of Christ.

That the authority of Christ was established by God and that God's desire is for all to heed to Christ makes it inevitable for us to pay attention to Christ. If Christ's authority were illegitimate, it would not matter what He said to His disciples or what commandments He gave them, because in the end nothing would come of what Christ demanded. However, because God was intimately involved in the plan to save man and put the plan together, making Christ its centerpiece, what Christ teaches and commands is just like the command and teachings of the one who put the plan together. As the centerpiece, Christ's commands should matter to us in all aspects of our relationship with Him as His disciples. How about us? Should we be limited to the authority of Christ? Are we to do only what Christ has commanded? What about what He has not commanded? No matter how the question is framed about the liberties one can take with scripture, I would like us to keep two scriptures keep in mind: "If you love me, you will keep my commandments" (John 14:15, ESV) and "teaching them to observe all that I have commanded you" (Matthew 28:20, ESV). If we take these scriptures to heart as we should, then we will seek to limit our liberties to what fits all that Christ has commanded.

Because Christ is our king . . .

What we do as Christians has to reflect His will—If we do not do what shows the will of Christ, how can we expect to stay in His grace? Surely we cannot expect to be looked upon with favor when we choose to not do His will. Although Paul tells us in Romans 6 that we cannot continue in sin and expect God's grace to abound, he also tells us in Romans 12 how we can learn and be trained to stay continuously in the grace of God. When we offer ourselves as living sacrifices set apart to God, we not only become acceptable to God but stay in His grace and are looked upon by Him with favor. We become like reader boards that God uses to demonstrate before the whole world. As God's demonstrations therefore we show the contrast between His will and the desires of the world, which are not according to God's will.

Without the authority of Christ His disciples cannot legitimately and effectively do the will of God—The best way to look at this is to take Christ out of the picture of salvation. This in essence takes away the King. A kingdom without a king is no kingdom at all. But a king can exist without his kingdom. He will have to build one, but before then he still exists. So it is with Christ and His kingdom. Without Him the salvation of mankind will be nonexistent. With Him, in fact, the first chapter of Hebrews said He existed before Creation, which means He existed before man encountered sin. All we do as His disciples ought to reflect submission to His authority and His commandments. Because Christ has all authority, He could delegate authority to His disciples to discharge duties in accordance with the King's will. It is never a good thing to exceed one's authority or undervalue that authority. Exceeding a given authority means doing what one has not been authorized to do, whereas failing to fulfill the duties of an authorized position only means shirking one's duties and responsibilities.

The teachings of the apostles were not from their own imagination—In fact Jesus told them not to leave the city of Jerusalem until they had received power and the Holy Spirit. From there on, nothing they did, taught, or said as far as God's work was concerned was a result of their own initiatives. Jesus said the Holy Spirit when He comes would take from what belongs to Jesus and give it to the apostles. Thus I believe everything the apostle taught derived its authority from Christ.

Our salvation is assured.

Our daily actions and decisions should reflect our new purpose—Paul told the brethren in Colossae to set their mind on things above where their king was seated at the right hand of God. We need to do the same.

The purpose of the church and the daily decisions by the church leaders ought to be the purpose of Christ.

Everything is under Christ, so we must not misuse or abuse the freedom He has given us. Doing so will lead us to fall out of favor before the Master.

Before we move on, let us observe that binding ourselves within the authority of Christ by submitting to His authority is not being legalistic. It is the right thing to do to stay in the grace of God. It is what we do when we understand that we have been accorded an immeasurable amount of favor. It is what we do when such understanding humbles our heart, mind, and thoughts and makes us refuse to think any more of ourselves than we are. It is what God would expect all of us to do if we love Him. And it is what we will teach others to do if we love God and love our fellow man and don't place ourselves lower or higher than them. It is what we do if we are to learn from Christ, who, even though he was the Son of God, humbled Himself and limited His will to what the Father had commanded. It is what we ought to do, because only by following what He has commanded can we become like Him. This is important!

In Luke 18:10-14, Jesus described legalism when He told the story of the two men who went to the temple to pray. In the story one man thought so highly of himself that when he went before God in prayer, he failed to recognize his own shortcomings. This man justified himself before God to the point where we might ask why he was praying in the first place. He seemed righteous in his own eyes. The other man could not even bear to look up to pray to God because he felt so guilty for his sins. Jesus declared that the man who could not bear to look up and pray, but beat his chest with regret for his waywardness, went home justified. How could that be? Doesn't God want righteous people? The issue is not that God is not interested in people who do right. The problem with the Pharisee in the story is that he was righteous in his own eyes and in the eyes of those like him. He used his own standard to condemn others. He thought because of His actions and goodness God ought to justify him as he had already justified himself. He had worked hard to please God. and God ought to have seen how great a person he was. Look at the two prayers and compare them with the model prayer given by Christ. It doesn't take too long to recognize which prayer fit the Lord's model. Legalism then is using God's word to set ourselves up as the standard by which God should judge others. It is when we set ourselves as better than all but fail to recognize the grace of God in our lives.

When someone comes along and challenges our scriptural stance on scriptural grounds, I don't think that is legalism, as long as they use the scriptures to make their points and we can verify what they are saying in the scriptures. In Acts 17, the Berean Jews were commended as noble compared with those Paul encountered in Thessalonica. Once the Bereans heard what Paul had to say, they searched the scriptures to make sure that what they were being told was what the scriptures said. We too need to search the scriptures eagerly whenever we hear something from God's word, and not take what we have been told for granted. If we don't understand an argument or a point that is being made, it is our duty to search the scripture to make sure that what is said is there. We need to test every teaching. That is not being legalistic. It becomes legalistic only when we fail to find out God's will and use our own standards to have God justify us.

Now that we have seen how significant the authority of Christ is, let us pay closer attention to the verse. Let's pay attention to each word in this segment of the Great Commission: "Teaching them to observe all things whatsoever I have commanded you" (KJV).

As we read the whole statement slowly and carefully, please keep the following in mind: 1) Making disciples involves repetitive instructions; generally these involve passing on precepts, traditions, and instructions that will lead the disciple to maturity. 2) How else is the new disciple going to learn, know, and do the will of the king if he or she is not taught continually?

The phrase διδασκοντες αυτους (*didaskontes hautous*) is the Greek phrase translated as "teaching them." In our discussion of verse 19 we looked at the Greek grammatical construct of the phrase Βαπτίζοντες αὐτοὺς *(baptidzontes hautous)*. In that analysis we identified the grammatical parts and the sentence structure that helped us understand Jesus's instruction or command to His disciples. The same exact treatment can and ought to be given to the phrase διδασκοντες αυτους in this early part of verse 20. Without repeating the same analysis let's delve into the study. The reader is encouraged to refer to the section on baptism for the analysis mentioned.

The Greek term τηρείν *(teerein)* is translated as "to observe" or "to obey" in most versions of the Bible as the infinitive of the word τηρέω *(teereo),* which has the following lexical meaning: "to keep watch upon, guard," "to watch over protectively," "to mark attentively," to heed," "to observe practically," "to keep strictly," "to preserve, shield," "to store up, reserve," "to keep in custody," "to maintain," or "to keep in a condition." As an exercise we can substitute each of these terms with whatever term our version of the Bible translation uses and ponder over what the verse says to us. The imagery here is that the new disciples should be all that Christ has commanded and the new disciple is to keep in custody all that Christ has commanded. The new disciples are to preserve these commandments, not tweaking or changing them to fit their needs. As the new disciples keep or preserve these instructions from the apostles, they pass on what they have received and maintained like Philip and Paul to others. By passing them on they take their turn to disciple others. That is, the commands of Christ do not change, so then what the apostles received and passed on ought no change from one disciple to another. Let us look at it this way: if we were given a trust to hold on to or keep in custody, the same trust is expected to be returned when it is required or requested of us. Paul delivered what he received to every disciple he made. Why can't we do the same?

What we need to look into as individual Christians is whether we are following what Christ commanded the apostles. Are we making disciples the way Jesus commanded? If we are doing anything different, then we are usurping authority or disobeying the King's command. Here silence of scripture does not mean permission. Just think about it: if Jesus knows it all and has all authority, and scripture is silent about an issue, then God has either decided that issue or act is irrelevant to our salvation and we don't need to worry about it, or to provide a means to test our faith and submission to Him, which will be a reason why the Holy Spirit did not reveal it to the apostles. We need to note that though God in the past allowed or sanctioned things His people desired, such as Israel's desire for a king during Samuel's time, He was not pleased yet let it happen. However, in the kingdom of God, engaging in things that have not been commanded by the King based on silence of scripture is a direct challenge to the King's authority. By the same token, to do what one wills can lead to chaos and insubordination. We need to teach only what Christ has commanded His apostles, because we have no idea what it will take or what it takes to live a life pleasing to God; only Christ does.

After the events in Acts 2 what happened to those who were converted and baptized? What did they do after the day of Pentecost, for example? To address questions such as these we need not look very far. In fact before Acts 2 ends, Luke's account tells us what happened to these disciples. As we investigate this new group, it will help to note that this group included people of Jewish background. As a result I will do my best to recall some things from the Old Testament that will put into perspective what is going on. Also, though this group was Jewish, we will see that the precepts they set applied to the Gentile brethren who came along later. This is important because both Jews and Gentiles who accepted the gospel were taught the same thing. The Jewish congregations had the same structure as the Gentile congregations. There were no differences spiritually speaking between the Jewish and Gentile congregations or churches, though culturally we note some behavioral differences. Let's search from Acts 2:41 on to the end of the chapter.

247

*The Early Disciples in Acts—A Direct Result of the Great
Commission*

Why is it important to learn about what the early disciples did?
There are many reasons why we will benefit from learning what the
early disciples did and follow them. I will give one simple reason
here. They were the first to be called Christians and were led by the
apostles, whom the Holy Spirit directed. Hence even though they
did not see or understood the whole picture perfectly, they gave us
the structure of the Lord's church and how it functioned.

We observe the following progressions:

Those who received Peter's word were baptized or immersed—Luke's
account makes it clear that not just anyone was baptized. Those
who were baptized were people who heard Peter preach the gospel
and asked what they needed to do. After Peter told them what
they ought to do, which was to repent and be baptized for the
forgiveness of their sins and to receive the gift of the Holy Spirit,
those who repented and stepped forward were baptized. We've
discussed this at length.

About three thousand souls were added that day.—We have an
idea to whom the three thousand souls were added from an earlier
verse in the account of Luke. The three thousand souls are probably
Jews who lived permanently in Judea and its surroundings and
those Jews from other countries who had gathered in Jerusalem to
observe the Pentecost festivities. Two questions need to be asked:

to whom were these three thousand souls added, and who did the adding?

The first part: We have established that when the Holy Spirit came at Pentecost, there could have been anywhere from 12 to 120 people present or even more. We do know from Acts 1:2 that before Jesus ascended to heaven, He commanded the apostles whom He had chosen during His ministry to remain in Jerusalem. We also know from Acts 1:3 that Jesus presented Himself alive to these apostles over a period of forty days. Luke said in Acts 1:4 that Jesus even stayed with them, the apostles—most likely the eleven at the time since Matthias was installed as an apostle later. While Jesus was with His apostles, He ordered them to stay in Jerusalem until the Holy Spirit came upon them. Obviously the 120 people are important because Mathias was chosen from them. That number probably also included Mary, the mother of Jesus, and probably Jesus's siblings, some of whom became very prominent in the church in Jerusalem and also some of his most loyal followers. Apart from the twelve any of these members could come and go anytime they desired, to take care of their chores or businesses needs, be it in Jerusalem or outside Jerusalem. However, the twelve because of Jesus's order had to, and I believe did, remain in Jerusalem in obedience to Jesus until the Holy Spirit came on them. Thus a conservative estimate is that the twelve were the ones to whom the nearly three thousand souls who were converted on the day of Pentecost were added.

The second part: Who could be doing the adding to the apostles? This is not hard to see if we follow the events leading up to this point. The apostles have stayed in Jerusalem, and the Holy Spirit came upon them on the day of Pentecost. In Acts 1:8 Jesus told the apostles that they would receive power when the Holy Spirit came upon them and they would bear witness to Him. Before saying this Jesus said to the apostles in Acts 1:7, "It is not for you to know times or seasons that the Father has fixed by his own authority." That is, the Father does things in His own time. The authority to save and when to save has to come from the source of our authority, our King, Christ Jesus. He is the only one who chose Matthias to take the place of Judas, and He is the only one capable of adding new disciples to the number of the apostles. How did the Lord add the new disciples? we might ask.

Again looking back to the events that took place in the ten days before the day of Pentecost, we see that Jesus had ascended to heaven as He finished giving the Great Commission to the apostles. The apostles received the Great Commission with the order to stay in Jerusalem and to not leave until the Holy Spirit came to them with power. On the day of Pentecost, the Holy Spirit came with power and the apostles preached the gospel of Jesus Christ, and those who heard the message, received it, repented, and were baptized were added to the apostles. One might observe that until the Holy Spirit came and Peter preached the gospel, nothing had moved the people. Obviously the people were in the neighborhood where the apostles were residing and were going about their normal life chores. The coming of the Holy Spirit upon the apostles drew attention to them, which caused the people to focus their attention on the apostles and drew them closer to hear what the apostles had to say. Some who heard the message and responded to it asked what they needed to do. The interesting observation here is that those who responded to Peter's prompting to repent and be baptized were the ones who were added. These were the folks who were added to their number. Is it possible that more that three thousand souls asked Peter and the other apostles, "Brothers, what shall we do?" My answer would be yes. Otherwise why will Luke use *those* and not *all* who heard the word? Later Paul will instruct us that the power to save is in the gospel. So then, those who hear the gospel and subject themselves to the requirements in the Great Commission are added to the number. That is, God through the authority of the Great Commission added to the apostles those hearers who yielded to its requirements and became disciples. The precedence here is that no one by his or her own will or accord can join the Lord's church or body as a member. This makes sense if we look at an earlier assertion we made that no one can approach God of their own accord, coupled with the fact that the disciples were baptized into Christ or the Godhead. In Acts 2:47 Luke makes it plain that the Lord added to the number or the church as He saved the souls who responded to the gospel message.

They devoted themselves to the apostles teaching—What are the apostles teaching? The New Testament, I contend. The apostles' teaching is what the apostles taught the early disciples under the direct supervision of the Holy Spirit. They were limited by the authority granted to them by Jesus Christ through the Holy Spirit and everything Jesus had commanded. The apostles could teach and do only what they were permitted by Jesus Christ through the Holy Spirit. Can anyone argue they went beyond that? I cannot.

The act of making disciples cannot end with telling people about Jesus Christ. If it ends with people only hearing about Jesus with or without the proper response of repenting, believing, and confessing the faith in what has been taught and believed, we have not fully discharged the duties assigned to us by the Great Commission. Neither can it end when the new disciple has been baptized. Again it leaves the commission partially fulfilled. The newly made disciple must be taught to live like a subject in the kingdom. He must be taught the will of the King in order to successfully serve the King. In this case, the new disciple needs to be taught to keep strictly all the things that Jesus commanded His apostles, who then handed it down to the first-century church.

The first-century church's authority in maintaining the apostolic teachings preceded canonizing the Bible document. Thus if the first-century church did not accept a doctrine or include a book in the New Testament, then no amount of persuasion should compel us to accept such a doctrine or book. It taints the purity of what Christ gave His apostles that was been handed down from generation to generation in the church. Really, it is in our interest to teach only what Christ has commanded, thus speaking where the New Testament speaks and being quiet where the New Testament is silent. Additionally, we add to Christ's command when we practice things that the first-century church did not do, or did not leave in the form of examples that we can follow. We become people who are inventing our own ways to please God and as such are no longer walking by faith. We reject God's will when we choose to do what we believe needs to be done to please God even if God has not sanctioned it.

They devoted themselves to the fellowship. Fellowship of the saints is something that needs to be encouraged greatly. We see that these new disciples in Acts 2 have come to a new faith, one that is perhaps different from that of their fathers. The Jews were religious people and people of faith. As such the proclamation of a new faith is bound to arouse all kinds of problems in the community. We see in Acts some of the challenges the church in Jerusalem faced from the onset. It is very likely also that people professing this life would be alienated from their families and relations. Also, most of these new disciples had traveled a long way to celebrate the Pentecost. Additionally, they had just begun a movement no one knew anything about, nor did anyone understand where God was leading it. Adding all of these together, it makes sense that fellowship with each other would be natural. Besides, the fellowshipping with each other would make it possible for these new disciples to be taught by the apostles. It is clear that they devoted themselves to fellowshipping with each other and enjoyed each other's company rather than the company of those who were not part of the movement. The idea of devotion is not one of a casual cause. It is intentional and purposeful. Their devotion to fellowship with each other is a lesson for us to do the same with each other, since we in many ways face the same or varied flavors of the challenges they faced.

They devoted themselves to the breaking of bread—The term breaking of bread is usually used to signify the Lord's Supper. But it can also mean sharing food in common. I believe that in this particular case Luke was referring to the Lord's Supper. This is because in a later verse he talked about the believers sharing their food.

Why the Lord's Supper

1) Christ instituted it and commanded the apostles to do it in remembrance of Him. "This is My body which is given for you; do this in remembrance of Me" (Luke 22:19, NASU). And Paul explains further, "This is My body, which is for you; do this in remembrance of Me . . . This cup is the new covenant in My blood; do this, as often as you drink it, in remembrance of Me" (1 Corinthians 11:24-25, NASU).

2) Jesus commanded the apostles to teach the disciples to observe all that He had commanded the apostles: "teaching them to observe all things whatsoever I commanded you" (Matthew 28:18-20, ASV).

It is important to note that this command has two parts to it. The apostles or disciple makers are to teach the new disciple all that Christ has commanded them. And the newly made disciple is to observe all that Christ commanded. To this effect the apostles and the early disciples observed the Lord's Supper on the first day of the week. "So then, those who had received his word were baptized; and that day there were added about three thousand souls. They were continually devoting themselves to the apostles' teaching and to fellowship, to the breaking of bread and to prayer" (Acts 2:41-42, NASU).

"On the first day of the week, when we were gathered together to break bread, Paul began talking to them, intending to leave the next day, and he prolonged his message until midnight" (Acts 20:7-8, NASU).

"For as often as you eat this bread and drink the cup, you proclaim the Lord's death until He comes" (1 Corinthians 11:26, NASU).

Let's imagine what the first Lord's Supper was like when the first Christians met after more than three thousand souls had been added to the Lord's body. What kind of atmosphere would we have witnessed had we been present? Can we imagine what it was like for those faithful disciples who followed Jesus Christ throughout His ministry? They probably had heard the apostles describe Jesus instituting the Lord's Supper without fully understanding its purpose at first. Yet with the help of the Holy Spirit leading the way and guiding the apostles, the apostles began to frantically prepare for the Lord's Supper at this first gathering, and things begin to click for them, such as Luke's reference to Jesus saying, "This cup poured out for you is the new covenant in my blood," and "Do this in remembrance of me," and many other things Jesus said. Imagine that as these things came together for the apostles and they were explaining them to the new disciples, the renewed emotional rush that must have overpowered all present. There couldn't be enough Kleenex for the group. Of those in the crowd, some of the apostles and those disciples who were not at the Lord's Supper when Christ instituted it but had witnessed all the events that had taken place in the previous fifty-plus days had heard Jesus preach His first sermon to the masses and followed Him faithfully. Can we imagine what that first Lord's Supper was like for those people?

For the apostles who knew, touched, heard, and were touched by Jesus, I imagine that taking the Lord's Supper brought back enjoyable memories, such as sitting at the table when Jesus instituted the memorial, and observing the Lord as He went through emotional swings. At one point noting the joy on the Lord's face showed that the occasion marked the beginning of the end. Of course at this point they had a better understanding than they did at the table. As a result they had come to appreciate the Lord even more now as they looked back, individually and collectively. For most of the faithful disciples who saw Jesus from the beginning of His ministry until He ascended to heaven, their emotions probably could not be contained. We can imagine the apostles sharing some of the stories at the table as they shared the Lord's Supper on the day of Pentecost. Imagine us in the crowd listening to one of the apostles. Perhaps John or Thomas or Matthew was leading the occasion and sharing his stories with the new disciples, some of whom never saw Jesus but had come to believe and took part in the breaking of bread. The disciples gathered together to take part in the Lord's Supper in the presence of the King, in His kingdom just as He had said. What a difference a few days makes! The apostles remembered Jesus saying, "But I say to you, I will not drink of this fruit of the vine from now on until that day when I drink it new with you in My Father's kingdom" (Matthew 26:29, NASU). The feeling might have been incredible!

Some of the apostles and disciples there had attended to Jesus's needs, and Jesus had touched some of them by healing, forgiving their sins, and in many other ways improving the quality of their lives. Hence, most of these disciples at the assembly remembered the Lord who had shown them so much love to the point of death and dying a cruel death for their sake and our sake. They remembered the Lord who died to make them free from sin. They remembered the Lord's tender touch and care toward each of them. They remembered the man Jesus, who loved perfectly. They remembered the divine Jesus, who saw beyond their ruggedness and loved them like they had never been loved. They remembered the divine Jesus who loved all and yet care for them individually. And on and on they each remembered the Lord.

Those of us who follow Christ today did not see him, so how do we remember him? It is true we never saw Christ, yet by faith we remember Christ! By faith we remember the Christ who loved us so much, He emptied Himself of His deity, sacrificing His life for us so that by believing in Him we might have life. By faith we remember the rich grace poured on us because of the cross. By faith we remember because the apostles taught it and we observe it. By faith we remember because by it we proclaim the Christ's death, burial, and resurrection. By faith we remember because it is the proclamation we make to each other to continue to be faithful to Christ whose sacrifice on the cross saved us. By faith we remember because we proclaim the death of the Christ that led to our birth, our redemption, and the forgiveness of our sins. By faith we remember because we proclaim the Christ as we partake of the Lord's Supper. By faith we remember because in partaking of the Lord's Supper we proclaim the Lord's death, burial, and resurrection. And in that proclamation, we are reminded that we are no longer beholden to sin. In that proclamation we are reminded that we died to our sins in baptism and that our sins have been cut away from us for good if we remain faithful to Him who died in our stead. In that proclamation also, we are reminded that our sins were buried with Christ Jesus in baptism and death's threat over us because of sin was rendered powerless. Finally in that proclamation, we are reminded that we were raised with Christ as He conquered the adversary, Satan, for good, and we are no longer beholden to sin as slaves to a master. Rather we now have a loving Master who knows and feels our pain and needs and has made us part of Him. He has made us anew in Him who is able to make us whole to walk according to the Father's will.

They devoted themselves to prayer—There is never enough that can be said about prayers. From the gospel accounts, we know that Jesus spent a lot of time praying. Sometimes He would remove Himself from the crowd just to go pray. In Acts 1 we read of the apostles that "All these with one accord were devoting themselves to prayer, together with the women and Mary the mother of Jesus, and his brothers" (Acts 1:14, ESV).

This was no casual onetime thing, I don't think. The example of Jesus's attitude toward prayers seems to have finally kicked in with the apostles. It is no wonder the new disciples were trained to acquire similar attitudes toward prayer.

What about us today? How do we approach prayer? Is it a casual thing we do when the saints come together or do we have a devoted attitude toward it? Do we pray because we love to or because we have to pray? Are we praying only when needs arise or are we praying regardless of our circumstance? How many of us actively and eagerly pray that the Lord Jesus will come quickly and that we will get to go home to the Father? Is our attitude toward prayer casual because we don't have any needs? Or do we become serious about it only when we have serious situations to deal with?

What will it take for us to appreciate that any time we enter into prayer, we enter the presence of the Almighty God who not only loves us, but has declared us His sons and is eagerly looking forward to what we have to say? Yes, He knows what is on our minds, but like the loving Father He is, He awaits with loving expectation to hear what we have to say. When I think of prayer I like to put the following verse in perspective

> *Therefore, brothers, since we have confidence to enter the holy places by the blood of Jesus, by the new and living way that he opened for us through the curtain, that is, through his flesh, and since we have a great priest over the house of God, let us draw near with a true heart in full assurance of faith, with our hearts sprinkled clean from an evil conscience and our bodies washed with pure water. (Hebrews 10:19-22)*

It humbles me to know that when I enter into prayer, God is not too far away and in fact is right near and very close. It makes me desire to pray more, but often I find myself weary and not investing as much time as I should. When I think of Jesus and His attitude toward prayer, the picture that comes to mind is one of a son who loves his father so much that he cannot wait to talk to him. Hence any given moment is a perfect excuse for him to engage his father's attention. I believe Christ loved His Father so much that He eagerly looked forward to each praying moment and made a lot of time for it. If we are to heed Paul's admonition to have the same attitude as Christ, then we ought to take hold of the avenue of prayer and learn to be like Christ and encourage each other to pray more often. In this respect I don't think the Father would mind at all if we turned out to be champs in our attitude toward praying. What I mean is that we become like Christ and seek our Father's attention frequently and often without apologies. That is, since through Christ Jesus we have direct access to the Father, let us approach Him in all humility and reverence with an attitude of immense appreciation toward Him and what He has done for us.

How about the believing community praying together? That is what this section is really talking about, isn't it? It is impossible to address the prayer attitude of the church without looking at the prayer attitude of the individual Christian. There has been a lot said and written about prayers and the prayer life of a Christian. I have also sat in discussions that involved teaching both old and new Christians how to pray and what to include in our prayer. The ACTS recipe for praying, where ACTS stands for *adoration, confession, thanksgiving,* and *supplication* is among the popular ones I have heard discussed. This prayer recipe has all the basic ingredients Jesus gave in His model prayer. My concern here is not so much about how to pray. We need to all pray as Christians like our Lord and Master Jesus Christ Himself did. Thus, if new or old Christians do not know how to pray, they need to be taught how! My concern here is our attitude toward prayers. I have not come across a brother or sister who does not see or feel the need to pray and pray frequently and fervently. But even though most brethren like and want to pray, they find very little or no time for it. A brother whom I admired during my early college years said of prayer that it is something we do to the point where it becomes second nature. I have also seen an attitude that makes it seem like going to God in prayer disturbs God!

The church cannot be a praying church if the individual Christian is not a praying Christian. An older preacher used the following scripture to teach about prayer; "For I say to you that unless your righteousness surpasses that of the scribes and Pharisees, you will not enter the kingdom of heaven" (Matthew 5:20, NASU).

That is, the righteousness of Christians is to exceed that of the Pharisees, so if the Pharisees gave a tenth of their income, the Christians had to give more than a tenth. If the Pharisees prayed three times a day, the Christians had to pray more than three times a day. The idea here is not to have a counting competition with the Pharisees. But in all of our efforts toward the works of faith that God has prepared for us, we in all sincerity seek to please God, so we work harder. Thus we maintain a serious relationship with God as we serve Him—a relationship filled with prayer to keep us in His favor, and a prayer life steeped in faith and desire to understand God's will and the sacrifice of the cross that draws us closer to God and keep us closer to Him. Add to that a consistent habit of studying God's word to help us know His will. This is a sure way to offer ourselves as living sacrifices, holy and acceptable to God. A habit of study combined with a praying habit will surely transform our way of thinking and help us not conform to the world, thus equipping us with the necessary knowledge and the ability to test and discern God's will as well as what is good, perfect, and acceptable to Him.

This is possible only by learning to do and be like Christ. In terms of prayer, we must learn to have Christ's attitude. As Christians, we don't have to pray only because tragedy has struck or harm has come our way. We pray because it is what we do to stay in tune with God. It is our life. In 1 Thessalonians 5:17 Paul said, "Pray constantly" (RSV) or "Continually be prayerful" (ISV) or "Pray continually" (NIV) or "Pray without ceasing" (ESV). He also told the Colossian saints in Colossians 4:2 to "Continue steadfastly in prayer" (ESV) or "Continue in prayer" (KJV) or "Devote yourselves to prayer." Our attitude toward prayers needs to be at the same level as our attitude toward studying the Bible. In fact they need to go hand in hand. We study the Bible so well. The question is, How successful have we been in applying the knowledge acquired? How successful have we been in applying the knowledge to outreach? How has that knowledge transformed us and moved us to yearn for the souls that are lost? How about using that knowledge to sincerely love and care for our Christian brothers and sisters, those struggling and those not struggling? Maybe we need to spend the same amount of time or more praying and with the same intensity so that we can effectively apply the knowledge we acquired through our studying.

We need to ask why Jesus prayed so often and for so long. I don't believe Jesus prayed because He was facing situations that were grave and He was uncertain about them. Certainly, the cross was grave, but I do not believe Jesus thought He could not overcome the situation. I believe Jesus prayed for our benefit. He prayed to teach us that we needed to keep in constant contact with the Father. Jesus prayed as a sign of submission to the Father, so we can also learn to be submissive to the Father. Jesus prayed and derived His strength from the Father. In fact before the cross, He prayed with such anguish that His muscles screamed out sweats like blood, according to the doctor Luke. Jesus prayed to teach us about the value of prayer. We need to learn to pray like Christ so we can derive our strength from the Father who is the true source of all power and comfort. When individual Christians have a prayer-filled life like the Master, the church as a whole is going to be a praying church. But it has to start with the leadership. When the leaders of the local congregation have the habit of praying, the tendency will be to steer the congregation in that direction. As Peter told the Jerusalem congregation, advancing the gospel and prayer has precedence over waiting on tables, and that should be the focus of the leadership. He did not say that waiting on tables is not important, else why did he suggest the appointment of the seven deacons? Waiting on tables has a different focus and can distract from the main mission of the church, which is reaching the world with the gospel.

When the elders are prayer champions, they will lead the local church in that direction. When the preachers and teachers love to pray, they will impress that on the local church. When the church prays, heaven rings and smells with fragrances of the requests from God's people. God the loving Father acts and things get done!

Attending the temple in Jerusalem was a Jewish tradition. Just about all the Jews in the society, whether good or bad, went there to pray and/or to listen to scriptures read. This is probably one of the scenes

Jesus described in Luke 18. The new disciples did not stop this practice as we see in Acts 2:46. They continued to attend the temple daily. The apostles themselves did too. They attended the temple, just like we read about Peter and John "going to the temple" in Acts 3. In the book of Psalms, David wrote about his desire to spend endless time in the house of God even though the temple was not yet built. It might have been that desire that prompted him to want to build the first temple in the first place. In any case the tradition was deep and strong. We also see in other places in Acts that these disciples prayed fervently in the homes where they met. They had met and were praying for Peter in one of these homes in Acts 12 when Peter came knocking on the door. In the first few chapters of Acts, we see this new group in its infancy. We also see them praying and having an active prayer life as a church and as individual members. As believing Gentiles we need to cultivate this tradition. As we look back at these early Christians and their examples, we need to make prayer the central part of our relationship with God just as they did. Let the church of our generation get excited about prayers. And let us fill heaven's throne room with requests for boldness, love, and learning how to love each other, showing love to the lost, and passion for spreading the message of salvation to the world.

The community was awed, and wonders and signs were done through the apostles—When God's hand is at work, we are left with nothing but wonder and amazement. As God saved these souls through the hands of the apostles, He supported the work of the apostles with signs and miraculous works. These signs showed the people in the community that God is at work. These miracles were not just any works of magic, trickery, and man-made initiatives.

As we see later in Acts 8, Simon, who charmed Samaria with his magical powers, realized the difference between his professed power and the power behind the new movement. Luke records that Simon became devoted to Philip and was amazed by the great miracles that Philip was doing. As news of the reception of the gospel by the Samaritans reached Jerusalem, the apostles Peter and John went to Samaria. Upon their arrival they imparted the Holy Spirit to the Samaritans. Through Simon's behavior, God made it clear that the wonders and signs done by the apostles were not from man. God was the source of their power, just like God set Himself apart through Moses with superior signs and miracles.

The language here needs some attention. The phrase "The Holy Spirit fell . . ." is used to describe how Cornelius and his group were affirmed by God as Peter was preaching the good news of salvation to them. Peter confirms that the way the Holy Spirit came upon Cornelius's group was the same way He came on them, the Jews. Thus, according to Peter, the Holy Spirit fell on the Jews in Acts 2 just like He fell on Paul. Some of the English Bibles use similar language to translate Luke's account describing what happened to the Samarian disciples: "who came down and prayed for them that they might receive the <u>Holy Spirit,</u> for he had not yet fallen on any of them, but they had only been baptized in the name of the Lord Jesus" (Acts 8:15-16, ESV).

Luke continues that these new disciples in Samaria received the Holy Spirit only after the apostles had prayed for them and laid their hands on them. In both Acts 2 and Acts 10, the Holy Spirit fell on both Jews and Gentiles, respectively, without any human interference. In the case of Acts 8 involving the Samarians there was human interference, for the apostles came and met these new disciples when they heard that the gospel had reached them. The apostles proceeded to lay their hands on the Samarian disciples before the Spirit "fell" on them. A clear difference is present in how the disciples in Samaria had the Spirit versus how the Spirit first fell on the Jews and the Gentiles. In order to understand this let us make a few notes:

1. The Samarians were not the first to experience the laying on of hands. In Acts 6 when the deacons were selected and presented to the apostles, the apostles prayed for them and laid their hands on them.

2. Before the apostles laid their hands on the deacons, a group that included Stephen and Philip, we note that Stephen was described as "a man full of faith and of the Holy Spirit." After the laying on of hands, Luke described Stephen as "full of grace and power, was doing great wonders and signs among the people" (Acts 6:8, ESV). Philip was also described later in Acts 8: "[W]hen they heard him and saw the signs that he did . . . And seeing signs and great miracles performed, he was amazed" (Acts 8:6-13, ESV).

3. We see that once the apostles laid their hands on the disciples in Acts 8 it was followed with a transfer of the Spirit. It is of utmost importance to note that though Philip did wonders and signs, he could not lay his hands on these new disciples in Samaria to transfer the Holy Spirit to them.

4. Simon, who had followed Philip around until the arrival of the apostles Peter and John, noticed that it was only by

the laying on of the apostles' hands on each new disciple that they received the Holy Spirit. As he witnessed that, he offered money so he could be given such power and do as the apostles were doing. Peter rebuked him and told him he had no share in performing that role. Simon might not have understood his calling, being that he was a new Christian. Yet what Peter told him was not just for him. Simon had no role in the laying on of hands for the transfer of the Holy Spirit from one saint to another. Philip, a more matured disciple who also had had the apostolic hands laid on him, could not lay his hands on the new disciples in Samaria to transfer the Holy Spirit to them. We read about many kinds of laying on of hands, such as laying hands on the sick and praying for them, and laying hands on Paul and Barnabas and praying for them before they were sent on their missionary journey. But as Paul explained to young Timothy ("For this reason I remind you to fan into flame <u>the gift of God, which is in you through the laying on of my hands</u>") (2 Timothy 1:6, NIV) the laying on of hands that transfers the Holy Spirit was something only the apostles could do. No other disciple had that capability, as Peter told Simon.

Before the days of Acts 6, Luke records in Acts 2 that God did wonders and signs through the apostles. Here Luke makes it clear that the apostles were the only ones doing wonders and signs. It was not until the days of Acts 6 that we read of other disciples such as Stephen and Philip. Stephen displayed extraordinary knowledge, and Philip is said to have done great wonders in Samaria. Anyone who is baptized in the name of Jesus receives the gift of the Holy

Spirit according to Acts 2:38, but through the laying on of hands by the apostles, God distributed extraordinary gifts to men who used them to do wonders in support of their ministries. In Acts we note that the apostles were the only ones who could lay their hands on the disciples to give them the gifts of the Holy Spirit, though there were other forms of laying on of hands, such as in Acts 13 when Paul and Barnabas were set apart for their missionary work.

The believers were together and had all their things in common. Those with possession sold them to support the new community of believers—This is a summary of Acts 2:44-46. Often when I look at these two verses, giving does not cross my mind. I focus on the idea that they had things in common and that those who had needs got them met. What I have failed to appreciate is that individuals who had possessions voluntarily sold them and contributed the proceeds toward helping care for the needs of the brethren. This is what Ananias and his wife attempted to do, but they failed miserably because they were not sincere. As Peter noted, the property belonged to them before they sold it. After the property was sold, the proceeds still belonged to them. If at any point their intention of contributing toward the welfare of the saints had changed, they could have held on to the money or made a decision that reflected their sincerity. Instead they chose to lie, and it cost them their lives. This act of giving toward God's work is not something new to the Jewish culture. It goes as far back as the days of the exodus. Also, when David was planning the building of the temple, the leaders and the people contributed generously. This practice of giving spread to the Gentile brethren, so Paul had to instruct them about how to give and the type of spirit that ought to accompany our giving—a spirit of sincerity and willingness. We see the evidence of this in his letters to the Corinthians, for example.

The Church

The Lord added to their number or the church daily those who were being saved—Luke's account continues by saying that the new converts praised God and were viewed favorably by all the people. At this point the number of believers had increased beyond the three thousand souls plus the apostles since the Lord kept adding more to the disciples. By the time Luke gets to Acts 4 the number of men alone in this new movement was at five thousand. One can conclude that the total number of those converted was more than ten thousand when women and children were counted. Who were these people? What was God doing with them?

We've already seen in earlier discussions that the Lord added three thousand to the apostles to begin this movement. This current discussion is only an affirmation of this fact. Here Luke records that the Lord added to the number, or the church, depending on whether one uses the Greek version of the New Testament or the English New Testament. As we continue this discussion, we will address why the number as this group is referred to as the church. The important fact here is that membership is directed by the Lord Himself. This is important because this little fact shows the importance of the message and what happens when hearers of the gospel respond as the message is heard. According to Mark's account, "Whoever believes and is baptized will be saved, but whoever does not believe will be condemned" (Mark 16:16, ESV).

This is the direct command Jesus gave to the apostles as He gave them the final orders to go make disciples of all nations. Couple this command with the fact that all authority has been given to Jesus. The apostles and the early disciples delivered the message they were sent to deliver. Those who respond to the message respond to Christ, whose message it is. As we respond to the apostolic message, we respond to Christ. Any actions we take because of hearing the message are taken in favor of Christ or against Christ. Thus as we receive the apostolic message, we receive Christ and the Father who sent Him. When we receive Christ through His message delivered by the apostles, He in turn receives us and adds us to His body, which is the church, according to Paul in Colossians 1:22. As Christ adds us to the church, He subjects us directly to His authority. This is not to say that the heaven and earth domain specified by Jesus in Matthew's account is not under Jesus's authority. Rather, these are who Christ has reconciled to the Father because of their acceptance of the gospel delivered by the apostles. These early disciples did as Christ commanded and came under Christ's personal protection. Paul said in Colossians 3 that their lives were hidden in Christ in God.

Let's look at some of the people who are possibly in this initial number or church. Before we do that, let's put things in perspective by looking at the bigger picture. Just over fifty-three days ago before Acts 2, Jesus was walking the grounds of the temple teaching, healing, rebuking, and caring for the people. He was arrested and killed by the Jewish leaders. He arose from the dead and after giving instructions to His faithful disciples ascended to heaven. Fast-forward to Acts 2, where the apostles preached the gospel. Those who heard the message and responded to it were added to the church. The point here is that Jesus is still fresh on the minds of the people. Luke recorded their first reaction when they heard Peter's presentation: "Now when they heard this they were cut to the heart" (Acts 2:37, ES).

Most of these hearers of Peter's message were locals from Jerusalem and the neighboring towns. Those coming from the Diasporas who heard the apostles speak in their native languages, if they had been to Jerusalem in the past three years, might have heard about Jesus at least once; there were a lot of disputes about Jesus during the Jewish festivals, which brought a lot of people to Jerusalem.

Apart from those who were in Jerusalem from the Diasporas, is it possible that some of the people present, the locals of Jerusalem and neighboring towns, had been affected by Jesus, especially those Jesus healed or whose sins he forgave? Remember the widow whose son Jesus raised? Remember the man whose convulsive son Jesus healed when the disciples could not heal him? Remember the prostitute who cleaned Jesus's feet with her tears, used her hair to wipe off the tears, and kissed His feet? How about the woman who poured the expensive perfume over Jesus's head? Remember also the tax collector whom Jesus went home with to eat? Remember the cripple, the lepers, the blind, the adulteress, the woman who had had more than five husbands, and the people

271

possessed by evil spirits, one of whom the society had bound at the outskirts of town? Remember Nicodemus the Pharisee who came to Jesus at night, the Centurion, the synagogue leader who came and requested healing for his sick child, and many more like them? There were also the Essenes, who were religiously pure. These are possibly the kinds of people Jesus added to the church that made up this new movement. Some were good and upstanding in the community, and others were rejected by the society. They were people who were first touched personally by Jesus and the signs God did through Him. They were possibly touched again by the gospel preached by Peter and responded to Christ again. These are the people who probably made up most of this initial group. This was a Jewish group. How about the Gentiles who also came to believe? Were they sinners like we have seen in the Jewish congregation in Acts? In most of Paul's epistle, he makes it a point to remind the Gentile believers that some of them were drunks, evildoers, homosexuals, prostitutes, and people involved in all kinds of sins and orgies. This is the state all of us are in before the gospel of Christ reaches us—sinners in a state of sinfulness!

The gospel of Christ, which is the apostolic message, is like a trumpet call to sinners. It is a call to awareness of our sinfulness. It is a call to repentance from our state of sinfulness to a state of forgiveness and redemption. It is a call to have a favorable conscience toward God. It is a call of reconciliation to God through Christ. It is a call to separate from a crooked and corrupt world into an eternal inheritance that is incorruptible. It is a call to righteousness and good standing before God. It is a call to follow Christ and to do as He desires and commands. It is a call to abandon the sinful ways of the world and to come and serve God. It is a call to deny oneself and pick up our cross and follow Christ. It is a call to bring our heavy burdens and trade them for rest. It is a call to discipleship and to be made a disciple.

The initial three thousand that the Lord added attained good standing with God. They were redeemed, saved, forgiven of their sins, and reconciled to God through Christ. Their sins no longer counted against them. Paul describes them as follows:

And you, who once were alienated and hostile in mind, doing evil deeds, he has now reconciled in his body of flesh by his death, in order to present you holy and blameless and above reproach before him, if indeed you continue in the faith, stable and steadfast, not shifting from the hope of the gospel that you heard, which has been proclaimed in all creation under heaven, and of which I, Paul, became a minister. Now I rejoice in my sufferings for your sake, and in my flesh I am filling up what is lacking in Christ's afflictions for the sake of his body, that is, the church . . . Him we proclaim, warning everyone and teaching everyone with all wisdom, that we may present everyone mature in Christ. (Colossians 1:21-24, 28, ESV)

In the above passage, Paul tells us the state from which the Christian was redeemed. The Christian is thus groomed through warnings and teaching into a state of maturity where he or she becomes blameless before God. These people have been reconciled to God through the blood of Christ and have been made part of the body of Christ, the church. What is the church? The Greek word translated as "church" is εκκλησια *(ekklesia)*. This same Greek word is translated as "assembly." In Acts 19 Luke uses the term to refer to the assembly that gathered at the call of Demetrius and his fellow businessmen to protest Paul's teachings. Demetrius was a silversmith in Ephesus who built artifacts of the Ephesians' goddess Diana, or Artemis. As the Ephesians received the gospel preached by Paul, they abandoned the goddess, and thus sales of the artifact went down. Demetrius realized that they were losing business because of this new sect. So he called together his fellow craftsmen and they raised a big ruckus, disturbing the whole city of Ephesus. The disturbance caused by Demetrius and his fellow businessmen caused the people of the city to pour into the theater. This gathering of the people is what Luke called the assembly, or the εκκλησια. They gathered at the theater because of the disturbance. As Luke records, the assembly was in confusion, and most of them did not know why they had gathered, yet they came to the gathering based on a call.

According to *Thayer's Greek-English Lexicon of the New Testament*, the term εκκλησια (ekklesia) means "a gathering of citizens called out from their homes into some public place, an assembly of people meeting in a public arena for deliberation." The term εκκλησια is a compound word, made up of two Greek words: εκ *(ek)*, which means "out," and κλησις *(klesis)*, which means a "call or calling, an invitation." Just as the gathering of Acts 19 was filled with confusion, the gathering in Acts 2 was not. In Acts 2 the initial gathering was caused by the coming of the Holy Spirit as He empowered the apostles to utter words that the hearers understood in their native tongues. As the people became intrigued and sought explanation, Peter and the other apostles rose and Peter explained what was happening. In the process he preached the gospel of Christ and baptized those who believed his message of God's salvation. Through Peter and all who proclaim the gospel of Christ, God calls out sinners to come for the forgiveness of sins and be reconciled to Him. God through the prophet Isaiah made a passionate call to the sinner to come to Him for forgiveness. With the message of the gospel God not only makes a similar passionate call to the sinner, but provides the vehicle and means by which the sins of the sinner are forgiven and the saved soul is provided with safekeeping. That safekeeping vehicle is the body of Christ. As the sinner is reconciled to God in the body of Christ by way of His death, Paul said in Colossians 3 that the sinner's life is hidden in Christ and will be revealed when Christ is revealed. The hearers of God's calling when they come together to meet and to fellowship as we read in Acts is the church. The church is not a place of meeting. It is the gathering of God's people who come together on a regular basis to fellowship, pray, sing, read, and discuss scripture and care for each other's needs.

This group of people, the church, Paul identified as follows (all of the following quotes were taken from the ASV):

> And he is *the head of the body, the church: who is the beginning, the firstborn from the dead; that in all things he might have the preeminence . . . Now I rejoice in my sufferings for your sake, and fill up on my part that which is lacking of the afflictions of* Christ *in my flesh for his body's sake, which is* the church*" (Colossians 1:18, 24); "the church of God *which is at Corinth, even them that are sanctified in Christ Jesus, called to be saints" (1 Corinthians 1:2); "the church of God" (1 Corinthians 10:32); "*the church of*

> *God" (1 Corinthians 11:22); "I persecuted <u>the church of God</u>" (1 Corinthians 15:9); "I persecuted <u>the church of God</u>, and made havoc of it" (Galatians 1:13); "<u>the church of God?</u>" (1 Timothy 3:5); "<u>the house of God</u>, which is <u>the church of the living God, the pillar and ground of the truth</u>" (1 Timothy 3:15); "Take heed unto yourselves, and to all the flock, in which the Holy Spirit hath made you bishops, to feed <u>the church of the Lord</u> which he purchased with his own blood" (Acts 20:28); "Salute one another with a holy kiss. All the churches of Christ salute you" (Romans 16:16). Paul ought to know this group well, for when Christ called him on his way to Damascus, Christ asked him, "Saul, Saul, why persecutest thou me? And he said, Who art thou, Lord? And he said, I am Jesus whom thou persecutest" (Acts 9:4-5).*

Were they perfect? Are they perfect today? Not by any means. Do they behave as if they are perfect? Sometimes! Look back at the characters we described who possibly constitute the initial three thousand. How many of them are outstanding in the community? One might be able to count them on one's hand. Yet is it possible that the tax collectors, the prostitutes, or any of the people in the different groups mentioned earlier were the ones selling their lands and sharing their properties in common? I'll say so. The fact is, God is perfect and Christ is perfect, but humans are not perfect. Christians, when they live like Christ desires, have the ability to demonstrate perfection. It does not mean they are perfect. They are just like any human being, with an exception. The exception is that they have answered God's call to come for forgiveness of sins. They do not have the heavy burden sin lays on us. They no longer carry the guilt of sin and the burden of seeking freedom. They are people whom God is grooming to perfection. Their sins have been forgiven!

Do Christians fail God's expectations at times? More than we will know! Christians are individuals who are walking in the good works that God has prepared for us. Christians are imperfect people in relationship with a perfect deity, God, who is molding us after His perfect Son, Jesus Christ. Christians are mortals who have been raised to live eternally. Christians come from weak, wicked, very evil, abused, and challenged backgrounds. A few come from respectable backgrounds. Christians have faults just like all human beings. We have come to God with such baggage that if one is privileged to see God's molding shop, he or she will not believe how hard and yet how tenderly and gently God pounds on the anvil to straighten us. With each pounding God skillfully removes the scars left behind by sin's long hold. As a superior expert surgeon, God through the teaching of His word carefully and gently removes each strain of rot that sin has left in our heart and mind.

The fact is, in the Lord's church, we witness broken souls who come to God and are restored and made whole. We see outcasts from the community who come to God and are molded into champions and bearers of God's word. We see sinners make a 180-degree turn to become righteous people. The continuous and gentle stroke of God's word that is taught and lands on the sinner's mind and heart has the potential to leave the saved sinner with a purified conscience that guides him or her into living the way God wills. Each time the sinner receives instruction and follows through with the required action, he or she is moved closer to God's objective. Are we perfect?

Not yet, but perfection is God's objective. Christians are the people who came to God as they were and are still coming to God as they are. And God molds them in His own image. I believe the musical instruments in heaven are far superior to anything the human ear has heard, yet these are the people whose voices God prefers, and they will chant the song of Moses and the Lamb before the throne of God in heaven. So I ask again, are they perfect? No, but God is busy getting them there. Paul said the following to the Philippian congregation:

Wherefore, my beloved, as ye have always obeyed, not as in my presence only, but now much more in my absence, work out your own salvation with fear and trembling. For it is God which worketh in you both to will and to do of his good pleasure. Do all things without murmurings and disputings: That ye may be blameless and harmless, the sons of God, without rebuke, in the midst of a crooked and perverse nation, among whom ye shine as lights in the world" (Philippians 2:12-15, KJV).

These are the people about whom it has been written in Revelation:

And they sang a new song, saying, "Worthy are You to take the book and to break its seals; for You were slain, and purchased for God with Your blood men from every tribe and tongue and people and nation." You have made them to be a kingdom and priests to our God; and they will reign upon the earth. (Revelation 5:9-10, NASU)

After these things I looked, and behold, a great multitude which no one could count, from every nation and all tribes and peoples and tongues, standing before the throne and before the Lamb, clothed in white robes, and palm branches were in their hands; and they cry out with a loud voice, saying, "Salvation to our God who sits on the throne, and to the Lamb." And all the angels were standing around the throne and around the elders and the four living creatures; and they fell on their faces before the throne and worshiped God, saying, "Amen, blessing and glory and wisdom and thanksgiving and honor and power and might, be to our God forever and ever. Amen." Then one of the elders answered, saying to me, "These who are clothed in the white robes, who are they, and where have they come from?" I said to him, "My lord, you know." And he said to me, "These are the ones who come out of the great tribulation, and they have washed their robes and made them white in the blood of the Lamb." For this reason, they are before the throne of God; and they serve Him day and night in His temple; and He who sits on the throne will spread His tabernacle over them. "They will hunger no longer, nor thirst anymore; nor will the sun beat down on them, nor any heat; for the Lamb in the center of the throne will be their shepherd, and will guide them to springs of the water of life; and God will wipe every tear from their eyes" (Revelation 7:9-17, NASU).

Then he showed me a river of the water of life, clear as crystal, coming from the throne of God and of the Lamb, in the middle of its street. On either side of the river was the tree of life, bearing twelve kinds of fruit, yielding its fruit every month; and the leaves of the tree were for the healing of the nations. There will no longer be any curse; and the throne of God and of the Lamb will be in it, and His bond-servants will serve Him; they will see His face, and His name will be on their foreheads. And there will no longer be any night; and they will not have need of the light of a lamp nor the light of the sun, because the Lord God will illumine them; and they will reign forever and ever. And he said to me, "These words are faithful and true"; and the Lord, the God of the spirits of the prophets, sent His angel to show to His bond-servants the things which must soon take place. (Revelation 22:1-6, NASU)

These are the people who make up God's church. Some have already fallen asleep. Christians are people of hope!

No one approaches God on his or her own terms. God has to invite us before we can approach Him. We read in the book of Esther the following about who is allowed to approach King Ahasuerus, a human king:

All the king's servants, and the people of the king's provinces, do know, that whosoever, whether man or woman, shall come unto the king into the inner court, who is not called, there is one law of his to put him to death, except such to whom the king shall hold out the golden sceptre, that he may live: but I have not been called to come in unto the king these thirty days. (Esther 4:11, KJV)

Although this might have all kinds of reasons, including security, God has no such problem. Paul said of God that God dwells in an unapproachable light. When Moses asked to see God, God told him that he could not see His face and live. So God covered Moses's face as He passed and allowed Moses to see His back. This is the God who interacted with the children of Israel on Mount Sinai in Exodus 19. I encourage the reader to read this chapter with a new appreciation for God. In describing the people's reaction Moses said, "The people trembled." The last paragraph of the chapter describes a terrifying situation as Moses narrates the scene when God came down to the mountain. This is the same God whose voice David describes in Psalm 29:

> *The voice of the Lord is upon the waters; The God of glory thunders . . . The voice of the Lord is powerful, The voice of the Lord is majestic. The voice of the Lord breaks the cedars . . . The voice of the Lord hews out flames of fire. The voice of the Lord shakes the wilderness . . . The voice of the Lord makes the deer to calve and strips the forests bare; And in His temple everything says, "Glory!" (Psalms 29:3-9, NASU).*

God indeed is an awesome God and is to be feared and revered! He is the God, the only one Christians serve and worship. As such, whoever takes any level of interest in Christians should take a look at the Christ who is perfect and the God who is awesome, whom Christians serve. Christians are not the ones who call new disciples. God calls the new disciple. The newly made disciple owes his or her allegiance to no one but God. In the end we have a perfect God who uses imperfect humans as instruments to reach out to other humans. Similarly, at a concert one does not focus on the drums beaten by the drummer or the drumsticks in the drummer's hands, but shares the music produced by the drummer who is using the sticks and the drum. We Christians are like drumsticks and drums that God, the master drummer, skillfully plays. The beautiful and marvelous tune that emerges ought to ring sweet melodies in the ears of any observers paying attention. As the Christians in Jerusalem won favor with all the people, so also I believe God wants the observers noting the lifestyle transformation of the individual Christian to enjoy the beautiful and pleasant fragrance of the person's new life. If we Christians are walking and loving as God has planned for us to do, our lives will ring like the beautiful music God plays. Then we will be a reason for onlookers to be attracted to our message. If we can let God mold us and be the master drummer He is, He can transform us into His image. Let us endeavor to make God the focus and center of our calling and kill, mortify, and render impotent the old self and make sin and pride ineffective in our lives so God can bend us to His will.

Paul said, "I am crucified with Christ: nevertheless I live; yet not I, but Christ who liveth in me and the life which I now live in the flesh I live by faith in the Son of God who loved me and gave Himself for me." Paul instructs us Christians to imitate him because he imitated Christ. We can arrive at the same conclusion Paul came to, so the world will not only see that but testify that Christ indeed dwells in him. The matured Christian then is a regenerated human being in Christ who strives to be just like Christ in every way. The matured Christian is one who has been transformed from the sinner who came to God into a spiritual being who is pleasing to God and is constantly in favor with God. He is like Paul the murderer transformed into Paul the example and a hero of faithfulness. He is like Peter the immature transformed into Peter the elder, who instructed fellow elders to be examples to the flock that had been placed in their care.

The matured Christian is like James, the Lord's brother, who might have had difficulties believing Jesus at first, but as a believer was transformed into one of the leaders in Jerusalem and referred to as one of the pillars by Paul. Remember how we said the shepherd smells like the sheep? Reverse that and you note that the matured Christian smells like Christ. He or she can say with Paul to the other flock, "[I]mitate me because I imitate Christ."

The good news is that Christians enter God's workshop as raw material. God, the master craftsman, molds each individual into the image of His Son. How does He do that? God works on each Christian's transformation through the church and the structure He has set up in His church. In the church each individual Christian receives teachings, instructions, and good examples on how to live in a world that no longer welcomes us. Every so often some of us get it and our molding shapes up faster. Often not all such saints were regarded as outstanding in the community, but when God is finished with them, they become more than outstanding in the community. Such saints are the ones who grasp what the Lord requires of them, make His will top priority, and shape up to maturity with noticeable changes in their lives. The rest of us, God keeps on the anvil a bit longer. As God keeps working on each Christian, He does not take us out of the sinful surroundings or the world. As we live out our new life and faith, we may fall sometimes. We may fail sometimes. But as we keep faith and stay faithful and stay on course, striving and staying focused, God is able to forgive our shortcomings and use those experiences to lead us into perfection. As the Christian matures, the transitions we go through are merely memorial markers, reference points, in a way. Our final target is to be like Christ. The onlooker of the Christian and the Christian himself need to fix their gaze on Christ, who is perfect and the final goal. The onlooker cannot use the shortcomings of unfinished work to judge and condemn God and His people.

In the church, God has set up a specific framework, a pattern to teach and mold the believer into the image of His Son.

> *And he gave some to be <u>apostles</u>; and some, <u>prophets</u>; and some, <u>evangelists</u>; and some, <u>pastors</u> and <u>teachers</u>; <u>for the perfecting of the saints</u>, unto the work of ministering, unto the <u>building up of the body of Christ: till we all attain unto the unity of the faith, and of the knowledge of the Son of God, unto a full-grown man, unto the measure of the stature of the fullness of Christ</u>: that we may be no longer children, tossed to and fro and carried about with every wind of doctrine, by the sleight of men, in craftiness, after the wiles of error; <u>but speaking truth in love, we may grow up in all things into him, who is the head, even Christ</u>. (Ephesians 4:11-15, ASV)*

The church in different flavors:

For the most part what we have discussed has been about the growth of the church in Jerusalem. This church was the first church formed from the preaching of the gospel of Christ. The membership was made up mostly of Jewish and proselytes, or people who had converted to Judaism. The church initially was led by the apostles. Later on in Acts 15, for example, we read about elders coming together to make decisions with the apostles. Before Acts 15 we saw in Acts 6 the installments of men to take care of the daily upkeep and needs of the church. These men served in the role of deacons in the church. The apostles Peter and Paul in their letters, Paul in particular, spelled out these roles. Peter in Acts 6 specified the character traits the Christian men should attain to serve in such roles, Paul in his letters to disciples Timothy and Titus provided definitive directives for men who desire to serve in such roles. As the first-generation church formed under the leadership of the apostles, they were guided by the Holy Spirit to form the organizational structure of the church that Paul laid out later in his epistles.

As we have seen in earlier discussions, the disciples in this church devoted themselves to the teachings of the apostles. The membership base was primarily Jewish, and the Jewish culture was prevalent. They continued to go to the temple to pray on a regular basis. They did not see the need to treat the Hellenistic Jews with the same level of care or love, and they criticized Peter for going into the house of Gentiles and spending time there. Even Peter, the spokesman of this new movement, had difficulty forgoing his Jewish tradition. Paul had to set him right, as Paul understood sooner that God has reconciled both Jews and Gentiles to Christ Jesus. The first church had her challenges. As a new church it did not fully understand the call at first. The Holy Spirit had to work on the people to transform them. As we read about the progression of this congregation, we note that this church had human challenges because they were saved, imperfect humans whom God was transforming. They progressed from being confrontational about things that didn't fit their understanding to becoming people God used to spread the gospel and to resolve issues on how Gentile believers ought to conduct themselves in their new life.

The church at Antioch was not started by an apostle or any prominent disciple we know. Instead disciples who fled Jerusalem as a result of the persecution of the church went to different cities, including Antioch, and started preaching. The account in Acts 11 notes that two groups of disciples preached in Antioch. One focused on the Jews and another preached to the Greeks. Luke did not record how the two groups came together, but he recorded the results of the intensive evangelical effort of the two: "And the hand of the Lord was with them, and a great number who believed turned to the Lord" (Acts 11:21, ESV).

We might argue that those disciples who preached only to the Jews were immature. That might be the case, yet when we read further, the Lord sends in more disciples who could rise above the race issues and spread the gospel to "all nations" to meet His initial command. Though circumstances might challenge us in answering His call, God is able to raise more disciples who will yet meet the needs of His commands. In any case, as the news reached Jerusalem that the gospel was spreading in Antioch, Barnabas was sent in to help just like Peter and John went to Samaria when the gospel reached that city. Here is what Luke recorded about Barnabas's visit: "When he came and saw the grace of God, he was glad, and he exhorted them all to remain faithful to the Lord with steadfast purpose, for he was a good man, full of the Holy Spirit and of faith. And a great many people were added to the Lord" (Acts 11:23-24, ESV).

Peter also visited the congregation later. It is possible that before Barnabas arrived, the two groups had already merged and were working together as a single unit. It is also possible that upon his arrival, Barnabas brought the two groups together. Whichever is the case, the important thing is that the Lord was directing their efforts, and with the additional manpower of Barnabas and Paul to these Christians, an already intensive effort of evangelism in the city was energized. For a year, these disciples evangelized Antioch and won more souls to the Lord. Makes you wonder about our three-day weekend evangelistic efforts. Reading further into the chapter, we note that the term *Christians* was first used to apply to this new movement in Antioch. This was the church that first received the resolution about whether or not Gentiles should be circumcised. This is the congregation from which Paul was called to go spread the gospel to other parts of the world. It was here that Paul rebuked Peter because apparently Peter forgot the lesson the Lord taught him when Cornelius was converted. Paul explains later why he had to rebuke Peter. Peter was all right when mixing with the Gentile brethren. But as soon as some brethren came to Antioch from Jerusalem, Peter withdrew himself from the Gentiles. His actions led to an awkward situation whereby the Jews were distancing themselves from the Gentile brethren to the point where trusted Barnabas fell into the same trap. This was why Paul had to set Peter straight.

Many other churches were established throughout Asia and beyond. As these evangelical efforts moved forward, the common thread was that the Lord was actively involved in the efforts of the disciples. He opened opportunities and closed others. The church in Corinth was one of these efforts. They were mostly Gentiles, and Paul had to address all kinds of issues to set them straight. Some of the issues were quite embarrassing. Paul said what was happening among the Corinthian brethren would embarrass those who were not Christians. These Corinthian Christians were living as if God had not called them or redeemed them and forgiven their sins. Their behavior showed that they did not understand why they had been called. When reading about these Corinthian brethren and many of the other congregations, the common trend we discover is that Christians are people God has called who have difficulty measuring up to the call—difficulty measuring up to the call if they try to live up to the calling on their own. Paul said in Ephesians 2 that Christians are God's creation in Christ Jesus, created for good works that God prepared before their time for them to walk in or live in accordingly. In other words, God had His expectations already set for Christians before our era began.

As God is the One who has set these expectations, it is therefore understandable that God would work in each individual in the church through them via the gifts He has given them. To know and understand these good works God desires for His people to walk in or live by, God's people, Christians, have to be taught and be trained continuously until we attain maturity. Jesus said, "<u>Teaching</u> them <u>to observe</u> ["to keep watch upon, guard," "watchful," "to watch over," "to mark attentively," "to heed," "to keep strictly," "to preserve, shield," "to keep in custody," "to maintain," "to keep in a condition"] <u>all things whatsoever I have commanded you</u>." This leaves out what Christ has not commanded and the apostles did not leave in the form of example, instructions, or record. This instructs us not to go beyond what is written, as Paul said to the Corinthians. As God works through each of us, we see in the church the need to continue to mature individually and as a whole. We can mature to God's expectations only by adhering to what Christ commanded the apostles and what they passed on to all generations of Christians. What we as Christians need to realize is that Christ has given us enough instructions through the apostles to develop us into the stature of the head who is Christ.

What is the Church?

Earlier we looked at the type of people God has called into the church. We also learned how Paul and the other apostles identified the church. The next question on my mind is, What is the church? According to Paul the church is the body of Christ and also the house of God.

> And he is *the head of the body, the church*: who is the beginning, the firstborn from the dead; that in all things he might have the preeminence . . . Now I rejoice in my sufferings for your sake, and fill up on my part that which is lacking of the afflictions of *Christ in my flesh for his body's sake*, which is *the church*. (Colossians 1:18, 24)

Also

> *[T]he house of God*, which is *the church of the living God, the pillar and ground of the truth*. (1 Timothy 3:15)

> But *now in Christ Jesus you who formerly were far off have been brought near by the blood of Christ*. For He Himself is our peace, who made both groups into one and broke down the barrier of the dividing wall, *by abolishing in His flesh the enmity*, which is the

Law of commandments contained in ordinances, so that <u>in Himself</u>
<u>He might make the two into one new man</u>, thus establishing peace,
<u>and might reconcile them both in one body to God through the</u>
<u>cross</u>, by it having put to death the enmity. And He came and
preached peace to you who were far away, and peace to those who
were near; for through Him we both have our access in one Spirit
to the Father. So then you are no longer strangers and aliens, <u>but</u>
<u>you are fellow citizens with the saints, and are of God's household</u>,
<u>having been built on the foundation of the apostles and prophets</u>,
<u>Christ Jesus Himself being the corner stone</u>, in whom the whole
building, being fitted together, is <u>growing into a holy temple in the</u>
<u>Lord, in whom you also are being built together into a dwelling of</u>
<u>God in the Spirit</u>. (Ephesians 2:13-22, NASU)

An in-depth discussion on the church will be reserved for another
time. Here I offer a rather brief discussion on the topic. The church
is not an idea that man came up with. What I mean is, the apostles
Peter, Paul, and the rest did not get together after winning many
souls and then decide they would organize the disciples into a body
and dedicate that organized body to Christ. No, that was not the
case! If the apostles had done that, they would have exceeded their
mandate in the Great Commission. If the church was an idea, it was
certainly an idea brought up by the Lord Jesus Himself. We see this
in Matthew 16: "I will build My church" (Matthew 16:18, NASU).

We can look up the whole exchange that led to this statement in
Matthew 16:13-20. Was this something that Jesus just brought up
to impress the apostles or was it also in God's plan? Old Testament
worshippers were familiar with the place of worship being called

the house of God, the temple of God, or God's dwelling place. This place of worship was physical, and it referred to a physical structure in Jerusalem. It was a place where God's people went and offered homage to Him. The difference in the New Testament is that there was no physical structure in a centralized location. As Christ said in John 4, God is spirit and His worshippers must worship Him in spirit and truth. This I contend takes place in the body of Christ. It is this body of Christ that Paul describes in Ephesians 2 as being fitted and growing into a holy temple, God's household and God's dwelling in the Spirit. In Matthew 16 Jesus told Peter and the rest of the apostles that "upon this rock I will build my church," referring to the confession Peter had made.

King David was the second king of Israel. When he sought to build a dwelling place for God, the God of Israel, His God, God sent the prophet Nathan to tell him that his descendant after him would build that house for God, a place of worship also called the temple of God. Solomon in the physical sense fulfilled this prophecy. He built the first temple for God's people to worship Him. Unlike Noah's ark, or the Ark of the Covenant, God did not give a blueprint for the temple Solomon built. We read in the following scripture that King David planned everything about this house of God he desired to build: "Then David gave to his son Solomon the plan of the porch of the temple, its buildings, its storehouses, its upper rooms, its inner rooms and the room for the mercy seat; and the plan of all that he had in mind" (1 Chronicles 28:11-18, NASU).

Man planned the house Solomon built. That temple of God in all its specifications and details was built by man with man-made materials.

Jesus in the flesh is a direct descendant of King David, according to the genealogical record given by Matthew. As a descendant of David, then, Jesus qualified to build a house for God. Thus when Jesus said to the disciples, "I will build My church," we might say that Jesus was talking about fulfilling the promise God gave King David many years ago. We might also say that Jesus said, "I will build my church," not a house. The Holy Spirit through the apostles taught that the church is the body of Christ. They also taught that the church is the house of God, a temple, a dwelling of God, as we have already seen. This is the church we have been discussing. This church is void of any human input and influence in building it. The only contribution from humans is the preaching of the gospel and teaching of the saints who make up the church. Christians are the individual building blocks with which Jesus is building His church.

In 1 Chronicles 28 we read the account of David entrusting his son Solomon in front of all the important people in Israel with the responsibilities of building the house for God. David had intended to build a house to house the ark of God and to serve as God's footstool. In this passage we note that the initiative to build the structure was solely on King David's part. David planned the structure and made preparations for its building. And even though God approved of such building, He elected for a descendant of David to erect the structure. Solomon had that honor in a physical sense. King David had wanted to build a permanent structure to honor God. But as history has it, the Babylonians destroyed the structure Solomon built many years later because of the unfaithfulness of the children of Israel. The structure was built again when the exiles returned to Judah before Christ was born, and it has remained destroyed since the first century. So far, that temple has been the only physical structure built in God's name that was planned by man and approved by God. Before this building, prophets like Samuel traveled across the land to judge and offer sacrifices and burnt offerings on behalf of the people. Why is this piece of information important? How does this information contribute toward the discussion of the church?

Let's review. King David wanted to build a permanent structure, a house of worship, a house where God's name would dwell. King David wanted to build that house of the Lord that he yearned to go into and never leave. He sang of such a house in his psalms. He sought to build a permanent house of God where he could go and dwell forever. God, knowing David's intentions, approved of the physical structure David sought to build and allowed it to be built. As sin increased in the land the building was built on, God allowed it to be destroyed. On the second destruction of the replacement structure built to replace the first one, God not only signaled the end of the old covenant and ushering in of the new one, but removed the worship place where His name dwelled for the more permanent one, which is a spiritual building in the body of His Son, the church. Why else would Christ tell the people to destroy the temple, the replacement of the original temple, and that He would erect it in three days? Combine this with Jesus telling the apostles that He would build His church! As a descendant of King David then on the cross, Jesus ended the old covenant and all its practices and united the Jews and the Gentiles in His body, His church. This is a permanent spiritual body that has as her members the people who are being saved. Each individual member that is added to the Lord's church, His body, is fitted in Christ's body into a holy temple, God's own household, and God's dwelling in the Spirit.

This new structure, unlike King David's structure, has a divine plan, thought of by God. According to the apostle Paul, the foundation for this building consists of the apostles and the prophets with Christ Himself as the chief cornerstone that supports the whole structure. This means that the church is not left for human tampering. The foundation laid is immutable; it cannot be changed. No human effort can destroy or change it. This is important because the apostles were charged by Christ Jesus to teach what He commanded. They were directed by the Holy Spirit. They expressed the will of Christ according to the dictates of the Holy Spirit. They were firsthand witnesses, and their testimony is very important to the mission of Christ. They received through revelation the blueprint for saving souls after Christ was resurrected. They preached the gospel first and taught the initial doctrines that Christ through the Holy Spirit revealed to them. According to Paul in Colossians 1, God qualifies people to share in the inheritance of the saints, those of whom Luke wrote as being saved and again wrote that they were called Christians in Acts 11. According to Matthew 28:20 and Paul's letters, God expects that Christians will maintain what they inherited from the apostles and teach others to do the same. Christians are to keep strictly, or keep in custody what the apostles have handed over to them. To do anything different is to change the will of God or, worse yet, reject God and revert to rebellion. We can reject God with our actions just as King Saul did. Samuel said to King Saul, "For rebellion is as the sin of divination, and presumption is as iniquity and idolatry" (1 Samuel 15:24).

The name *church of Christ* is not a term or brand name owned by a person or group of people. To say "the church of Christ" is just like we have said "the body of Christ." It is Christ's body. It is the term used to identify God's household. We have seen other names used by the apostles to identify the body of Christ, such as the "church of God," "church of the Lord," and so on. The Lord's church is not a human idea, and its implementation was not under the directive of any human efforts. The Lord's church is a spiritual organization put in place by God. God has set Christ as the head of His church just as Christ is first in everything and all authority. In the Lord's church, God has outlined a structure for the maturing of the saints. Each church in each geographic location is independent of the other. Each local church is directly under Christ. The local leadership of elders, deacons, preachers, and teachers are all under the direct headship of Christ. In the absence of the outlined leadership set forth by God, for example, a newly started congregation is still under the direct headship of Christ. That is, the church has no human head.

The Church of Christ is not a brand of another Christian religion, nor is it another organized church put together by human ideas and/ or ideals. No human or group of people for that matter has a claim to the name as their own. Only Christ and His church own the name. The name identifies the collection of people who, as it was in the apostles' day, believed the gospel message, submitted to the Lord in baptism, and gathered together at appointed times at different geographical locations. There are many other names the Bible uses for the church, but for identification purposes *church of Christ* is widely used.

Hence the church as described in the New Testament is not a hodgepodge of man-made organizations put together to please God. The church is a collection of the people who are being saved. The church is all of the following:

- The house of God. (What shall we call the house of God?) There are those who say the name is not important, but if that were the case, why did God give names to every family according to Paul in his letter to the Ephesians? If name is not important, why did God reveal to us that Jesus inherited a name far superior to any in this age and the age to come? Was God interested in giving a superior to Christ just for the sake of it?

- The body of Christ. (What shall we call the body of Christ? If Christ has a superior name both in this age and the one to come, should His body be called something different?)

- A collection of people who come together in the name of Christ.

- The church is a spiritual organism. It grows and has body parts that work together.

- Christ purchased or obtained the church with His own blood.

- Churches are in specific geographic locations.

- Christ is taught in the church.

- Member parts of the body of Christ are not individual churches in different geographical locations. They are individual members whom Christ expects to function properly for the growth of the church into maturity. Let's think about this for a moment. Christ is the one who adds each individual member to the church, His body. Each member is a part of His body according to Paul in 1 Corinthians 12. If the individual members are parts of Christ's body, then Christ, who added that member to that specific body part, expects that part, him or her, to perform specific functions according to the ability or abilities He has given to that part of His body. Paul said to the Corinthians that it is God who works in all of us through the gifts He has given each individual member in the church. Thus it is incumbent upon the individual member of Christ to avail himself or herself of the full potential that God has given him or her, or make use of the full functionalities and abilities of the parts God has placed in them. Then Paul's argument that no one member part is more important than another is much clearer, since all the body members functioning properly is what makes the whole body function properly. If some body members start claiming superiority over others or apathy is found among us because of what we do or don't do in the body, the body cannot be whole. This is because a sense of superiority causes division, envy, and unhealthy jealousy that cannot be good for the body. Apathy leads to lukewarm that can or make the Lord's body mediocre or worse yet kill the Lord's body. This is why Christ warned the Laodicean congregation about being lukewarm.

Thus the individual Christian does not exist in isolation. He or she is a member of the body of Christ and is firmly secured in Christ because Christ added each member to His church, His body. Is the church flawed? Far from it! Does the church contain people who are flawed? Yes! The church is not flawed because it is the house of God and the body of Christ. It is incorruptible by human action. However, the people who make up the church may be fallible, but they are being raised to be perfect and flawless. Christians have been called out of a corrupt world as we saw earlier. We enter God's workshop by means of the Lord's body for molding and shaping. As we mature in Christ, we learn to live and behave like Christ for as long as we remain faithful to His teachings. It is unfortunate when Christians' actions sometime lead the world to believe otherwise. Yet Christians are saved; they have to obey the gospel. With time we will grow to be like Christ. It is therefore a serious mistake for any one soul saved or lost to abandon the body of Christ on the grounds that the church's actions are hypocritical. That might be, but we will all be accountable for our individual actions in the end, both offender and offended.

How is one added to the Church? Baptized into one body by one Spirit

Let's review a section of the earlier discussion on baptism. In the discussion on baptism, we made the observation that the participation of the one being baptized is passive, although he or she is making an active decision in submitting to God's will. Before we proceed any further, let's define a couple of terms to help clarify this part of the discussion. The first term I want us to agree on is to call the person doing the baptism, that is, the one dipping another person in the water, the *baptizer*. The second term is to call the person being dipped into the water the *baptizee*. Furthermore, the baptizee is one who has heard the gospel message either from the baptizer or another disciple maker. The baptizee becomes a subject for baptism after believing the gospel message, repenting of his or her sins, and making that known by expressing the desire to submit to God. Thus as far as baptism goes, the baptizer dips the baptizee into water to baptize him or her. We noted also that the baptizee does nothing except present his or her body as a subject for baptism because 1) the baptizer does the dipping of the baptizee's body into the water, and 2) once the baptizee is in the water, whatever takes place physically and spiritually takes place outside the control of the baptizee and baptizer alike. According to both Paul and Peter in baptism the following takes place:

> *[A]nd in Him you were also circumcised with a circumcision made without hands, in the removal of the body of the flesh by the circumcision of Christ; having been buried with Him in baptism, in which you were also raised up with Him through faith in the working of God, who raised Him from the dead. (Colossians 2:11-12, NASU)*

> *Or do you not know that all of us who have been baptized into Christ Jesus have been baptized into His death? Therefore we have been buried with Him through baptism into death, so that as Christ was raised from the dead through the glory of the Father, so we too might walk in newness of life. (Romans 6:3-5, NASU)*

> *For even as the body is one and yet has many members, and all the members of the body, though they are many, are one body, so also is Christ. For by one Spirit we were all baptized into one body,*

whether Jews or Greeks, whether slaves or free, and we were all made to drink of one Spirit. (1 Corinthians 12:12-13, NASU)

For *you are all sons of God through faith in Christ Jesus*. For *all of you who were baptized into Christ have clothed yourselves with Christ*. (Galatians 3:26-28, NASU)

But when the kindness of God our Savior and His love for mankind appeared, He saved us, not on the basis of deeds we have done in righteousness, *but according to His mercy, by the washing of regeneration and renewing by the Holy Spirit*, whom He poured out upon us richly through Jesus Christ our Savior. (Titus 3:4-6 NASU)

Peter said to them, "Repent, and *each of you be baptized in the name of Jesus Christ for the forgiveness of your sins; and you will receive the gift of the Holy Spirit*" (Acts 2:38-39 NASU).

Corresponding to that, *baptism now saves you—not the removal of dirt from the flesh, but an appeal to God for a good conscience*—through the resurrection of Jesus Christ (1 Peter 3:21, NASU).

[T]hat, in reference to your former manner of life, *you lay aside the old self*, which is being corrupted in accordance with the lusts of deceit, and that *you be renewed in the spirit of your mind, and put on the new self, which in the likeness of God has been created in righteousness and holiness of the truth*. (Ephesians 4:22-24, NASU)

To summarize these scriptures, according to apostles Paul and Peter in baptism we participate in the death, burial, and resurrection of Christ. We experience the circumcision of Christ, which is the removal of the body of flesh, the old self, that which is in competition with our spiritual body and draws us ever so strongly toward sin. By one Spirit we are baptized into one body, the body of Christ, which is his church. We are clothed with Christ as sons of God. We receive forgiveness of sin and the promised gift of the Holy Spirit, a seal and God's down payment to His pledged inheritance to us to claim us as His own possession. We are washed not for removal of dirt from the body, but for a renewing regeneration by the Holy Spirit. It is an appeal to God for a good conscience. And last but not least, we are saved by baptism. We can find more in the scriptures to add to this list. The baptizee has no control over any of these listed above; as he or she submits in baptism, God through the Holy Spirit does all of these in the Savior Christ Jesus.

Now let's connect a few things. In the scriptures above we have learned and reviewed some important facts and truths about baptism. In the following scriptures we seek to elaborate more on one of the important truths mentioned above, which is that by one Spirit we were baptized into one body. This truth carries the idea of placement into the body of Christ, or being placed into the possession of Christ. That is, baptism places the baptizee into the body of Christ or into the possession of Christ. To elaborate on this, let's look closely at the following scriptures:

> And he said, "<u>Into what then were you baptized?</u>" And they said, "Into John's baptism." Paul said, "John baptized with the baptism

of repentance, telling the people to believe in Him who was coming after him, that is, in Jesus" (Acts 19:3-4, NASU).

For <u>He rescued us from the domain of darkness</u>, and <u>transferred us to the kingdom of His beloved Son</u>, in whom we have redemption, the forgiveness of sins. (Colossians 1:13-14, NASU)

[P]raising God and having favor with all the people.<u> And the Lord was adding to their number day by day those who were being saved</u>. (Acts 2:47, NASU) or [P]raising God and having favor with all the people. And <u>the Lord added to the church daily those who were being saved</u>. (Acts 2:47, NKJV, depending on which translation one uses)

I find Luke's choice of words in Acts 2:47 curious. Why didn't he say for example that the number or the church grew as more and more people were saved? What was important about the Lord adding to the church? Was Luke's intention only to point out that the church grew as people came to faith and were saved? How does the Lord add to His church? How does transfer into the kingdom of God's beloved Son happen?

If Luke's desire was to tell us about the speed with which the church grew, he could have mentioned that without telling us about how the church grew. Instead he not only mentions the growth of the church in Jerusalem but tells us how the church grew. He tells us that the church grew by the Lord adding to the church those who were being saved. Why is this piece of information important? Before we answer this last question, we must take into consideration the following:

Luke was a careful historian who took great care to investigate and accurately record his accounts. By the time he wrote Acts, he was one of Paul's closest allies. He had access to all the apostles who could affirm or discourage what he recorded as far as accuracy and its truthfulness were concerned. Coupled with the fact that the baptizee is a passive participant in the process of baptism, I believe what Luke reveals to us in Acts 2:47 is the fact that no one joins the Lord's church by his or her own choosing. That is, the Lord is the one who adds to the church, and He adds to the church those who are saved. Same idea: the baptizee is passive in the process of baptism, and he or she is passive in becoming a part of the body of Christ! The significance of this is that the growth of the church is not in human hands. God personally controls that. As such, if Christopher does not like a particular baptizee, he cannot relegate that person to a different group. Once a person has accepted the gospel message and made it known by confessing his or her faith and is ready to submit to the will of God in baptism, God takes control of what happens in making the disciple a Christian, from baptism to being added to the body of Christ. The information Luke provides in Acts 2:47 is important because he tells us how we become part of Christ's body, the church. We become part of Christ's body, His church, through baptism, a process that is beyond man's control.

As Paul traveled through Ephesus, he came across a group of disciples who had been baptized by John the Baptist. As Paul did not know about their background, he asked them, "Into what were you baptized?" Upon hearing their answer he explained to them what needed to take place and baptized those disciples in the name of the Lord Jesus. Paul's question to these disciples and his actions in response to their answer indicates that baptizees are baptized into Christ Jesus. This is consistent with what Paul said in his letter to the Corinthians in 1 Corinthians 12:12-13, which is that by one Spirit we are baptized into one body. Collectively the individual baptizees become individual members of Christ's body. With this part of the discussion in mind, let's reflect on the passages below:

> [F]or *through Him we both have our access in one Spirit to the Father. So then you are no longer strangers and aliens, but you are fellow citizens with the saints, and are of God's household*, having been built on the foundation of the apostles and prophets, Christ Jesus Himself being the corner stone, *in whom the whole building, being fitted together, is growing into a holy temple in the Lord, in whom you also are being built together into a dwelling of God in the Spirit.* (Ephesians 2:18-22, NASU)

> Therefore, brethren, since *we have confidence to enter the holy place by the blood of Jesus, by a new and living way* which *He inaugurated for us through the veil, that is, His flesh,* and since *we have a great priest over the house of God, let us draw near with a sincere heart in full assurance of faith, having our hearts sprinkled clean from an evil conscience and our bodies washed with pure water.* Let us hold fast the confession of our hope without wavering, for He who promised is faithful; and *let us consider how to stimulate one another to love and good deeds, not forsaking our own assembling together,* as is the habit of some, but encouraging one another; and all the more as you see the day drawing near. (Hebrews 10:19-25, NASU)

The call to return to the Bible and teach only what the Bible teaches ought not to be looked at as "I am right and you are wrong." Instead it should be looked at from the point of view that the Bible is right and sufficient for our salvation. Neither should it be looked at with a view for or against one-size-fits-all. When Christopher uses a one-size-fits-all model for everyone, then there is a problem—a problem because Christopher has tunnel vision, and is partial and biased. He favors those he likes even if they are evildoers and hates those he dislikes even when they are good people. However, God is impartial. He is merciful and loves justice. So when He said, "Thou shall not covet," it was a one-size-fits-all, wasn't it? This is just one example. One can find many situations of one-size-fits-all in God's word. We cannot compare our one-size-fits-all to God's. I don't think God has a one-size-fits-all anyhow. I believe God sees our needs and knows exactly what needs to be done to correct that situation. In any case if God's plan seems like a one-size-fits-all, then He must have His reasons, given that He sees the whole spectrum of mankind from beginning to end. He is the only one who can resolve the difficulties and challenges facing man, the ultimate of which is sin.

In my opinion, teaching only what the Bible says about the church should be looked at with questions such as, Does God knows what He is doing, and can we trust that God has worked all this out beforehand? What role does the church play in our salvation? Why the church—what is the church? Does the church have a pattern, and if so does God intend for that to be the case? If God does not know what He is doing, then I think He ought to welcome contributions and changes from us humans. We, like Him, can come up with some incredible solutions to our needs and can contribute to His plan at a high level. After reading these last two sentences we might exclaim, "Really?! I don't blame anyone who says such a thing." The truth is, we humans have a way of messing things up. We have done it over and over again throughout time. Adam could not hold on to the garden of Eden. His immediate descendants failed to live up to God's will and expectations and ended up being destroyed. The Israelites could not abstain from idol worship, which the people they evacuated from the land of Canaan were known to have practiced. They rejected God as their king and engaged in all the things God had warned them not to do. Is it likely God will welcome our help? I don't think so, because men in previous generations and even now have demonstrated that we know how to do one thing well: mess up our relationship with God. So, then, does God know what He is doing?

If God knows what He is doing, then it is ultimately better for us to leave His plans intact and submit to His will. I know I have the tendency to think God is too slow, His plans sometimes looks to be insufficient, and I feel the need to tweak them to make them more perfect. For example, what is wrong if I make disciples and do not baptize them? What if I make disciples by telling them that God will save if only they will pray for forgiveness, and not submit to baptism as Christ commanded? What if I told people that the church does not matter, God will save anyway and anyhow? The questions that should be ringing in our head ought to be, Is that right? Is that what God's words say? Is that God's will? If one cannot find any consistencies between what I am teaching and what God's words teach, then God's words ought to be upheld. God's words ought to be upheld because in the end it is God's word that will sustain and save.

To this effect we not only need to be watchful, but to continuously examine what people are telling us about God's word. We need to search and draw our own conclusions. The fact is, the preachers and teachers we listen to are going to face judgment just like us. Paul said that each of us is going to give his or her own account, whether we did well or badly. For we must all appear before the judgment seat of Christ, so that each one may be recompensed for his deeds in the body, according to what he has done, whether good or bad" (2 Corinthians 5:10, NASU).

In the end, "But my preacher said so" or "But my Bible teacher said it was okay" might not be enough. We work out our own salvation.

> So then, my beloved, just as you have always obeyed, not as in my presence only, but now much more in my absence, work out your salvation with fear and trembling; for it is God who is at work in you, both to will and to work for His good pleasure. (Philippians 2:12-13, NASU)

The apostle Peter said God knows how to save the righteous. God has been in the business of saving souls for more than six thousand years. That is what I call experience. Most employers like employees with lots of education, but the majority like and want to hire people with experience who have done the same job or a similar one for years. Thus the majority of employers might hire a person with less education but many years on the job. If I may put it in human terms, God has both the knowledge of how to save and the experience. He has done it on several occasions. God saved Enoch from the midst of his generation. And the apostle Peter wrote about punishment:

For if God spared not angels when they sinned, but cast them down to hell, and committed them to pits of darkness, to be reserved unto judgment; and spared not the ancient world, but preserved Noah with seven others, a preacher of righteousness, when he brought a flood upon the world of the ungodly; and turning the cities of Sodom and Gomorrah into ashes condemned them with an overthrow, having made them an example unto those that should live ungodly; and delivered righteous Lot, sore distressed by the lascivious life of the wicked (for that righteous man dwelling among them, in seeing and hearing, vexed his righteous soul from day to day with their lawless deeds): the Lord knoweth how to deliver the godly out of temptation, and to keep the unrighteous under punishment unto the day of judgment. (2 Peter 2:4-9, RV)

God and only God retains the power to punish evildoers, both angels and mankind, permanently. He also retains the power to save souls that in the face of evil acts seek to please Him and stay away from sin. If God knows how to rescue His people, then in my estimation, He knows what He is doing by establishing the church. In Matthew 16, Jesus told the apostles that He would build His church on the rock, the confession that Peter had made. Since Jesus did nothing outside the will of the Father, it tells me that Jesus and the Father knew all along that the church was going to play a role in the salvation plan. From what we know of God, He is not a God who reacts to things. He already has His plan and is working it to His perfect will. Because God has kept His word through the generations, I can trust Him and rely on Him that He knows exactly what He is doing.

The Church has a structure

Bishops, overseers, pastors, elders, and *shepherds* are all words used interchangeably to talk about the same role in the Lord's church. These names or titles are not different positions that represent a hierarchy or different functions in the Lord's body. The men who fill this role are disciples who have backgrounds similar to that of any other disciple in the Lord's church. As local members in each local congregation, these disciples of Christ lead the local congregation. Paul warns that new disciples are not to be selected to serve in this role. Thus the men who serve have attained a level of maturity and understand better the counsel of God than most Christians. God placed them in a trusted role by giving them responsibilities for safekeeping Christ's flock, which includes themselves. They keep these responsibilities by teaching, instructing, and being examples to the flock of Christ. The burden on these men is not light, and everyone in this position ought to view the opportunity to serve in this capacity as a great honor. Because of their role, what they say and do has significant influence on the other disciples. The decisions they make in leading the church ought to reflect the fact that they understand their submission to Christ's authority. We do not have the apostles and prophets in the Lord's church today to fend off false teachings and maintain the word of God as inherited from the apostles. These men have a role in seeing to it that the purity of the word of God is maintained and is accurately taught. It is an enormous task that requires not only that they know God's word well, but, as Peter observed in Acts 6, that they stay in tune with God through constant prayer and make sure the church is focused on advancing the gospel. They in fact are leaders who pray and set the tone in leading the local church in adopting a Christ-centered and Christ-filled life.

Paul instructed his disciples Timothy and Titus on the character traits they should look for in a man before he is appointed to serve as an elder. As this study has focused on the Jerusalem congregation, a Jewish congregation, I want to bring some Old Testament perspective into the study to help us grasp the magnitude entailed in manning the elder role. When we look as far back as Jacob and his sons, we often read that they will meet and make decisions. This went on throughout their sojourning years. During the years in Egypt we read of the sons of Jacob getting together to make decisions. An example of this is seen after Jacob died. His sons got together and planned on what to say to Joseph, their brother. When Moses came back to Egypt on God's word, he and Aaron gathered "the elders" to tell them about Moses's mission. The involvement of the elders with Moses as well as Joshua's decisions during the Exodus are well documented. As the Israelites settled in cities in Canaan, we read of the role these groups of men played in the local communities. These men usually convened at the gate and settled all kinds of issues between fellow citizens. For example, the elders would meet and talk to a man whose brother had passed away and left behind a wife about fulfilling the customary requirements of raising children in the dead sibling's name. If this brother refused to honor his widowed sister-in-law by performing husbandly duties, the elders will supervise the required punishment for that brother as prescribed by the Law. We saw this play out before Boaz was able to marry Ruth. Undisciplined children were also brought before the elders for proper action. If an offender came to a city for refuge, the city elders were responsible for investigating and keeping that soul safe until a viable conclusion had been determined. We could go on and on listing the duties entrusted to these men. In a nutshell, they were responsible for keeping the community safe and ensuring that God's laws were obeyed. When these men became corrupted and were not watching over God's sheep—the people—as God had instructed, God sent the prophets to warn them. When the corrupted leadership failed to repent, they became examples for the people, who became corrupted themselves. As the people became corrupted, they rejected God, and God sent them into exile.

The church in Jerusalem had apostles, prophets, elders, deacons, teachers, and so on who took care of the needs of the saints. As far as the new movement, Christianity, it is not until Acts 11 that we first read that the gift sent to Jerusalem by the church in Antioch was given to the elders of the church in Jerusalem. Before that there are mentions of elders referring to the Jewish leadership, which wasn't part of the Christian movement. For Luke to record that the elders, not the apostles, were the ones who received the gift brought to the Jerusalem church is a bit peculiar to me. I use the word *peculiar* because until Acts 11 we did not know of the elders in the Jerusalem group. It seemed that the apostles did everything before then. However, the mention of the elders' role under this circumstance suggests to me that not only was the structure of the church being put into place but the proper leadership of the church was as well. This is not to say that the apostles were not the proper leaders of the church; rather what I am trying to say here is that the role of the apostles was specific and temporary. Christ chose all the men who served in that role Himself. After their deaths He did not replace them. The only possible reason for that was that their work of laying the foundation and first principles for the Lord's Kingdom would be finished with their deaths. The role of the elders in the church—men selected from the members in each local congregation—on the other hand, was part of the permanent nature of the church as the Lord had intended, I might add.

It seems to me that what we observed in Acts 15 was that the disciples were following the traditional Jewish practice over many years of resolving issues. That is, the community leaders got together and deliberated the issue at hand, using God's word as their frame of reference to arrive at the appropriate conclusion. In Acts 15 we read about issues facing the Gentile church because some Jewish brethren said the Gentiles needed to observe the law of Moses and be circumcised to be saved. After Paul and Barnabas had battled those teaching these doctrines for a while, it became necessary for them to go to Jerusalem and meet with the apostles and elders to address this issue. On this occasion we see that the leadership of the Jerusalem congregation consisted of the apostles and the elders. The group of men included James, the Lord's brother, whom Paul called one of the pillars at the time. Since James was not an apostle, we can safely say that he must have been one of the elders. The words of Peter and James based on God's words led to the conclusion of the matter at hand. This tells me that the role of the elders is not a trivial role in the church, or an afterthought. It is a very serious role that requires maturity and greater understanding of God's will. As important as the apostles were to the first-generation church, the elders were just as important in the daily affairs, decision making, and the well-being of the flock of Christ—the church—as indicated by Acts 15. Why is it important to note that the elders in Jerusalem shared in the decision-making process with the apostles at this time in the growth of the Lord's church? It is important because for the first time, we observe people who were not apostles becoming part of God's calling in the leadership role.

Notice the following progression: (1) Luke did not give us a time line of when the elders were first appointed in Jerusalem. The only possible time line I can imagine is that the elders had been included in the leadership long before Barnabas left Jerusalem for Antioch to help the brethren there on their evangelism campaign, possibly afterward (Acts 6). (2) Until the mention of elders in Acts 11, the only other designated role we know of were the deacons appointed in Acts 6. These deacons were appointed to serve a specific function—to take care of the logistical needs of the members in the Lord's body, to wait on tables, according to Peter. (3) Acts 11 is the first time we read about elders in the Jerusalem congregation. On behalf of the Jerusalem church, they received the gifts sent by the Gentile church in Antioch. (4) In Acts 15, the apostles and the elders are together in the decision making for the church. This puts the elders in a role as leaders of the church. On the other hand, when we carefully consider what Peter said to the whole group of disciples in Acts 6, we are left with a clear impression that the role of the deacons is different from that of the elders. (5) Paul clearly specified these two roles in his letters to Timothy and Titus. Paul also told the elders in Ephesus in Acts 20 that God made the elders overseers of His flock, which He purchased with His own blood. Paul also wrote to the Ephesians about people such as apostles, prophets, evangelists, pastors, overseers, bishops, elders, preachers, teachers, and many others with gifts the Lord has given to individual members to see to the proper functioning of His body and the development of the saints.

How do we go about appointing elders today? Imagine if Paul had not outlined the qualities to look for in men to be appointed to minister in the role of elders. How would we have gone about appointing men to serve in this role? Let's go back to the Jerusalem church. If Acts 6 is the only example we have for appointing men to serve or minister in the Lord's body, how will we go about selecting men to serve in the various roles? Note what Peter said to the whole congregation in Jerusalem: "[L]ook ye out among you seven <u>men of honest report,</u> <u>full of the Holy Ghost</u> and <u>wisdom,</u> whom we may appoint over this business" (Acts 6:3, KJV). Below are other translations of the same verse.

> *Look ye out therefore, brethren, from among you seven <u>men of</u>* > *<u>good report,</u> <u>full of the Spirit</u> and <u>of wisdom,</u> whom we may appoint* > *over this business. (Acts 6:3, ASV)*

> *[P]ick out from among you seven <u>men of good repute,</u> <u>full of the</u>* > *<u>Spirit</u> and <u>of wisdom,</u> whom we will appoint to this duty. (Acts 6:3,* > *ESV)*

> *[S]earch out, and elect from among you, seven <u>men of whom there</u>* > *<u>is good testimony,</u> <u>men full of the Spirit of the Lord,</u> and <u>of wisdom;</u>* > *that we may place them over this business. (Acts 6:3, Murdock)*

[L]ook out . . . seven <u>men of you who are well testified of, full of</u>
<u>the Holy Spirit</u> and <u>wisdom</u>, whom we may set over this necessity.
(Acts 6:3, YLT)

[C]hoose seven of your <u>men who have a good reputation. They</u>
<u>must be full of wisdom</u> and <u>the Spirit</u>. We will give them this work
to do. (Acts 6:3, ERV)

With this proposal by Peter, these first-generation Christians appointed seven men to serve as deacons. How did these Christians know that among them were seven men of good report, or men of good reputation, or men of honest report, or men well testified of? How did they know that men such as Stephen and Philip were full of the Spirit and of wisdom? I will contend that the disciples knew because they knew each other well through the interactions via fellowshipping they had had with one another since the beginning of the Christian movement. Luke describes it thus:

And <u>they devoted themselves to the apostles' teaching</u> and <u>the</u>
<u>fellowship, to the breaking of bread and the prayers</u>. And awe came
upon every soul, and many wonders and signs were being done
through the apostles. And <u>all who believed were together</u> and <u>had</u>
<u>all things in common</u>. And <u>they were selling their possessions and</u>
<u>belongings and distributing the proceeds to all</u>, as any had need.
And day by day, <u>attending the temple together</u> and breaking bread
in their homes, they received their food with glad and generous
hearts, praising God and having favor with all the people. And
the Lord added to their number day by day those who were being
saved. (Acts 2:42, ESV)

Luke said they devoted themselves "to the apostles' teaching . . . the fellowship, to the breaking of bread and the prayers . . . all who believed were together, had all things in common . . . they were selling their possessions and belongings and distributing the proceeds to all . . . attending the temple together and breaking bread in their homes." With such commonality, I think we can easily infer that these disciples knew each other well. Thus it will be easy to identify seven out of more than three thousand to fill the role of deacon. Let us go back to the assumption that Acts 6 was all we had to learn from to appoint elders. We note however that the criteria described in Acts 6 were used to appoint only deacons, not elders. Our attempt here is purely an exercise to try to understand things from the point of view of the early disciples. As the church had grown before Acts 11, where we first read about elders, what standard or criteria could they have used to appoint the men who served as elders and shared in the leadership of the Jerusalem church? I will submit that it will be a bit higher standard than what we just read in Acts 6. Not only did they have to be men of "good report," "good reputation," "honest report," or "men well testified of" and "full of the Spirit" and "of wisdom," but they would also have had to display a consistent spiritual lifestyle, spirit-led qualities, and perhaps abundant display of both knowledge and understanding of God's word. Members of the whole congregation who testified that those men could shepherd the Lord's body would have known of such qualities in them.

James, the Lord's brother, spoke to the group that had gathered to learn how to instruct the Gentile brethren on how to live the new life they had been called into. Close examination of what James said to the group in Acts 15 clearly demonstrates that he was well versed in God's word and spirit led. James also had a very pronounced reputation among the believers in Jerusalem at the time. His reputation was so huge that I wonder if anything went around among the early disciples in Jerusalem without his knowing or involvement or approval. He was referred to as one of the pillars in Jerusalem. The others were Peter and John. Paul met James when he went to Jerusalem absent the apostles. James must have prayed a lot, for he cited Elijah's prayer habits and also said, "[T]he prayer of a righteous man is powerful and effective." He could not have said something like this if he had not been a praying man. Besides his knowledge of scripture, James would have had to live a life worthy to be an example to the other disciples to relate to others the essence of praying. In his letter to his fellow saints he described himself as "Christ's bond-servant." Such might have been the caliber of men chosen to serve in the role of elders in the Jerusalem church. Thus, in the absence of Paul's letters to Titus and Timothy, we would have to glean for men like James to serve as elders. Again, how do we search for and appoint men to serve in this role?

Do we search out men among us to serve because of their business successes or because they are of honest report among the brethren, full of the Spirit and wisdom and meeting all the criteria Paul outlined? The truth is that just because one succeeds in a business, that person will succeed in everything he attempts. We are influenced by our culture and its practices. Thus in our culture today successful businesspeople, though they might lack good repute, are well looked upon and well regarded purely because of their business successes. The temptation for us is to bring that into the

317

Lord's church and try to make that work in the church context. But what we need to understand is that the church is a spiritual being. And we are being transformed into spiritual beings. Therefore it is only appropriate that we be full of the Spirit as we worship in spirit and in truth. Hence our leaders be men full of the Spirit and led by the Spirit.

How many of our brethren will hire a degreeless man filled with the Spirit who clearly demonstrates wisdom and insight into God's word to minister in the pulpit versus a graduate who is not full of the Spirit but has a perfect GPA, is filled with lots of ideas, and has the tendency to know it all? We all like success and should look for it at all costs while emphasizing spirituality. We need to make it our top priority to find men to serve who are not just looking for a career but are passionate for God and full of the Holy Spirit and wisdom. I am convinced we can find such men among us if we fellowship more frequently with each other and make getting to know each other our priority. Am I condemning preachers who have worked hard to acquire an excellent education? By no means at all; education of the people of God is important. Otherwise why would Christ command that new disciples be taught to observe all He has commanded the apostles? My point is that although academic education can give us a handle on God's word, God is able to enrich His people with the ability to aptly handle His word. Therefore we need to look within our congregations for such men who might or might not have an academic degree yet are full of the Spirit and passion for God to minister to the Lord's body. My general point here is that whether we are academically polished or not, we are disciples subjected to Christ and His will. As such we are teaching as well as being taught all that Christ has commanded. We absorb the teachings of Christ and hence the teachings of the apostles so we can be filled with the Spirit as we learn and walk humbly before Christ.

How do we find such men? The same way the early disciples did, by fellowshipping with each other and getting to know each other. We might inquire from others, but because the choice comes from among us, we need to identify these men through their exposure to the church.

God has a unique role for all of us in his kingdom. Let us pick people who will meet the needs of God's work and have the desire to do so. As people of faith who serve God in spirit and in truth, should we not lean heavily on God for our choices and decisions? Christ's body has a culture of its own. It is a culture wherein we walk by faith, we worship God in truth and in spirit, we forgive each other's offenses, we count trials and tribulations as joy, we love those who hate us, we do good to our enemies, we love each other as Christ has loved us, our bodies are presented to God as living sacrifices holy and acceptable to God, our minds are renewed, and we possess a very sensitive conscience favorable to God. Our culture as Christians is different from that of the cultures we have been called from. Let us shine in the new culture like light to a lost world. Let us fellowship with each other more and often so we can identify men of good report, good reputation, honest report, men well testified of and full of the Spirit, of wisdom, and more to serve the Lord's body well and shepherd the flock of the Lord.

Why is the discussion of the early disciples and the church important to the Great Commission? In Acts, we see that the apostles discharged the Great Commission. They preached the gospel and won the hearts and minds of the hearers, and those who responded favorably were commanded to be baptized for the forgiveness of sins and reception of the Holy Spirit. We could say that up to this point, Matthew 28:19 has been accomplished, which led directly to the establishment of the church. We see in Acts 2:42 onward that the disciples continued in the apostles' teachings. That is, the apostles taught the new disciples and the new disciples observed what the apostles taught them. I believe we can easily make such a case directly from Matthew 28:20. In Acts, we see clearly the beginning of the Christian movement and its growth into maturity. By Acts 14, Paul and Barnabas were appointing men into these roles on their missionary campaigns. For the purpose of continuity and permanence in the absence of the apostles and the prophets, the Lord's body needs to be well formed or defined so that successive Christian generations will know what to do. Better yet, with all the permanent roles in places, doctrines will be well defined, the Lord's body could be known for what it is and stands for, and the pattern of doctrine Paul admonished his students to note and maintain can be well described. Also, since the disciples taught by the apostles were to keep strict continuity of the Great Commission—making disciples and maintaining them through all that Christ had commanded the apostles, that is, maintaining the apostolic doctrines—could proceed. Otherwise, after the death of the apostles, the work would die and no one would know what to do or expect.

Today's elders in the church have difficult challenges as relativism dominates our societies, and authorities are trampled upon and not respected. Add to that people's desire to do as they please. We see authorities dishonored and disrespected. These men are thus challenged to hold the line by keeping the church faithful to Christ and under the authority of Christ.

There are many more duties and responsibilities that God has given to individuals in the church. These are gifts God is using to develop the saints. They might not be teaching or preaching, but they are all just as important in the upkeep of the church. We might not mention the janitor, for example. But the person who takes on the church janitorial work, paid or not, plays a significant role that enables the church to meet in a conducive place—a place where God meets His people because His people meet there! They might not be the face of the church, yet their role is vital to the proper functioning of the church when she meets. Who knows, maybe God is fine-tuning the brother or sister who is performing the janitorial duties today for His own purposes tomorrow.

In many ways, our teachers and preachers become the face of the church as they go out and reach out. These men have the responsibility to tell the rest of us what God's word is saying, what it means, and how we are to apply it to our lives. Often as I think about this, I am frightened by the responsibility. In a way these men are God's mouthpiece to us today. Their role is probably the most important when it comes to making disciples and developing disciples through continual teaching as mandated by Christ. To fill this role those called to it need to be students of God's word and as Paul said to Timothy, "study to show thyself approved unto God, a workman who needs not be ashamed but rightly dividing the word of truth." Studying does not apply to these men only. As Peter also said, we all ought to be ready to defend our faith when questioned about it. How do we do so in a competent manner? By being like Timothy, with study and constant prayer. As the teachers and preachers teach and preach, the Master's expectations as stated in this commission statement are for the new disciple to keep strictly, or keep in custody, or to observe and obey what has been taught. James said God is interested not in the one who hears and does nothing with what he or she has heard. Rather God is interested in the one who hears and does what they have heard. James similarly warns the teachers and preachers that they will be held to a much higher standard of accountability. Paul warns both Timothy and Titus to watch carefully what they teach and to make sure their lives reflect their teachings. This way their conduct will not distract from their work and the message of Christ. This way, mockers cannot mock Christ.

The attitude and conducts of our teachers are so important because they can convey anything but the attitude of Christ. Perception can annul any meaningful inroads we make in reaching out. As such, teachers and preachers alike need to be careful about the unintended messages we can portray through perception. Yes, perception is a subject to the call of the perceiver or even the hearer. But can we afford as disciples of Christ to leave any negative impression anywhere we are? The world we live in is brutal. As it condemns us based on perception, it tells us we cannot mention the actual sinfulness of the world. If we do, we are the meanest people planet Earth ever saw. If our attitude as Christ's disciples is perceived as people who know so much, in fact as ones who know it all, and if we are coming off as prideful because of the role we have in God's greater plan, then here are a few things we teachers and preachers need to think about. The talents we have: How did we get them? Are we using them to glorify God or to make ourselves important in our own eyes? What about the rest of the church: Are those people's roles insignificant to God's work? What do we have that was not given to us? Are we perceived as ones who are beyond receiving instructions? Do we know because God gave us the knowledge and the skill to relate His message, or did we acquire our gifts without God? In a nutshell, we desperately need to adopt the attitude of Christ, who although in the form of God, emptied Himself for our sake. He loved us so much that he even died on the cross. Can we empty ourselves and put on Christ and His attitude and see ourselves as servants faithfully discharging a duty? In the end when our work is done or even as we continue to discharge our duties, we say, "We are only vessels in God's hands and are being used to His glory."

As teachers and preachers handle God's word, the spiritual sword, we need to remind ourselves that the one working in us is gentle, kind, and compassionate. As this spiritual sword is swirled around, we need to be mindful that we are God's tender surgical hands that gently heal the sinner with each tender cut. The objective is to make the sick whole, not to thrust the sword in to kill. Each tender stroke God makes through us ought to reflect the skillfulness of the master surgeon who is working through us. We need to be guided by a clear understanding that we are under the authority of Christ. We understand the sacrifice of Christ, so we reach out to save, not push away. I can understand the need for the numbers. But in the end God is the one who provides the growth. Still we are only instruments in God's hand, and nothing we do is about us. It is all about God. We need to keep at the forefront of our minds that God requires us to love one another and to love the sinner enough to gently snatch them from Satan's hand.

In general, our attitude ought to be one that reflects unity with each other. Take for example the brother who prays for a little more than five minutes or the song leader nicknamed Speedy because by the time he is through with the first stanza, the whole church feels as if they have just finished a marathon. Or the slower song leader who drags the song out so slowly that an elastic cord cannot stretch any longer. How about the preacher or teacher we cannot stand because his demeanor is boring? Or consider the brother who says a long prayer for one reason or another. That brother better be ready with some good professional lawyers on his side, ready to put out all the fires his action will cause. Of cause I have exaggerated a bit here with the lawyers, but the poor brother must be ready for all the complaints that might come his way for making the congregation stand too long or sit too long, or even—mercy on him—for making them kneel while he prayed that long prayer. As for the song leader, his style is so fast that people cannot properly sing the notes or breathe properly to sing out as they should. Or his style is so slow that by the time the first stanza is done, everyone is ready to go to sleep. Not to mention that the preacher followed all that up with a long sermon that made people uncomfortable. There are many more such complaints we could list, but these make the point.

They are all legitimate issues that might require minor to major corrections through training to improve the qualities and styles of the men who lead the congregation during different sections of the Christian worship. However, what will happen if we adopt a sincere and genuine attitude that eliminates complaints and instead offers support by making sure that at the end of the day we can say we did our very best to make the worship experience, which takes place in the presence of the Almighty God, a positive one? What we need to keep in mind is that when we come together as disciples, or better yet as people who have become sons of God, we have come before God, the Father of our Savior and Lord Jesus and our Father. When we are together as people of God, we come to the presence of Jesus Christ, the One who has made our meeting and salvation possible. The host of heaven looks in on us, perhaps, as we offer up a worthy fellowship that sends a fragrance that is pleasant to God and acceptable before Him.

Keeping this in mind, we ought to adopt the posture toward our fellowship meetings that seeks to do everything possible to please God. Our meetings can show reverence to God, which in turn shows we understand that He is present in our midst and that our gatherings are not just gatherings of mere mortals. Another thing is that with such an attitude, we show love, unity, and support. If we can eliminate most or all of our complaints about irritants and throw our lots in as if we have nothing to lose—and we truly have nothing to lose, really—then our worship will be inviting to our visitors and God will be glorified in it. Remember David and how he behaved in the presence of God? Really, nothing did matter to him when it came to setting the example for the people that he was excited before God.

It was contagious. When his wife complained about his behavior not being acceptable for a king, he said, "It was before the Lord . . . and I will make merry before the Lord. I will make myself yet more contemptible than this, and I will be abased in your eyes. But by the female servants of whom you have spoken, by them I shall be held in honor" (2 Samuel 6:21-22, ESV).

If a visitor walks into our meeting, should he or she not leave with an impression that these folks surely have unity only because they observed it from our actions and contributions toward worship? Think of the powerful message that sends and the effect that might have on our visitors. Let us adopt David's mind-set that has nothing to lose or to fear, truly participate in our fellowship with all of our being, and make each experience before God one that pleases Him. I don't mean showing improper behavior or doing inappropriate things during our worship—far from it. What I mean to suggest is that we actively participate in our worship assembly and leave no room for distractions. If we have time to focus on irritants and distractions, then we probably are not focused on praising and adoring God and paying Him the proper homage due Him even though He is present in our midst.

In Acts 2 Luke's record indicates that the three thousand disciples devoted themselves to the apostles' teaching. What did the apostles teach, and how did the people respond to those teachings? I believe we have addressed the first part of this question above. The New Testament is where we find the apostles' doctrines. In the New Testament we understand from the apostles themselves that there is a pattern to their teachings. For example, in this study we have looked at the message the apostles and the other disciples preached when they made disciples. We have seen that the messages preached by Peter, Paul, Philip, and the like were drastically similar. In fact when we look at Peter's message in Acts 2 and Paul's message in Acts 13, we might think Peter gave the message template to Paul. But we note that Paul says in his letters that the Lord Jesus Himself gave His message to him, not man. Here is a caution: If Moses was warned to carefully follow the pattern given to him when he was instructed to build the tabernacle to an inferior covenant, wouldn't God have a pattern for a more superior covenant? God's commands do not change. Hence what the apostles taught is what Matthew's account records Jesus saying to the apostles: "all things whatsoever I have commanded you." Thus, a more appropriate answer to the question about the apostles' teachings is what they were commanded by Jesus Christ, the only one to die and arise never to die again, the only one with all authority, and the only head of the church, which is His body.

The second half of the question is, What did the disciples do in responding to the apostolic teachings? The answer to this question was clearly stated by Luke. Luke in Acts 2:42 said that the new disciples devoted themselves to the apostolic teachings. This is consistent with Jesus's expressed desire in the commission statement. Jesus's charge was for the newly converted disciple to adhere to the apostles' teaching, or to keep strictly, or keep in custody, or observe, or obey what they have been taught by the apostles. Matthew's account records that Jesus's expectation of the newly converted disciple is to "observe all things whatsoever I have commanded you." The Greek infinitive τηρῖν *(teerein)* translated as "to observe" can also be translated using the following English terms: "to keep watch upon, guard," "watchful," "to watch over," "to mark attentively," "to heed," "to keep strictly," "to preserve, shield," "to keep in custody," "to maintain," "to keep in a condition." When we substitute any of these other terms in place of *to observe,* one understands why Luke used the term *devoted* to describe how the disciples responded to the apostolic doctrines. The new disciples were not impartial to what the apostles taught. They did not take some of the teachings and leave those that made them uncomfortable. Instead they devoted themselves to what the apostles taught. Thus Paul instructed his disciples Timothy and Titus to hold on to sound teachings as well as to the form of teaching or the pattern of teachings they received from the apostles. Something to dwell on: How did the disciples who scattered around Judea and all Asia know what to preach? How did Philip know what to tell the Samaritans and the Ethiopian eunuch? How about the two different teams that went to Antioch to spread the gospel as a result of prosecution—how did they know what to preach to make disciples? It sounds to me like the apostles did a bang-up job teaching the fundamentals of how to become a Christian and instilled in the minds of the new disciples that they had a share in spreading the gospel to all nations!

We can argue about whether or not there is a pattern of the teaching taught by the apostles in the New Testament. But the truth is that expectations are not fluid. That is, expectation from Jesus Christ the King of king, the savior who died on the cross, the One who does not change, has expectations that the commands He gave will be obeyed. He desired and commanded that the early disciples to keep strictly what they were taught by the apostles. He has not changed His expectations of any new disciples, not even in our age. He expects us to hold on to what the apostles taught. That is what He charged them or commanded them. It is thus safe to conclude that if we fail to hold on to what the apostles taught, we fail to obey what Christ Jesus directly commands and desires. This is not a condemnation. It is a plea and an encouragement to all who seek to please God the Father and Christ Jesus—the King and our Savior. We need to diligently search the scriptures, study hard, and pray for clear direction and understanding into the Lord's will. What the apostles taught was, according to Matthew, what Jesus commanded.

And behold I will be with you always unto the end of the age.

This last point is not a task. Let us observe that Christ the King has fully sanctioned the work of His disciples. Think of how we would feel if we were in a fight for our king and all of a sudden we observed from the corner of our eye that he was right there, cheering for us to fight on. That is the picture this part of the commission conveys to me. The assurance here is that He is right there with us as we present Him to the world. Christ is with us spiritually as we present Him to the world. It is important that we correctly present His word and accurately teach His commandments to the lost world. What is noteworthy here for us is that if there is any conquest or fighting, the King, who in my mind's picture is cheering us on, has already conquered. Joining Him makes us conquerors. In a way we are only collecting the bounty after His conquest. We are gathering the harvest and bringing in the sheaves. The King who did the conquest and is sitting on the right hand of the Father is also the main cheerleader waiting at the finish line for each of us personally. He will personally welcome home each faithful soul who persevered to reach the finish line through strife and hardships, and trials and persecutions. He welcomes them to a home where tears will no longer count, where rest has true meaning, where the Father is not covered with clouds and our eyes can behold Him, and where death and pain no longer exist. This is the hope that awaits the Christian.

In my sophomore year in college, I had the privilege of sitting in on a lecture about the expanding universe. The lecturer was a renowned mathematician and cosmologist. He wasted no time in impressing his mathematical understanding on us. He explained a lot of things that day. With time I have forgotten most of the details pertaining to most of the hypothesis and theories he presented. However, I did not forget some of the main theories he presented as more plausible than others. Among them were these: 1) The universe has no origin and will keep expanding forever. 2) The universe originated sometime in the distant past and has been expanding for some time. It will keep expanding until it collapses. 3) The universe has an origin, but it will keep expanding forever with no forecast of a collapse. Of these theories, the lecturer spent more time on the second one. His explanations were based on the sun's radiation and detections through Doppler effects. It was exciting stuff to those with scientific inclinations and to science students. As I listened to the lecture with great interest, I noted that though this professor was not proving scripture, a chunk of what he was saying made sense and was consistent with scripture. The Hebrews writer says the universe will be rolled away. Peter wrote of "waiting for and hastening the coming of the day of God, because of which the heavens will be set on fire and dissolved, and the heavenly bodies will melt as they burn!" (2 Peter 3:12, ESV).

God is going to bring this universe to an end someday. When? No one knows, and no one has the ability to predict when God will bring that day about. According to Jesus, only the Father knows what time He has set for that day. For now, those of us who follow Jesus and are waiting for His return need not engage in predicting when He will return. Our focus needs to be on spreading the gospel and winning as many souls as God would make possible.

As we await the return of the King, the segment of the commission tells us that Jesus is not distant from His disciples. He is not impartial to His own cause. He intimates Himself with His disciples and to the tasks He has sent us to accomplish. This is not the first time Jesus has indicated His ever presence among His disciples. After instructing the disciples on conflict resolution in Matthew 18, He concludes with the following: "For where two or three are gathered in my name, there am I among them" (Matthew 18:20, ESV).

When Saul who later became known as Paul was persecuting the church in Jerusalem, Christ intervened and had the following dialogue with Saul: "And falling to the ground he heard a voice saying to him, 'Saul, Saul, why are you persecuting me?' And he said, 'Who are you, Lord?' And he said, 'I am Jesus, whom you are persecuting'" (Acts 9:4-5, ESV).

Later on Paul wrote about how close Christ is to the Christians: "Keep your life free from love of money, and be content with what you have, for he has said, 'I will never leave you nor forsake you.'

So we can confidently say, 'The Lord is my helper; I will not fear; what can man do to me?'" (Hebrews 13:5-6, ESV).

This is significant because not only has the king commissioned disciples to be made, but the source of that authority comes from Him and as the head of His body. He assures us that His closeness to His disciples is evermore present until He returns. The literal translation of this segment reads, "and behold I am with [together with, on the same side, party with, in aid of] you all the days until the completion [end, consummation] of the age." That is, "and behold I am with, or together with, or on the same side, or party with, or in aid of, you all the days until the completion or end, or consummation of the age."

C: Conclusion

Summary

Summary of the Great Commission statements:

The following exercise should not be taken as a replacement for any of the Great Commission statements in the gospel account. This is only an exercise to understand the statements all together; thus it is not a replacement. The author of this text holds dear to scripture as written and has no intention now or ever of seeing them changed by this author or any other human being. I defer all authority and references to scripture as revealed by the Holy Spirit to the apostles, the prophets, and all who recorded the scriptures.

And Jesus came to them and spake unto them, saying, All authority hath been given unto me in heaven and on earth. Go ye therefore, and make disciples of all the nations, baptizing them into the name of the Father and of the Son and of the Holy Spirit: teaching them to observe all things whatsoever I commanded you: and lo, I am with you always, even unto the end of the world. (Matthew 28:18-20, ASV)

And he said unto them, Go ye into all the world, and preach the gospel to the whole creation. He that believeth and is baptized shall be saved; but he that disbelieveth shall be condemned. And these signs shall accompany them that believe: in my name shall they cast out demons; they shall speak with new tongues; they shall take up serpents, and if they drink any deadly thing, it shall in no wise hurt them; they shall lay hands on the sick, and they shall recover. (Mark 16:15-18, ASV)

And he said unto them, These are my words which I spake unto you, while I was yet with you, that all things must needs be fulfilled, which are written in the law of Moses, and the prophets, and the psalms, concerning me. Then opened he their mind, that they might understand the scriptures; and he said unto them, Thus it is written, that the Christ should suffer, and rise again from the dead the third day; and that repentance and remission of sins should be preached in his name unto all the nations, beginning from Jerusalem. Ye are witnesses of these things. And behold, I send forth the promise of my Father upon you: but tarry ye in the city, until ye be clothed with power from on high. (Luke 24:44-49, ASV)

¹All three passages, ²Matthew 28:18-20, ³Mark 16:15-18, ⁴Luke 24:44-49

In the Great Commission statement, we see the following truths:

¹Jesus spoke to the disciples, or the apostles, to be specific.

⁴Jesus reminded the disciples that He had taught them that all the things written in the law of Moses, the prophets, and the psalms about Him, the Messiah, had to be fulfilled.

²Jesus told the apostles, "All authority hath been given unto me in heaven and on earth." Comments: We have discussed this at some length in the section discussing authority.

⁴In opening the minds of the disciples to understand what Jesus was telling them, Jesus also explained to them that "the Christ should suffer, and rise again from the dead the third day." Comments: Note that this explanation came after Jesus had opened their minds to understand the scriptures. Here again we see Jesus exercising power over His disciples in opening their minds. Notice that in the text Luke writes, Jesus opened the mind of the disciples before He uttered the words, "the Christ should suffer, and rise again from the dead the third day," which I contend here is an explanation of the events that had just happened.

Jesus further explained that it is written "that repentance and remission of sins should be preached in his name unto all the nations, beginning from Jerusalem." Comments: Neither the apostles nor the prophets at the ushering in of the New Testament era had any control over the message or who got saved. Subsequently, no other human being has control over what message is heard. Only God does. Before time began, God had determined how the sinner would be saved and the content of the saving message. No human determines who hears the message or how it is processed after it is heard. The message is to be preached to everyone. Anyone who hears the message of the death, burial, and resurrection of Christ has to process the message and determine what they want to do after hearing it. He or she might need some persuasion and have questions answered. In the final analysis, the hearer is the only one to respond in obedience or disobey. No man can tell hearers whether they are fit to respond in obedience and submit to baptism. God has already outlined what He expects once a person hears the message of the cross. According to Luke's account, "repentance and remission of sins should be preached in his name." According to Mark's account, "He that believeth and is baptized shall be saved; but he that disbelieveth shall be condemned."

[4]Jesus informed the apostles and disciples that they were witnesses to these things. Comments: This is not insignificant. A witness's testimony weighs much more heavily in a court of law than any expert testimony. Added to that is the fact that their testimony was supported and revealed by the Holy Spirit. That is, the Holy Spirit took from what was Christ's and revealed it to, or reminded, the apostles, according to the gospel of John. The apostles were initial vessels God used to accomplish His purposes. They obeyed Jesus's order to stay in Jerusalem until they received the Holy Spirit, who led them to accomplish the task for which God had called them. They stayed in Jerusalem and preached the first gospel message

in Jerusalem. What they preached and taught was revealed to them by Christ through the Holy Spirit.

[2,3]Go therefore [2,3,4]into all nations and [2]make disciples [3,4]preaching the gospel. Comments: We might ask how the apostles knew what message they were to preach. 1) Jesus told the apostles what had been written in the law of Moses, the prophets, and the psalms, which was [4]"that the Christ should suffer, and rise again from the dead the third day; and that repentance and remission of sins should be preached in his name unto all the nations, beginning from Jerusalem." This is what the apostle Paul referred to in the first four verses of 1 Corinthians 15. 2) Since the prophets saw this coming, it could mean only one thing. God had planned this long before revealing it to the prophets and thus long before Christ came to earth. 3) The message of salvation is not about personal stories of coming to Christ, though they might help as real-life examples. The message of salvation is Christ, the cross, and what it means to us as forgiven Christians and yet-to-be forgiven people—that is, those yet to believe. 4) The apostles were not in charge of the message. God had the message outlined before the apostles were sent out. God controlled the message. It will help us to note this point and preach the same message the apostles preached.

The command is [2]"baptizing them into the name of the Father and of the Son and of the Holy Spirit:" Comments: In Matthew's account this is a command. It is a command given to the apostles to obey and by default to anyone making disciples today. In Mark's account it reads, [3]"He that believeth and is baptized shall be saved; but he that disbelieveth shall be condemned." The Greek word βαπτισθείς (*baptistheis*) is what Mark uses and is translated as "is baptized" in this version of the text. In the Greek grammatical structure, this word is a participle in the nominative case, singular, aorist tense in the passive mode. The nominative case is the subject in English. Thus using this little piece of information one could translate this section of Mark's account as "He that believeth and is the subject of baptism shall be saved; but he that disbelieveth shall be condemned." The sense here is that the hearer of the gospel who believes the message and makes himself or herself available to be baptized shall be saved. From Luke's account we read that repentance and remission of sins are preached to sinners so they can come to God. In Mark's account we read that belief of the gospel message is expected from the hearer of the message. In both Matthew's and Mark's accounts we read that the hearer who has believed the message of the gospel of Christ is required to be the subject of baptism. The obedience of the apostles to obey the command to baptize the believer and the believer yielding because of his or her response to the gospel are not mutually exclusive events when we go to make disciples. They are continuous events that need to happen one after another. They have to be done or kept together in keeping the command that Christ gave.

Mark's account gives us a clear choice about what to do with the gospel message when we hear it. In the end when we hear the gospel message, we have two clear choices available. Mark's account spells out the choices: Believe, be baptized, and be saved, or disbelieve and be condemned. The hearers of the gospel have very clear choices. By believing, we acknowledge that God is faithful and His word is true and worthy of acceptance. Also by believing, we accept God's testimony about His own Son. This is because God was the primary witness to Jesus's work and God supported His work by allowing signs and wonders to be done. The gospel writers, most of whom were firsthand witnesses, testified that God Himself bore witness to the hearing of the people. When we disbelieve, we discount God's witness and make God who is true look like a liar. By not believing God, we reject Him. As God's word stands, it does not and cannot be changed by the compassionate work of man. It will vindicate or condemn according to how we respond to God's will. Yes, God is merciful, loving, kind, just, and so on and so forth. But God through Samuel has this to say about obeying His will:

> *Samuel said, Hath Jehovah as great delight in burnt-offerings and sacrifices, as in obeying the voice of Jehovah? Behold, to obey is better than sacrifice, and to hearken than the fat of rams. For rebellion is as the sin of witchcraft, and stubbornness is as idolatry and teraphim. Because thou hast rejected the word of Jehovah, he hath also rejected thee from being king. (1 Samuel 15:22-23, ASV)*

In the end, if we reject God like King Saul rejected God, with the unfaithfulness of his actions that Samuel said amounts to rejecting God, God will reject us as a result. Samuel instructs us that obeying God's word is of more interest to God than what we choose to do in our efforts to please Him. As God's word is spoken, it stands, and it will accomplish God's intended purposes. This is the case here as indicated by Mark. Thus we do what the word says and are saved, but if we do anything else, we disobey God, which is a rejection of Him. No man can cause God's word to change. Any attempt or attempts to do anything different from God's expressed will leaves us in a position like Saul and leaves us rejecting God. Not believing God and doing anything different from what God has directed amounts to unfaithfulness and rejection of God.

[2]The new disciples are to be taught "to observe all things whatsoever I commanded you." Comments: This also is not insignificant. 1) The new disciples are to be taught. One might ask, what are they to be taught? Well, Jesus in giving this command made it a point to add that the apostles are to teach the new disciples only what He has commanded them. I point this out only because Jesus leaves no doubt about what He desires to be taught, which is, all that He has commanded. This is important because Jesus always did only what the Father had commanded Him. Besides, He is the only one who can instruct us on how to please the Father. Hence it makes sense to follow His commands if we are to be like Him. 2) The new disciples are to observe, hold on to, and preserve what the apostles teach them. This is why Luke in Acts 2 recorded that the disciples devoted themselves to the apostles' doctrines. Luke did not use the word devoted by mistake. He understood Jesus's command and recorded for us that the new disciples held on to the apostles' teachings, thus obeying what Jesus had commanded.

[3]The new disciples will have the capability to do wonders and extraordinary things.

[4]Jerusalem is the starting point of this mission. Comments: This is important because it is written by the prophets. Acts 2 saw the fulfillment of this prophecy.

Christ and the Godhead are intimately involved with the disciples
in this mission or quest.

Without the Great Commission we do not have the authority to make
disciples or save souls. Within the Great Commission or in executing
the Great Commission we fail to make disciples or save souls if
we pick and choose which part or parts of the charge to follow for
whatever reason or reasons, and which not to follow. In other words,
we cannot say that certain parts of the Great Commission are more
important than others. Or that some parts are deserve to be followed
more than others. We make disciples only by doing what we see the
apostles do in Luke's accounts in Acts. This is because they received
the charge first and set the pace for discharging the responsibilities
therein. If we have questions or concerns about what to do with regard
to the Great Commission, the apostolic authority and examples in
my opinion will be the foremost authority and examples to address
our concerns. We thus make disciples according to God's will only
by following the outline in the Great Commission.

A lot of things have been discussed or touched on in the course of our
attempt to examine the Great Commission. We have been careful to
accurately relate a thorough understanding of scripture in this effort.
Ultimately, however, it is the duty of every Christian to examine
carefully what has been presented here with study of the scriptures
and prayer for understanding to make sure what has been presented
here is scripturally accurate. Our desire is to save lost souls and
snatch them from the damnation that God has prepared for all those
who reject Christ Jesus. It is our belief that this can be achieved only
by holding on to what God gave the apostles, and teaching that only.

But perhaps the most important reason that compels us here is the need to recognize that we do not go beyond the authority of Christ Jesus. That is, as disciple makers or evangelists or anyone involved in soul winning at any level, we do not preach or teach what Christ has not commanded.

We saw earlier in the discussion of verse 18 of Matthew 28 that Jesus showed proofs of His divine power over anything He chose, be they events of nature or afflictions to the human condition. Jesus showed that He had power to overcome anything. Despite all His power Jesus did nothing that was not approved by His Father. In other words, Jesus submitted His will to His Father's will and in His own words did as His Father had commanded. Or He did as He saw His Father do. We also looked at the kingship of Jesus Christ and the fact that God enthroned Him as King. God has established Jesus as the king of heaven and earth. Paul puts it as follows: "and you have been filled in him, who is the head of all rule and authority" (Colossians 2:10, ESV).

> *Being found in appearance as a man, He humbled Himself by becoming obedient to the point of death, even death on a cross. For this reason also, <u>God highly exalted Him, and bestowed on Him the name which is above every name</u>, so that <u>that at the name of Jesus every knee will bow, of those who are in heaven and on earth and under the earth</u>, and that <u>every tongue will confess that Jesus Christ is Lord</u>, to the glory of God the Father. (Philippians 2:8-11, NASU)*

By confessing that Jesus is Lord, we indicate our willingness to submit to His Lordship and to His authority. And as we submit to His authority, we show loyalty by following His command and instructions. It will be impossible to say that we are under Christ's authority and not do what He has commanded. We will obey His commandments if we love Him. Furthermore, we do as the king wills because His love toward us and our love for Him compels us. That is loyalty!

Does Jesus intend for us to submit only to His authority? If He did not desire for us to be limited to His authority, then what other sources of authority can we heed to? Let's look at a few things. Before Jesus started His ministry, the authority for God's people was derived from the law of Moses, the words of the prophets, and the psalms. Jesus referenced these sources often when He spoke to the people. For instance, in Matthew 5, Jesus cited and explained the magnitude of these authorities to the crowd:

> *Do not think that I came to abolish the Law or the Prophets; I did not come to abolish but to fulfill. For truly I say to you, until heaven and earth pass away, not the smallest letter or stroke shall pass from the Law until all is accomplished. Whoever then annuls one of the least of these commandments, and teaches others to do the same, shall be called least in the kingdom of heaven; but whoever keeps and teaches them, he shall be called great in the kingdom of heaven. (Matthew 5:17-19, NASU)*

Later on in Mark 13 Jesus said of His own words, "Heaven and earth will pass away, but My words will not pass away" (Mark 13:31-32, NASU).

In Luke's version of the Great Commission statement, we read the following:

> *Now He said to them, "These are My words which I spoke to you while I was still with you, that <u>all things which are written about Me in the Law of Moses and the Prophets and the Psalms must be fulfilled</u>." Then He opened their minds to understand the Scriptures, and He said to them, "Thus it is written, that the Christ would suffer and rise again from the dead the third day, and that repentance for forgiveness of sins would be proclaimed in His name to all the nations, beginning from Jerusalem. You are witnesses of these things. And behold, I am sending forth the promise of My Father upon you; but you are to stay in the city until you are clothed with power from on high" (Luke 24:44-49, NASU).*

Luke's account records Jesus citing these same sources. In Luke's citation, Jesus points out the finality and purpose of these sources. These sources pointed to Jesus and His mission to reconcile man back to God. Once Jesus had fulfilled all they had said about Him, they were referred to in the past. Matthew's accounts records Jesus no longer focusing on these authoritative sources. Having fulfilled all in the law of Moses, the prophets, and psalms, Jesus is now the one and only source of authority as we saw in the transfiguration. God removes all the other sources of authority and consolidates all the authority pertaining to salvation and how man is reconciled to

God in Jesus, the Christ. This does not mean we cannot cite the law, the prophets, or the psalms any longer. We still need these sources for teaching and proving God's word. We also need them for historical references and purposes. But we do not dwell on them as the Jews did as their source of authority. Our source of authority today comes only from Christ and what He commanded His apostles. Hence when Matthew's records have Jesus citing His own authority, Matthew's account does not contradict Luke's account. Instead, by carefully studying the two accounts, we can conclude that because Jesus had truly fulfilled all that was written about Him in the law of Moses, the prophets, and the psalms, it was only fitting that God set those sources aside and set the focus on Christ. Christ is the one God wants all of us to listen to and obey. There is no competition or contradiction here. God is working the plans He had laid out since before the beginning of the earth into perfection. Hence I believe that not only does Jesus desire for us to keep His commands but that God the Father commands it. How are we able to do this? We are able to keep Christ's word through faith and a desire to stay under God's rich and bountiful grace. I don't remember who related this visual to me about God's grace, but it is as follows: Our attempt to please God is like trying to clean up a big mess with a fork. We try, but nothing really gets cleaned up. God comes behind us with a big fat shovel and sweeps up all the mess like it never happened. This in essence gives us a clean slate each time.

Jesus addressed his command to go make disciples to a group of people. We have identified the responsibilities that those receiving these instructions from Jesus had to go and perform. These responsibilities were twofold. The first responsibility was to preach or teach the gospel. The second responsibility rests with the hearer of the gospel.

The preacher or teacher of the gospel

1. is to go make disciples by preaching the gospel of Christ. The gospel informs the world about God reconciling man to Himself because of the sacrifice of Christ on the cross. The gospel informs all hearers that God is redeeming man and forgiving their sins through Christ Jesus. is to baptize the hearers who believe the gospel. This is part of the command to make disciples. It is not separate and apart from the Great Commission. God has His reasons for doing things the way He commands and wills. The hearers are to be baptized into the Godhead, or, as Peter put it, to "be baptized into Christ." Paul said in his letter to the Colossians that it pleased God to place all the fullness of the Godhead in Jesus. And also in Jesus the fullness of the deity dwells, whether one is baptized in the name of Jesus Christ, or in the name of the Father, the Son, and the Holy Spirit. At this point in my growth, I will say that the same mission is accomplished. However, for consistency's sake if a local congregation agrees to use one statement or another, this ought not lead to division or contentions. If problems result, then let's resort to prayer and study to resolve our differences as brothers and sisters, not as enemies. Once we have decided on a solution as a church, it is proper for us to understand that we have a responsibility to each other to present a united front. If questions remain,

then the issue is not settled. It needs to be addressed and settled.

2. Those who have submitted to the authority of Christ through baptism after hearing the gospel are to be taught all that Christ has commanded. What Christ has commanded is seen in the teachings of the apostles and the examples the apostles left for us. The same encouragement Barnabas gave to the brethren at Antioch holds for us too: "he exhorted them all to remain faithful to the Lord with steadfast purpose" (Acts 11:23-24, ESV).

3. We can do this by devoting ourselves to the apostles' teachings just as the early disciples did. By doing that, we devote ourselves to what Christ has commanded.

To the hearers of the gospel:

1. Anyone who hears the message of the gospel of Christ is being called by God to come into union with Him. God is calling the hearer to safety, to be redeemed, and to come receive forgiveness of sins. God is calling the hearer to come under His grace and become free of sin's bondage. God is calling the sinner who is currently the subject of God's wrath to redemption from His wrath to safety. This is the time for all sinners to choose to come to Christ and escape the day God has set aside to avenge Himself on His enemies and the children of wrath.

2. God expects hearers to believe and to repent of their sins.

3. God desires for hearers to submit to baptism for the remission of their sins.

4. God desires for hearers to observe and to keep strictly what Christ has commanded.

Paul told the Corinthians not to go beyond what is written. He also said to his trainees, "But as for you, teach what accords with sound doctrine" (Titus 2:1, ESV).

For this reason I remind you to <u>fan into flame the gift of God</u>, which is in you through the laying on of my hands, for God gave us a spirit not of fear but of power and love and self-control. Therefore do not be ashamed of the testimony about our Lord, nor of me his prisoner, but share in suffering for the gospel by the power of God, who saved us and called us to a holy calling, not because of our works but because of his own purpose and grace, which he gave us in Christ Jesus before the ages began, and which now has been manifested through the appearing of our Savior Christ Jesus, who abolished death and brought life and immortality to light through the gospel, for which I was appointed a preacher and apostle and teacher, which is why I suffer as I do. But I am not ashamed, for I know whom I have believed, and I am convinced that he is able to guard until that Day what has been entrusted to me. <u>Follow the pattern of the sound words that you have heard from me</u>, in the faith and love that are in Christ Jesus. By the Holy Spirit who dwells within us, <u>guard the good deposit entrusted</u> to you. (2 Timothy 1:6-14, ESV)

If anyone teaches a different doctrine and does not agree with the sound words of our Lord Jesus Christ and the teaching that accords with godliness. (1 Timothy 6:3, ESV)

> *Know ye not, that to whom ye present yourselves as servants unto obedience, his servants ye are whom ye obey; whether of sin unto death, or of obedience unto righteousness? But thanks be to God, that, whereas ye were servants of sin, ye became obedient from the heart to that form of teaching whereunto ye were delivered. (Romans 6:16-17, ASV)*

Why do we need to devote ourselves to the apostolic doctrines? For one thing God desires it so and Christ commands it. In addition, the apostles were direct witnesses to all that Christ did and said. In any court of law their testimony surpasses any expert testimony if the expert was not at the scene of the incident. Moreover, Christ personally picked out the apostles for the very purpose of using them to lay the foundation of His church. Their teachings and instructions are vital to our salvation. If we follow the apostolic doctrine and build on the foundation they laid, we will end up building the same structure they built in terms of Christ's body. If we fail to follow the apostolic doctrine, we cannot replicate what the apostles built. This is why we need to heed them. What they passed on to the earlier Christians as well as today's Christians is what Christ desired for the church to know. Furthermore, Christianity is an inheritance. We inherit what Christ gave the apostles, which they in turn passed on to every generation of Christians. There might be confusion every now and then, but it is up to each generation of Christians to maintain what we inherited in its purity and submit to the will of God. This is the only way we can successfully keep and maintain God's will pass along the pattern taught by the apostles.

As Christians our mission is to preach about the king. We do not hold the position of the judges. The king is the savior and the judge. He will judge those who receive His message of repentance and forgiveness of sins. God desires all to come to Him and accept His extended hand of reconciliation through the blood of Christ Jesus. He is not interested in the perishing of sinners. Christ sacrificed His life for that. As a result, rejection of the gospel message is a rejection of God's extended hand and of His offering for peace. Condemnation of those who reject the gospel message becomes possible only because of their own choice for condemnation. The appeal here is to make God the desired choice and settle for His offer of peace, reconciliation, and salvation for the sinner. Also, Christians cannot concede ground to Satan with excuses such as "people have rejected God." That might be, yet we need to be reminded that Christ said, "[T]he gates of Hades shall not prevail against the church." Also, according to Paul, we are conquerors and are smashing all kinds of meaningless human arguments and ways of thinking. The battle has already been won. Dangerous and treacherous the task might be, but to us, to die is to gain and to perish is to go home and be with the Lord Jesus.

Concluding thoughts

Did Jesus limit Himself in giving the Great Commission?

Did Jesus limit Himself to His commandments in the Great Commission? Or, if Jesus has all authority, does the Great Commission limit Him? Or, if Jesus is all powerful like His Father, can He be limited? Can we put Jesus in a box called the Great

Commission? What is the difference between the way I limit God and the way God limits Himself? These are all reasonable questions to ask, and an attempt to answer any of them needs to be carefully thought through.

One Sunday I was listening to my Bible class teacher talk about a visit to an orphanage that the local church supports. They had taken a group to tour the orphanage as well as do maintenance work that was badly needed. As part of his narrative, the teacher talked about the rules and regulations that the children in the orphanage were expected to live by. As I listened to the description by the teacher of the challenges the children face, the situations that arise from everyday life, and the rules and regulations instructing them on how to deal with their immediate challenges, it dawned on me that we are like those children. When we come to God or heed His calling and respond, we come broken, and God provides us with a way to become sound again. We come bearing a heavy load. All of us come to God in a wretched state of one form or another. We need structure to help us live like God would have us live. The rules and regulations provide the children in the orphanage with a structure that helps them rebuild their lives.

Consider the law given to the Israelites, for example. God did not give the Israelites the law to benefit Himself or to limit Himself, He gave the Israelites the law so they could live up to God's expectations. The law for the most part contained values that were characteristics of God, such as love and holiness and kindness. These were values that are not predisposed to our nature. In a way, the law was a limitation set forth by God for the Israelites to have so they would know what was expected of them in their covenant relationship with the Holy God. The limitation did not bind God, it bound the Israelites in terms of what they could and could not do in their relationship with Him. So although God cannot be and is not limited, He limits Himself. Better yet, He provides limitations for the sake of His relationship with His people so we can function within them.

Let's ask ourselves why the scriptures say that without faith it is impossible to please God. If God is all powerful, why should He require faith to be pleased? The requirement of faith according to Hebrews 11:6 is not a limitation that put God in a box called faith. Nor does it limit God to faith. The requirement is such that those who respond to God's calling will have a framework or a structure that tells us what God expects or requires of us. Just as the law was for the Israelites, faith is for us, and God is the object of our faith. Through faith we obey and fulfill God's will. God need not have faith in Himself. He knows who He is, and He is all knowing!

Another way to consider this is to think of a situation where God did not make the law available or faith did not exist. What would our relationship with God look like? How could we know or understand God's will in order to serve Him? So then, the law, faith, baptism, and any of the revelations of God serve as a guide, or a framework in which we can function, to properly keep His word.

We would all agree that Jesus died so that all mankind can be saved. The Great Commission says Jesus has all the authority, and to "make disciples of all nations." So why did Jesus not declare that all mankind are saved? Instead He said, "Go make disciples of all nations, baptizing them in the name of the Father and of the Son and of the Holy Spirit, teaching them to observe everything that I have commanded you." Even though Jesus has all authority in heaven and on earth, by commanding that disciples be made, He restricts His grace to those who hear and accept the gospel about Him and become His disciples. That is, humans are not robots; we all have free will to choose and do as we wish. We make decisions for our own self-interests, good or bad. Also by asking for the disciples to be baptized, in the name of the Godhead, He provides a boundary within which His will is specified. Yet again by commanding that the disciples be taught everything He has commanded, He restricts what the disciples can be exposed to. When all is said and done, we see that in the Great Commission Jesus provides a framework for His disciples to function in order to meet His expectations. I have a lot more questions to ask Jesus about this whole arrangement, but I did not die on the cross to save all mankind, and I have it only in my interest to obey the one through whom God's grace and forgiveness has been extended to me. That one is Jesus, the Christ.

Who is responsible for the Great Commission today?

I mentioned in the opening paragraph that I see the Great Commission as my charge as a faithful Christian. We might wonder if that really is the case. Is the Great Commission charged to today's Christians? Let's look at one of the Great Commission statements:

> *And Jesus came and spoke to them, saying "All authority has been given to Me in heaven and on earth. Go therefore and make disciples of nations, baptizing them in the name of the Father, and*

the Son and the Holy Spirit, teaching them to observe all that I commanded you; and lo, I am with you always, even to the end of the age. (Matthew 28: 18-20)

To think that this responsibility is not our concern is to think that disciples like Philip, Apollos, and many others who left Jerusalem during the persecution of the church and spread the gospel message had no business doing that. These were not apostles; they were just disciples converted by the apostles. Paul gave his disciple Timothy the following instructions:

I solemnly charge you in the presence of God and of Christ Jesus, who is to judge the living and the dead, and by His appearing and His kingdom: preach the word; be ready in season and out of season; reprove, rebuke, exhort, with great patience and instruction . . . But you, be sober in all things, endure hardship, do the work of an evangelist, fulfill your ministry. (2 Timothy 4:1-5, NASU)

We noted earlier that the message preached by both apostles and non-apostles was the same. To this extent Paul notes that after preaching the gospel, if he came back to change the message he first presented, he should be accursed. Paul's conclusion applies to anyone who preaches anything but the gospel or anything other than what the apostles preached, and who is accursed. My point here is that as the apostles first received the charge and discharged the responsibilities. In Acts, the Holy Spirit led different disciples to spread the good news. It is important to keep in mind that the Lord directed the activities of the church. To understand this is to understand that the church was working directly under the authority of Christ. Moreover, Paul also told the disciples at Ephesus that the church is to make known the mysteries of God to the world. Among these mysteries is that God through Christ has brought both Jews and Gentiles together as His sons—a mystery that was hidden until the time was right. Furthermore, we note that as the apostles taught people the gospel of Christ and believers were converted, these believers were taught all that Christ had commanded. The new believers then took the message to places as they were directed, led, or prompted by the Spirit. This way the gospel spread throughout the world. The church today is responsible for seeing to it that this mission continues by maintaining and teaching what the apostles taught. The cyclical nature of making disciples who then go out to make yet more disciples need not change the gospel message. The apostles were entrusted with leading the way in making disciples. In that sense, they had the blueprint for making disciples according to the will of the Savior and King, Christ Jesus. Any other method or methods apart from the gospel fail in making disciples or give people false hope.

When we say the church is responsible for seeing to it that the gospel continues to spread today, does that free the individual Christian from spreading the gospel message? We might note that individuals make up the church. Also we might note that God gave gifts to the church's individual members. The gifts God gave were not collective gifts. There might be many in the same congregation who can teach exceptionally well, for example, but they are different individuals. And though God uses all these gifts to achieve His purposes and to mature the church, He is the one who works in each individual separately and in all collectively. It is true that one person alone cannot meet all of these responsibilities. As a body, the church must work together as a unit. At the same time these functions and gifts are specialized and must all work together to attain unity and bring the Lord's body to maturity. Each unit of the body, the individuals, must bear their own burden and function properly and in unison. As Paul said, there cannot be division, with the hand saying it is not the leg and so it is unimportant or vice versa. All the body parts must play their own role properly and effectively to keep Christ's body, the church, advancing the gospel. Thus outreach to the community is not the job of only the preacher or teacher but the whole body.

The impossible is possible to God

Usually when we insist on following the apostles' teachings and stress the need for baptizing the newly converted, we are presented with questions that challenge the human mind. Such questions usually present situations that are impossible for humans to deal with or find solutions for. Usually such questions are, What if the gospel is preached in the desert? If there is no water, how do we baptize the person who has believed? Often it is impossible for the gospel preacher to come up with reasonable or satisfactory answers to these questions. I was recently in a discussion with a couple and was asked such a question. To further complicate the situation, I was told that if I insist on baptism, I discourage young people who might otherwise have believed the gospel message and prayed for forgiveness of their sins. "Do you mean they are not saved?" I was asked. My initial reaction was that it is not my job to judge any soul.

My task is to teach the gospel as Christ has commanded and teach what the apostles taught.

I have since taught about this question a bit more and reflected on it quite a bit. As one who would like to win millions of souls for God, I felt saddened by that question, for it made me feel I was taking people's hope away. As I thought about these questions and many like them, I wondered about what it meant to be given false hope. What is false hope? False hope can come in all kinds of shapes and forms. Say, for example, that I know of a rich man who is giving out his wealth and I choose to direct people to the location where his money is being dispersed. If I give the wrong directions, whether intentionally or unintentionally, I can be considered to have given false hope to people. Maybe the rich man requires that the people who come to be enriched ring a specific doorbell or approach him only through his front door to be given a million dollars. Say I fail to pass that information on and as a result none of the people I send receive any money from the rich man. Again I can be considered to have given false hope. The rich man is still giving out the money. But those I send did not get to him or those who get to the house fail because I neglected to give them a vital piece of information that would have taken them to the right chamber where he was waiting with the check. The folks I sent will leave empty-handed. Their hopes will be dashed. However, if I give them the proper direction and accurate pieces of information and they act on it appropriately, they will meet the rich man and be made rich. If the folks I send with the proper information and direction decide they do not care for the rich man's property and fail to act on my information, or they fail to follow the rich man's instructions properly, they will have themselves to blame if they remain poor. In that case, I could not be blamed for giving false hope. If in informing people about the rich man's intentions and invitation I stress to them that they should pay close attention to the instructions, then it is probably because the rich man impressed that on me as being his will, or I know how important that piece of information is to getting them closer to a million dollars.

In a similar manner when we stress following God's will, we are trying and working hard to eliminate false hope. Our desire for everyone who comes to God is to provide them with the proper information that will lead them to Christ, following what Christ Himself gave to His disciples. It is not because we want to see people condemned. On the contrary we, with all the might God has given us, desire to bring people to Christ and leave them with no doubt. It is a painful thing to get to the end of the line or the end of a race before learning that one is disqualified. It is too late then. If we have any reason to stress the importance of keeping God's command, it is that we don't want people to be disqualified at the finish line. Most important, we stress obedience to God's command because His love compels us and we love the sinner, not the sinful ways.

As I have pondered these questions, I have also been enlightened that we are walking with God by faith. And because of that faith we respond to God's will and urge others to do the same. By faith we believe God's word and trust His faithfulness that if we do what His has commanded, He will save us and do as He has promised. Because of that faith we take God at His word, trusting that He knows what He is doing. I have also come to the realization that what God has

357

commanded perfect or imperfect ought to be fine with me. I don't need to ask what-if questions. God's test of Abraham to sacrifice Isaac, the promised son, is a well-known story. I have heard all kinds of discussions about this story. Yet in this story Abraham's faith in God is shown to be at its zenith. There is no hint of false hope in the story, nor is there any pretense. Abraham found himself in a bind: do as God asks and sacrifice Isaac, his only heir by his wife, Sarah, or say no to God and save his son's life. Furthermore, what would he tell Sarah when he got home without their son, who was born to them at a very advanced age? Surely Sarah is more than a hundred years old at that point, and it would have been inconceivable to think of her having another child. How would he explain to Isaac that he was the lamb for the sacrifice? Perhaps these and many other insoluble questions were the kinds of thoughts running through Abraham's mind as he trekked the road to the place God had chosen for the sacrifice. Abraham responded to an impossible situation in faith, reasoning that the same God who had asked of him an impossible request had the answers and solutions. So, in obedience of faith, Abraham took God's request on, and when Isaac finally asked about the sacrificial lamb, he told Isaac God would provide it. Whether there was going to be a sacrificial lamb other than Isaac is insignificant at this point. The fact is that Abraham did not know that. Abraham believed God, and was willing to give to God what God asked of him without any ifs or buts. He just did what God asked of him. He responded to God in faith, and God did not disappoint him. The fact is, if we trust in God and are willing to yield our will to His, He will make a way even when the task is impossible.

The story begins with God asking Abraham to sacrifice His only son with his wife, Sarah. The sacrifice was to take place at a designated location God would show Abraham. Abraham woke up in the morning and made all the necessary arrangements for the sacrifice and for the journey. He set out on the journey with Isaac and one of his servants. I don't know how Abraham slept through the night. And I don't know what he might have been thinking all that morning as he got ready. I can only guess how emotionally drained and physically worn out he was. Who knows what he was thinking as he walked the uncertain path in faith to sacrifice his only son? He might have been figuring out a way to explain himself to Sarah if things didn't turn out as planned. All of a sudden he felt the pull from his son disrupting his thoughts. Isaac had been trying to get his attention for a while now. Isaac asked Abraham a logical question: "My father . . . Behold, the fire and the wood. But where is the lamb for a burnt-offering?" (Genesis 22:7, ASV).

The question is logical, all right. They had the fire, and they had the wood that the fire would burn, but . . . but no sheep or goat or cow. Something was definitely missing, and it was Isaac's doing. Isaac hadn't packed the stuff. We have no indication of how far they had traveled before Isaac posed the question. It is entirely possible that at his age Abraham had forgotten to select one of the finest and choicest among the lambs for the sacrifice. But was that the case? Abraham responds as follows: "God will provide himself the lamb for a burnt-offering, my son" (Genesis 22:8, ASV).

The Holy Spirit will later reveal to us Abraham's thought process: "He considered that God is able to raise people even from the dead, from which he also received him back as a type" (Hebrews 11:19-20, NASU).

In his answer we learn several things about Abraham, including the state of his mind and faith. Abraham had not forgotten the lamb as his son or we might have suspected. He knew exactly what he was doing. Though Abraham might not have seen God raise the dead, he reasoned that God is able to do just that. But going back to his answer to his son, we learn where Abraham was with his faith. He believed God would provide the lamb for the sacrifice and give him back his son. It was a no-win situation from a human perspective. But it was possible for a man like Abraham who was walking before God in faith. If we will listen to God and be ready to do as He has commanded, all the what-if scenarios and questions will evaporate. And we can respond in like manner as Abraham, that no matter the situation and what God's will is calling for, "God himself will provide" for our needs to meet the demands of the situation. He provided water for Hagar and Ishmael because He is also the God who sees. He does see our needs. Paul said He would make way for us to overcome our situations. And God will not subject us to a situation that we cannot overcome. It necessarily means that God is able to resolve any challenges that interfere with His children. It also means that with God we are not going to run into impossible situations. And even if we do, we have God's assurance that He has the answer. With God all things are possible. We need to keep this in mind as we walk with God in faith. We also need to remember that Jesus taught that we manifest our love for Him by keeping His commandments. We might find logical and reasonable ways to take care of some needs that might look impossible to us, yet to momentarily meet our needs in a way that God has not commanded could lead to rejecting God and offering false hope.

In the book of 1 Samuel, we read about the leaders of Israel going to Samuel, the prophet and judge at the time, to ask him for a king. Before Samuel's era, the people of Israel spent more than two hundred years in an up-and-down relationship with God. They forsook God and engaged in idol worship and all kinds of sins. God then allowed one of the surrounding nations to reign over Israel and oppress them. The people of Israel called on God for redemption and forgiveness. God then chose a leader from the ranks of the people and used that individual to redeem His people. This cyclical relationship was the type of relationship the children of Israel had with God after Joshua and all the elders God used to bring Israel to the land of Canaan had passed away. One of the people God chose to use was Samuel. Samuel was a bit different from all the other leaders. He had grown up under the direction of Eli the priest. Samuel went around Israel judging the people and leading them before God. He restored a healthier relationship between God and Israel. When all the elders of Israel came to visit Samuel at his home and asked for a king, Samuel's reasonable reaction was one of disappointment and rejection. The following scripture sums up the essence of Samuel's reaction at this request: "But the thing displeased Samuel when they said, 'Give us a king to judge us.' And Samuel prayed to the Lord. And the Lord said to Samuel, 'Obey the voice of the people in all that they say to you, for they have not rejected you, but they have rejected me from being king over them'" (1 Samuel 8:6-7, ESV).

Samuel followed God's directions and gave them a king. Under these kings the same cycle that Samuel had broken resumed. The people of Israel had great or good kings at one point or another, and then they had a king who dishonored God and led the people into sin. After many years of these cycles repeating over and over again with the nation divided into two kingdoms, the people under the leadership of the kings drifted from God and God sent both nations into exile. God did not abandon His people even though He had sent them into exile. Rather, God used His people to reveal Himself as the only one who enthrones and dethrones kings and kingdoms. The prophet Daniel made this known to the great King Nebuchadnezzar as King Nebuchadnezzar was elevated by God, humbled by God, and shown grace by God. This summary spans more than a thousand years of relationship between God and Israel.

This story teaches us a lot of lessons, among which are these:

> » God gives us freedom to do whatever we want in our relationship with Him. He might not stop us when we reject Him with our actions.
> » God will allow us to do what we want even when that means rejection of Him.
> » We can reject God's leadership and put in place human leadership, and God might or might not react.
> » Though God was rejected, He still used Israel to bring about the Christ to save the world.
> » God's faithfulness still holds strong even when we reject His will and directions.

» Though God rules over human affairs, He does not offer false hope. What He offers is real. If we accept His will through faith and follow God's will, He will keep His word despite our unfaithfulness. If we do not keep His word, He is still faithful.

» The prophet Daniel recorded for us that God is ultimately the one in charge of human affairs, and He deals with kings and kingdoms.

Finally

We all know that Hebrews 11 talks about the heroes of faith. In the last part of the chapter Paul makes a note that all these heroes did not receive the promise God made them for a simple reason: "[S]ince God had provided something better for us, that apart from us they should not be made perfect" (Hebrews 11:39-40, ESV).

Ooh, the thought that God was waiting for you and I all along, for you and I to become part of His plan! All this time He held off His judgment, prolonging His patience, waiting, delaying His judgment to give us a chance to become His children! What a thought! To think that before He created the universe, He anticipated the day we will yield to His will and become part of His plans. Narrow the thought down to only yourself. Think about it: God desired long before we were thought of as a baby to become His own. Hold that thought, and add to that the thought that God has prolonged His promise to some serious and very faithful people, so that you and I living today will receive the same invitation to be part of His plan. That is, all those heroes mentioned before this passage are waiting, because God desires for us to receive the reward together with them. Just think about it: Noah, Abraham, Isaac, Jacob, Joseph and his brothers, Joshua, Caleb, Samson, Samuel, David . . . all died without receiving the promise of God, though they saw it from afar and welcomed it. These mighty men and women are all waiting for you and I to become part of what they spent their life looking forward to receiving.

To come to the knowledge that for more than six thousand years God has anticipated this generation's participation in His plans. To come to know, appreciate, and live in the love that made it all possible. To imagine God's joy looking forward to the day that we will believe the gospel. Such joy to my imagination is as intense as the intensity of the agony God felt throughout Christ's suffering and Christ's death on the cross. Such intense joy that I imagine excites God to no end, as each of us are created anew or born again through baptism and added to the Lord's body. To imagine that with each passing moment in our lives He was waiting and looking forward to that day we will call His Son "my Lord and my God." To imagine His joy on that day that we made the great confession that "Jesus is Lord and the Son of God," submitting to baptism to be born anew into Christ as part of the body of Christ. To imagine the delight in heaven as we were born anew in Christ! A new creature! To note how the all-powerful God, the all-knowing God, the Almighty God, and the all-seeing God patiently awaited our participation in His plan, waiting just for you and me! To wonder about the depth of the love that set it all in motion and compels His continuing patience in the face of rejection, disappointments, rebellion, and sinfulness of the very people He has so deeply loved, planned for, and waited for before the conception of time. To imagine the intensity of the love that put the plan to save mankind together. To imagine the love that executed the cross and to appreciate the love that sent the Savior to the cross and that continues to hold all the heroes of faith in their graves just because you and I are being expected. Still yet to think that some of these heroes lost their lives and the evildoers have not been avenged yet. To observe that this delay is all for you and me, yes, you and me—such love is too amazing and too wonderful for me to comprehend.

To wonder about such love! The excitement and joy it brings to the heart that God in all of His majesty and riches and might would love us so much. He saw you and me from afar. Far before we were even thought of to be conceived, let alone born. To wonder about the love for you and me that causes Him to delay His judgment and to wait for us, delaying reward for those who many years ago chose to forfeit their own interests in this life and serve Him faithfully. Some served to the point of death, others losing all they had, and still others thought of themselves as strangers and chose to live as strangers even in the land where they were born. All these people did not receive the promise just because God saw you and me coming and chose to keep them waiting so they would not enjoy the promise without us. Just think about that! All those great men we've read about in scripture are all waiting on us, yes, you and me, to make the last entrance! Now, that ought to make humble us and leave us with a sense of overwhelming love! Think of it this way: We went to a party at the invitation of our king. As we entered the banquet hall, we realized that all the important dignitaries we had heard of but had never seen were present. Furthermore, we noticed that all of these dignitaries were standing by chatting with each other and waiting to be seated. As we entered the hall, they all looked in our direction with joy and excitement, perhaps thinking, "These are some of the last ones." It wasn't that we are late, only that they were there a little earlier than us! Just think that as soon as we entered, the king also entered and ordered the party to commence. All along, we were the ones they were waiting for. This is the imagery this last passage in Hebrews 11 conjures in my mind. Yes, such is the way you and I have been loved. Such love is indeed beyond human understanding and comprehension.

ADDENDA

A

Baptism

The Jewish tradition had all kinds of ceremonial washing. Immersion was not part of their ceremonial washing. For the most part the washing included washing one's clothes, washing one's hands and feet, and washing one's body. The purposes of these ceremonial washings varied from general cleansing after coming in contact with the carcass of an animal to priestly cleansing so the priest could appear before God and enter areas designated as holy in the temple. God outlined other requirements for the children of Israel to wash under certain conditions. Immersion was not part of the kinds of washing one reads about in the Jewish traditions. The only thing about immersion one can find in relation to Israel is what the Holy Spirit revealed to Paul in the following scripture: "[T]hat our fathers were all under the cloud and all passed through the sea; and all were baptized into Moses in the cloud and in the sea" (1 Corinthians 10:1-2, NASU).

Immersion was not part of Jewish custom and practice. Given this piece of information, then, we might ask why John was baptizing by immersing in water and who sent him. And who gave him the authority to do something different from the normal cultural practice? John the Baptist answered these questions himself in the following passage:

> *The next day he saw Jesus coming to him and said, "Behold, the Lamb of God who takes away the sin of the world!" This is He on behalf of whom I said, 'After me comes a Man who has a higher rank than I, for He existed before me.' I did not recognize Him, but so that He might be manifested to Israel, I came baptizing in water." John testified saying, "I have seen the Spirit descending as a dove out of heaven, and He remained upon Him. I did not recognize Him, but He who sent me to baptize in water said to me, 'He upon whom you see the Spirit descending and remaining upon Him, this is the One who baptizes in the Holy Spirit.' I myself have seen, and have testified that this is the Son of God" (John 1:29-34, NASU).*

John the Baptist was a prophet, and his source of authority was God. Jesus submitted Himself to God's will as He went to be baptized by John the Baptist. Just think about it: if Jesus had not come to be baptized by John, John could not have introduced Jesus to Israel as "the Lamb of God who takes away the sin of the world"! This is especially important when one notes that the mothers of John and Jesus are related. Is there a chance these cousins might have met during one of the Jewish festivals in Jerusalem or during a visit by either side of the families? I think it is possible or highly likely that these cousins might have met during a visit to Jerusalem, given that both sets of parents were very religious. The gospel writers did not record this piece of information, so we can only speculate. This is important because John said of Jesus, "I did not recognize Him." It is entirely possible that the two never met each other. It is also possible that John, being a prophet of God, took nothing for granted. That is, even if he had knowledge of who Jesus was, he needed a confirmation and certainty so he wouldn't introduce the wrong person as the savior to Israel. The sure sign was for him to do as God had told him to do and look for the signs God had given him. This is why John's testimony about Jesus is crucial, for he was a great prophet. John was a prophet who, like all the prophets, received God's word and told it to the people. He was an authority who represented God before the people of Israel.

Jesus, on the other hand, was the Son of God. He did and said what the Father had commanded. In that respect He was no different from the other prophets. The difference is that God crowned Him King after His suffering and gave Him a name above all names. As Peter puts it, "Let all the house of Israel therefore **know for certain** that **God has made him both Lord and Christ, this Jesus whom you crucified**" (Acts 2:36, ESV).

God has made Jesus Lord by giving Him all authority. God has made Jesus the first in everything, everything in both heaven and earth, according to Paul's letter to the Colossians. God has made Jesus the Christ, the Anointed One, the Savior, the only one who can save. Hence one might ask where Jesus got the authority to command the disciples to go make disciples and baptize them. For one thing, Jesus said He had been given all authority. For another, He always said He did as the Father commanded. So when Jesus commanded His disciples to baptize the newly made disciples, He not only moved

369

away from old Jewish traditions of washing, but put in place a new system, immersion. Did He have the authority to do that, and was that pleasing to the Father? I will answer both questions yes! If Jesus sought to please the Father all the time He was on earth, He wasn't going to depart from that just because His status changed. I don't believe that! Besides, the Father testified that He was pleased with Jesus. Not only was the command to baptize pleasing to the Father, but He had planned all this before the beginning of the universe. Like always, Jesus, though He had been given all authority, was discharging the Father's plan according to the Father's will. It will serve us well to not only learn from Jesus, but to do as He commands. Hence John baptized because God commanded him to. Jesus commanded that His disciples be baptized because He knew what the plan of God the Father was and how to please the Father.

By forsaking baptism we disobey the King's direct orders, a direct order given by the King Himself. The order is part of the command to go make disciples; it is not separate and apart from the command to go make disciples. The requirement is to believe and be baptized. No one can tell the potential disciple who has believed and repented when He or she can be baptized. If I were to teach an unbeliever the gospel of Christ and he or she were to believe, repent, and make known by confession that Christ is the Son of God, the command is that I baptize him or her. It is not my call to determine when this new disciple is baptized. In other words, if one has come to believe the gospel message, repented, and made that known, they are to be baptized as Mark's account outlines. It is not anybody's position to determine when a disciple is ready to be baptized. God knows the heart of each of us. Just as He requires us to have faith in walking with Him, He is capable of taking us at our word and working with us. He sees, He knows, and He will save!

With the command to make disciples and baptize them, Jesus set the term for entry into the new covenant. Under the circumcision covenant, one had to be born into a Jewish household or be bought as a slave by a Jewish master. It is important to note that though the prophets prophesied about reaching all nations with the news of the Savior, repentance, and the forgiveness of sins, they did not tell us how one was going to enter the kingdom of God. Jesus did. The Jews with their familiarity with ceremonial cleansing could understand the relevance of baptism better than Gentiles, who had no concept of such cleansing. Baptism thus was not difficult to understand from their perspective. Is it too difficult to understand that the Holy God desires union with sanctified sinners—washed and cleansed sinners, that is?

B

Why the Apostolic Doctrine Is Important

Jesus said, "If you love Me, you will keep My commandments" (John 14:15, NASU).

He also told the apostles to teach the disciples all that He, Jesus, had commanded the apostles. By deduction, then, the apostles were not to teach what He, Jesus, had not commanded them. To ensure this, Jesus told them the Holy Spirit would take from what is His and give to the disciples, as well as remind them of all things He had taught them.

"But the Comforter, [even] the Holy Spirit, whom the Father will send in my name, he shall teach you all things, and bring to your remembrance all that I said unto you" (John 14:26, ASV).

"He shall glorify me: for he shall take of mine, and shall declare [it] unto you. All things whatsoever the Father hath are mine: therefore said I, that he taketh of mine, and shall declare [it] unto you" (John 16:14-15, ASV).

"But when the Comforter is come, whom I will send unto you from the Father, [even] the Spirit of truth, which proceedeth from the Father, he shall bear witness of me" (John 15:26, ASV).

» Thus the first thing important about the apostles' doctrine is that they taught only what Jesus has commanded.
» Second, what they taught was directly controlled by the Godhead. The Holy Spirit revealed to the apostles as well as reminded them what Jesus desired to be revealed as He reminded them what Jesus had taught earlier.
» Third, they were eyewitnesses to Jesus's ministry and His teaching. They heard Him before and after His resurrection, they saw Him before and after His resurrection, they touched Him before and after His resurrection.
» They laid the foundation of the church, and they are that foundation, with Christ as the cornerstone.

» They were led by the Holy Spirit to express and manifest God's will in the pattern or the form of doctrine handed down to the apostles.

An important point to keep in mind is that the early disciples had only the Old Testament to go on. It is thus easier to see that most of the doctrinal problems in the church stemmed from that background. Take for example the problems with circumcision in the flesh, Jewish brethren having a difficult time after Peter visited Cornelius, and a whole host of issues. The Jews had the teachings of the old covenant, whereas the Gentiles came in mostly with the idol worshiping. The Jews were to be weaned off the old covenant, and the Gentiles were to be taught the one true God. Both Jews and Gentiles were to be united in Christ and taught about God and His great and immeasurable kindness toward us. There were new things to be taught and understood. For example, God did not regard the Gentiles as different from the Jews anymore. Other things pertained to God's church, how to live in the kingdom of God, and a host of new instructions about our relationship with God and how to serve Him faithfully together. In essence, what the apostles taught the first-century Christians is what the church preserved in the New Testament text and passed on. Following the apostolic doctrines will lead to the same the goal: pleasing God. Not following the apostles' doctrines leads to division and something totally different from God's will.

C

Bibles Cited

RSV	Revised Standard Version
RV	Revised Version
NKJV	New King James Version
KJV	King James Version
NIV	New International Version
ESV	English Standard Version
ASV	American Standard Version
ISV	International Standard Version
NASB	New American Standard Bible
NASU	New American Standard Bible—Updated Edition
ERV	Easy to Read Version
YLT	1898 Young's Literal Translation
Murdock	James Murdock New Testament

Sources

Thayer, Joseph H. Thayer's Greek-English Lexicon of the New Testament: Coded to Strong's Numbering System. Peabody, Massachusetts: Hendrickson, 2007

Perschbacher, Wesley J. The New Analytical Greek Lexicon Peabody, Massachusetts: Hendrickson, 2006

Vine, W. E., Unger, Merrill F., White, William Jr. Vine's Complete Expository Dictionary of Old and New Testament Words with topical Index, Nashville: Nelson, 1984, 1996

Wallace, Daniel B. Greek Grammar Beyond The Basics: An Exegetical Syntax of The New Testament. Grand Rapids, Michigan: Zondervan, 1996

Benner, Jeff A. The Ancient Hebrew Language And Alphabet: Understanding the Ancient Hebrew Language of the Bible Based on the Ancient Hebrew Culture and Thought. College Station, Texas: Virtualbookworm.com, 2004

Weingreen, J. A Practical Grammar For Classical Hebrew: Second Edition. Oxford: Oxford, 1959

Pratico, Gary D. and Van Pelt, Miles V. The Basics of Biblical Hebrew Grammar. Grand Rapids, Michigan: Zondervan, 2001, 2007

Thank You

I will like to express my deepest gratitude to my wife and three girls whose time I choose to spend on this work over the past year and two month undertaking this study. Without my wife's support and corporation this work would not have been brought to completion. I also want to thanks my instructor at The Theological University of America who allowed me to use the study as part of my Greek classes and posed some difficult questions that directed my studies and encouraged making this study public. I also thank Rowena Hanson whose hard work created the graphics for the cover of the book. I also want to thank the folks at AuthorHouse whose fine work made the script into a book. Last but not the least, I thanks all those who saw pieces of the script and urged me on.